George Manville Fenn

The Adventures of Don Lavington

George Manville Fenn

The Adventures of Don Lavington

ISBN/EAN: 9783337177096

Printed in Europe, USA, Canada, Australia, Japan

Cover: Foto ©ninafisch / pixelio.de

More available books at **www.hansebooks.com**

OF

DON LAVINGTON.

BY

GEORGE MANVILLE FENN,

AUTHOR OF
"CORMORANT CRAG," "FIRST IN THE FIELD," "STEVE YOUNG,"
"THE CRYSTAL HUNTERS," "THE GRAND CHACO,"
ETC., ETC.

LONDON
S. W. PARTRIDGE AND CO., LTD.
OLD BAILEY

NEW EDITION

CONTENTS.

CHAP.		PAGE
I.	FOUR FOLK O' BRISTOL CITY	9
II.	BLIND AS BATS	17
III.	AN AWKWARD GUINEA	26
IV.	MIKE BANNOCK HAS A RIDE	33
V.	A STUBBORN DISPOSITION	41
VI.	JEM WIMBLE TALKS SENSE	50
VII.	DON AND JEM GO HOME TO TEA	55
VIII.	KITTY CHRISTMAS SITS UP	64
IX.	A SOCIAL THUNDERBOLT	70
X.	GONE	76
XI.	THINKING BETTER OF IT	80
XII.	PRISONERS	89

CONTENTS.

CHAP.		PAGE
XIII.	HOW TO ESCAPE?	102
XIV.	WORKING UNDER DIFFICULTIES	110
XV.	A DESPERATE ATTEMPT	118
XVI.	PRISONERS AGAIN	126
XVII.	ON BOARD	132
XVIII.	JEM IS HUNGRY	135
XIX.	A CONVERSATION	141
XX.	A NATURALIZED NEW ZEALANDER	145
XXI.	AN INVITATION	154
XXII.	DON'S DECISION	166
XXIII.	BEFORE THE CAPTAIN	180
XXIV.	TOMATI'S PROMISE	187
XXV.	THE ALARM	196
XXVI.	WHAT MR. JONES THOUGHT	203
XXVII.	THE FUGITIVES	211
XXVIII.	FRIENDLY ATTENTIONS	220
XXIX.	AN UNWELCOME RECOGNITION	231
XXX.	A DETERMINED ENEMY	239
XXXI.	GOOD FOR EVIL	244

CHAP.		PAGE
XXXII.	CLOSE SHAVING	248
XXXIII.	ANOTHER ALARM	253
XXXIV.	AMONG FRIENDS AGAIN	259
XXXV.	LEFT BEHIND	264
XXXVI.	SOMETHING TO DO	271
XXXVII.	A PERILOUS DESCENT	281
XXXVIII.	DON'S REPORT	291
XXXIX.	WAR	298
XL.	DEFEATED	314
XLI.	PRISONERS OF WAR	319
XLII.	TOMATI ESCAPES	332
XLIII.	A SEARCH IN THE DARK	336
XLIV.	AFTER SUSPENSE	344
XLV.	IN THE WOODS	353
XLVI.	AN UNTIRING ENEMY	359
XLVII.	A DANGEROUS PHASE	367
XLVIII.	NGATI'S DISGUISE	373
XLIX.	UNWELCOME ACQUAINTANCES	377
L.	HOW TO ESCAPE	385

CHAP.		PAGE
LI.	NGATI'S GOAL	389
LII.	DON HAS A HEADACHE	393
LIII.	DON SPEAKS OUT	401
LIV.	HOME	413

THE ADVENTURES

OF

DON LAVINGTON.

CHAPTER I.

FOUR FOLK O' BRISTOL CITY.

"MIND your head! Crikey! that was near. 'Nother inch, and you'd ha' crushed him like an eggshell."

"Well, you told me to lower down."

"No, I didn't, stupid."

"Yes, you did."

"No, I didn't. You're half tipsy, or half asleep, or——"

"There, there, hold your tongue, Jem. I'm not hurt, and Mike thought you said lower away. That's enough."

"No, it arn't enough, Mas' Don. Your uncle said I was to soop'rintend, and a nice row there'd ha' been when he come back if you hadn't had any head left."

"Wouldn't have mattered much, Jem. Nobody would have cared."

"Nobody would ha' cared? Come, I like that. What would your mother ha' said to me when I carried you home, and told her your head had been scrunched off by a sugar-cask?"

"You're right, Mas' Don. Nobody wouldn't ha' cared.

You aren't wanted here. Why don't you strike for liberty, my lad, and go and make your fortun' in furren parts?"

"Same as you have, Mike Bannock? Now just you look ye here. If ever I hears you trying to make Master Don unsettled again, and setting him agen his work, I tells Mr. Chris'mas, and no begging won't get you back on again. Fortun' indeed! Why, you ragged, penny-hunting, lazy, drunken rub-shoulder, you ought to be ashamed of yourself!"

"And I arn't a bit, Jem Wimble, not a bit. Never you mind him, Master Don, you strike for freedom. Make your uncle give you your father's money, and then off you goes like a man to see life."

"Now lookye here," cried the sturdy, broad-faced young fellow who had first spoken, as he picked up a wooden lever used for turning over the great sugar hogsheads lying in the yard, and hoisting them into a trolly, or beneath the crane which raised them into the warehouse. "Lookye here, Mike Bannock, I never did knock a man down with this here wooden bar, but if you gets stirring Mas' Don again, has it you do, right across the back. Spang!"

"Be quiet, Jem, and put the bar down," said Lindon Lavington, a dark, well set-up lad of seventeen, as he sat upon the head of a sugar hogshead with his arms folded, slowly swinging his legs.

"No, I sha'n't put the bar down, Mas' Don. Your uncle left me in charge of the yard, and—what yer sitting on the sugar-barrel for when there's a 'bacco hogshead close by? Now just you feel how sticky you are."

Don got off the barrel, and made a face, as he proved with one hand the truth of the man's words, and then rubbed his treacly fingers against the warehouse wall.

"Your mother 'll make a row about that, just as my Sally does when I get molasses on my clothes."

"You should teach her to lick it off, Jemmy Wimble," said the rough-looking, red-faced labourer, who had lowered down a sugar hogshead so rapidly, that he had been within an inch of making it unnecessary to write Don Lavington's life, from the fact of there being no life to write.

"You mind your own business, Mike," said Jem, indignantly.

"That's what I'm a-doing of, and a-waiting for orders, Mr.

"'WHY DON'T YOU GIVE 'EM THE WORD AND HAVE ME PRESSED'?" (*p*. 12).

Jem Wimble. He's hen-pecked, Mas' Don, that what's the matter with him. Been married only three months, and he's hen-pecked. Haw-haw-haw! Poor old cock-bird! Hen-pecked! Haw-haw-haw!"

Jem Wimble, general worker in the warehouse and yard of

Josiah Christmas, West India merchant, of River Street, Bristol, gave Mike the labourer an angry look, as he turned as red as a blushing girl.

"Lookye here," he cried angrily, as Don, who had reseated himself, this time on a hogshead crammed full of compressed tobacco-leaves from Baltimore, swung his legs, and looked on in a half-moody, half-amused way; "the best thing that could happen for Christmas' Yard and for Bristol City, would be for the press gang to get hold o' you, and take you off to sea."

"Haw-haw-haw!" laughed the swarthy, red-faced fellow. "Why don't you give 'em the word, and have me pressed?"

"No coming back to be begged on then by Miss Kitty and Mas' Don, after being drunk for a week. You're a bad un, that's what you are, Mike Bannock, and I wish the master wouldn't have you here."

"Not such a hard nut as you are, Jemmy," said the man with a chuckle. "Sailors won't take me—don't want cripples to go aloft. Lookye here, Mas' Don, there's a leg."

As he spoke, the great idle-looking fellow limped slowly, with an exaggerated display of lameness, to and fro past the door of the office.

"Get out, Mike," said Don, as the man stopped. "I believe that's nearly all sham."

"That's a true word, Mas' Don," cried Jem. "He's only lame when he thinks about it. And now do please go on totting up, and let's get these casks shifted 'fore your uncle comes back."

"Well, I'm waiting, Jem," cried the lad, opening a book he had under his arm, and in which a pencil was shut. "I could put down fifty, while you are moving one."

"That's all right, sir; that's all right. I only want to keep things straight, and not have your uncle rowing you when he comes back. Seems to me as life's getting to be one jolly row. What with my Sally at home, and your uncle here, and you always down in the mouth, and Mike not sticking to his work, things is as miserable as mizzar."

"He's hen-pecked, that's what he is," chuckled Mike, going to the handle of the crane. "Poor old Jemmy! Hen-pecked, that's what's the matter with him."

"Let him alone, Mike," said Don quietly.

"Right, Mas' Don," said the man; "but if I was you," he murmured hoarsely, as Jem went into the warehouse, "I'd strike for liberty. I knows all about it. When your mother come to live with your uncle she give him all your father's money, and he put it into the business. I know. I used to work here when you first come, only a little un, and a nice little un you was, just after your poor father died."

Don's brow wrinkled as he looked searchingly at the man.

"You've a right to half there is here, Mas' Don; but the old man's grabbing of it all for his gal, Miss Kitty, and has made your mother and you reg'lar servants."

"It is not true, Mike. My uncle has behaved very kindly to my mother and me. He has invested my money, and given me a home when I was left an orphan."

"*Kick!*"

That is the nearest approach to the sound of Mike's derisive laugh, one which made the lad frown and dart at him an angry look.

"Why, who told you that, my lad?"

"My mother, over and over again."

"Ah, poor thing, for the sake o' peace and quietness. Don't you believe it, my lad. You've been werry kind to me, and begged me on again here when I've been 'most starving, and many's the shillin' you've give me, Mas' Don, to buy comforts, or I wouldn't say to you what I does now, and werry welcome a shilling would be to-day, Mas' Don."

"I haven't any money, Mike."

"Got no money, my lad? What a shame, when half of all this here ought to be yourn. Oh dear, what a cruel thing it seems! I'm very sorry for you, Mas' Don, that I am, 'specially when I think of what a fine dashing young fellow like——"

"Don't humbug, Mike."

"Nay, not I, my lad; 'tarn't likely. You know it's true

enough. You're one of the young fellows as is kep' out of his rights. I know what I'd do if I was you."

"What?"

"Not be always rubbing my nose again a desk. Go off to one o' them bu'ful foreign countries as I've told you of, where there's gold and silver and dymons, and birds jus' like 'em; and wild beasts to kill, and snakes as long as the main mast. Ah! I've seen some sights in furren abroad, as what I've told you about's like nothing to 'em. Look here, Mas' Don, shall I stop on for an hour and tell you what I've seen in South America?"

"No, no, Mike; my uncle doesn't like you to be with me."

"Ah, and well I knows it. 'Cause I tells you the truth and he feels guilty, Mas' Don."

"And—and it only unsettles me," cried the boy with a despairing look in his eyes. "Get on with your work, and I must get on with mine."

"Ah, to be sure," said the scoundrel with a sneer. "Work, work, work. You and me, Mas' Don, is treated worse than the black niggers as cuts the sugar-canes down, and hoes the 'bacco in the plantations. I'm sorry for you."

Lindon Lavington thrust his little account book in his breast, and walked hurriedly in the direction taken by the man Jem, entering directly after a low warehouse door, where rows of sugar hogsheads lay, and there was a murmur and buzz made by the attracted flies.

Mike Bannock stood with his hands clasping the handle of the crane winch against which he leaned without moving, but his eyes were hard at work.

He followed Don with them till he had disappeared through the low dark doorway, then glanced at the closed gate leading into the busy street, and then at the open office door, a few yards away.

All was still, save the buzzing of the flies about the casks on that hot midsummer's day, and without the trace of a limp, the man stepped rapidly into the office, but only to dart back again in alarm, for, all at once, there was a loud rattling noise of straps, chains, and heavy harness.

There was no cause for alarm. It was only the fat, sleepy horse in the trolly shafts, who, at the same time that he gave his nosebag a toss, shook himself violently to get rid of the flies which preferred his juices to the sugar oozing from many a hogshead's seams.

Mike darted into the office again; the flies buzzed; the horse munched oats; the faint sound of Don's voice in converse with Jem Wimble could he heard; then there was a faint click as if a desk had been shut down softly, and Mike stepped out again, gave a hasty glance round, and the next moment was standing dreamily with his eyes half-closed, grasping the handle of the crane winch as Don returned, closely followed by Jem Wimble.

"Now, Mas' Don, I'll just mark another," said Jem, "and we'll have him out."

He took a lump of chalk from a ledge close by, and ascended a step ladder to a door about six feet above the spot where Mike stood, and Don stood with his book under his arm, his brow rugged, and a thoughtful look in his eyes.

Just then the small door in the yard gate was opened, and a sturdy-looking grey-haired man in snuff-coloured coat and cocked hat, drab breeches and gaiters, entered unseen by the pair, who had their backs to him.

"I 'member, Mas' Don, when I were out in the *Mary Anne* five year ago. We'd got to Pannymah, when the skipper stood with his glass to his eye, looking at a strange kind o' hobjick ashore, and he says to me, 'Mike, my lad——'"

"You idle scoundrel! How many more times am I to tell you that I will not have my time wasted over those lying stories of yours? Lindon, am I ever to be able to trust you when business takes me away?"

The words came in short sharp tones, and the speaker's dark eyes seemed to flash.

The effect was marvellous.

Mike began to turn the handle at a rapid rate, winding up

the rope till the pair of hooks used for grasping the great hogsheads rattled with their chains against the pulley wheels of the crane, and a shout came from the warehouse,—

"Whatcher doing of? Hold hard!"

"Stop, sir!" cried the stern-looking man to Mike, just as Jem appeared at the upper doorway and looked down.

"Oh!" he ejaculated. "Didn't know as you was there, sir."

"It is disgraceful, Lindon. The moment my back is turned you leave your desk to come and waste the men's time. I am ashamed of you."

Lindon's forehead grew more wrinkled as Josiah Christmas, merchant of Bristol city, and his maternal uncle, walked into the office, whither the lad followed slowly, looking stubborn and ill-used, for Mike Bannock's poison was at work, and in his youthful ignorance and folly, he felt too angry to attempt a frank explanation.

In fact, just then one idea pervaded his mind—two ideas—that his uncle was a tyrant, and that he ought to strike against his tyranny and be free.

CHAPTER II.

BLIND AS BATS.

THAT same evening Don Lavington did not walk home with his uncle, but hung back to see Jem Wimble lock up, and then sauntered slowly with him toward the little low house by the entrance gates, where the yardman, as he was called, lived in charge.

Jem had been in the West India merchant's service from a boy, and no one was more surprised than he when on the death of old Topley, Josiah Christmas said to him one morning,—

"Wimble, you had better take poor old Topley's place."

"And—and take charge of the yard, sir?"

"Yes. I can trust you, can't I?"

"Oh, yes, sir; but——"

"Ah! yes. You have no wife to put in the cottage."

Jem began to look foolish, and examine the lining of his hat.

"Well, sir, if it comes to that," he faltered; and there was a weak comical aspect in his countenance which made Don burst out laughing.

"I know, uncle," he cried, "he has got a sweetheart."

"Well, Master Don," said the young man, colouring up; "and nothing to be ashamed on neither."

"Certainly not," said the merchant quietly. "You had better get married, Wimble, and you can have the cottage. I will buy and lend you old Topley's furniture."

Wimble begged pardon afterwards, for on hearing all this

astounding news, he rushed out of the office, pulled off his leather apron, put on his coat as he ran, and disappeared for an hour, at the end of which time he returned, went mysteriously up to Don and whispered,—

"It's all right, sir; she says she will."

The result was that Jem Wimble looked twice as important, and cocked his cocked hat on one side, for he had ten shillings a week more, and the furnished cottage, kept the keys, kept the men's time, and married a wife who bore a most extraordinary likeness to a pretty little bantam hen.

This was three months before the scene just described, but though Jem spoke in authoritative tones to the men, it was with bated breath to his little wife, who was standing in the doorway looking as fierce as a kitten, when Jem walked up in company with his young master.

"Which I will not find fault before Master Lindon, Jem," she said; "but you know I do like you to be home punctual to tea."

"Yes, my dear, of course, of course," said Jem, apologetically. "Not much past time, and had to shut up first."

"That's what you always say when you're late. You don't know, Master Don, what a life he leads me."

"'Tain't true, Master Don," cried Jem. "She's always a-wherritting me."

"Now I appeal to Master Don: was it me, sir, as was late? There's the tea ready, and the bread and butter cut, and the watercresses turning limp, and the flies getting at the s'rimps. It arn't your fault, sir, I know, and I'm not grumbling, but there never was such a place as this for flies."

"It's the sugar, Sally," said Don, who had sauntered aimlessly in with Jem, and as he stared round the neat little kitchen with the pleasant meal all ready, he felt as if he should like to stay to tea instead of going home.

"Yes, it's the sugar, sir, I know; and you'd think it would sweeten some people's temper, but it don't."

"Which if it's me you mean, and you're thinking of this morning——"

"Which I am, Jem, and you ought to be ashamed. You grumbled over your breakfast, and you reg'larly worried your dinner, and all on account of a button."

"Well, then, you should sew one on. When a man's married he does expect to find buttons on his clean shirts."

"Yes, and badly enough you want 'em, making 'em that sticky as you do."

"I can't help that; it's only sugar."

"Only sugar indeed! And if it was my last words I'd say it—there *was* a button on the neck."

"Well, I know that," cried Jem; "and what's the good of a button being on, if it comes off directly you touch it? Is it any good, Mas' Don?"

"Oh, don't ask me," cried the lad, half amused, half annoyed, and wishing they'd ask him to tea.

"He dragged it off, Master Don."

"I didn't."

"You did, Jem, and you know you did, just to aggravate me."

"Wasn't half sewn on."

"It was. I can't sew your buttons on with copper wire."

"You two are just like a girl and boy," cried Don. "Here you have everything comfortable about you, and a good place, and you're always quarrelling."

"Well, it's his fault, sir."

"No, sir, it's her'n."

"It's both your faults, and you ought to be ashamed of yourselves."

"I'm not," said Sally; "and I wish I'd never seen him."

"And I'm sure I wish the same," said Jem despondently. "I never see such a temper."

"There, Master Don," cried the droll-looking little Dutch doll of a woman. "That's how he is always going on."

"There, Jem, now you've made your poor little wife cry. You are the most discontented fellow I ever saw."

"Come, I like that, Master Don; you've a deal to brag about, you have. Why, you're all at sixes and sevens at home."

This was such a home thrust that Don turned angrily and walked out of the place.

"There!" cried Sally. "I always knew how it would be. Master Don was the best friend we had, and now you've offended him, and driven him away."

"Shouldn't ha' said nasty things then," grumbled Jem, sitting down and attacking his tea.

"Now he'll go straight to his uncle and tell him what a man you are."

"Let him," said Jem, with his mouth full of bread and butter.

"And of course you'll lose your place, and we shall be turned out into the street to starve."

"Will you be quiet, Sally? How's a man to eat his tea with you going on like that?"

"Turned out into the world without a chance of getting another place. Oh! it's too bad. Why did I ever marry such a man as you?"

"'Cause you were glad of the chance," grumbled Jem, raising his hand to pour out some tea, but it was pushed aside indignantly, and the little woman busily, but with a great show of indignation, filled and sweetened her husband's cup, which she dabbed down before him, talking all the while, and finishing with,—

"You ought to be ashamed of yourself, Jem."

"I am," he grumbled. "Ashamed that I was ever such a stupid as to marry a girl who's always dissatisfied. Nice home you make me."

"And a nice home you make me, sir; and don't eat your victuals so fast. It's like being at the wild beast show."

"That's right; go on,' grumbled Jem, doubling his rate of consumption. "Grudge me my meals now. Good job if we could undo it all, and be as we was."

"I wish we could," cried the little woman, whose eyes seemed to say that her lips were not telling the truth.

"So do I," cried Jem, tossing off his third cup of tea; and then to his little wife's astonishment he took a thick slice of bread and butter in each hand, clapped them together as if they were cymbals, rose from the table and put on his hat.

"Where are you going, Jem?"

"Out."

"What for?"

"To eat my bread and butter down on the quay."

"But why, Jem?"

"'Cause there's peace and quietness there."

Bang! went the door, and little Mrs. Wimble stood gazing at it angrily for a few moments before sitting down and having what she called "a good cry," after which she rose, wiped her eyes, and put away the tea things without partaking of any herself.

"Poor Jem!" she said softly; "I'm afraid I'm very unkind to him sometimes."

Just at that moment Jem was sitting on an empty cask, eating his bread and butter, and watching a boat manned by blue-jackets going off to the sloop of war lying out toward the channel, and flying her colours in the evening breeze.

"Poor little Sally!" he said to himself. "We don't seem to get on somehow, and I'm afraid I'm a bit rough to her; but knives and scissors! what a temper she have got."

Meanwhile, in anything but a pleasant frame of mind, Don had gone home to find that the tea was ready, and that he was being treated as a laggard.

"Come, Lindon," said his uncle quietly, "you have kept us waiting some time."

The lad glanced quickly round the well-furnished room, bright with curiosities brought in many a voyage from the west, and with the poison of Mike's words still at work, he wondered how much of what he saw rightfully belonged to him.

The next moment his eyes lit on the soft sweet troubled face of his mother, full of appeal and reproach, and it seemed to Don that his uncle had been upsetting her by an account of his delinquencies.

"It's too bad, and I don't deserve it," he said to himself. "Everything seems to go wrong now. Well, what are you looking at?" he added, to himself, as he took his seat and stared across at his cousin, the playmate of many years, whose quiet little womanly face seemed to repeat her father's grave, reproachful look, but who, as it were, snatched her eyes away as soon as she met his gaze.

"They all hate me," thought Don, who was in that unhappy stage of a boy's life when help is so much needed to keep him from turning down one of the dark side lanes of the great main route.

"Been for a walk, Don?" said his mother with a tender look.

"No, mother, I only stopped back in the yard a little while."

His uncle set down his cup sharply.

"You have not been keeping that scoundrel Bannock?" he cried.

"No, sir; I've been talking to Jem."

"Ho!" ejaculated the old merchant. "That's better. But you might have come straight home."

Don's eyes encountered his Cousin Kitty's just then, as she gave her head a shake to throw back the brown curls which clustered about her white forehead.

She turned her gaze upon her plate, and he could see that she was frowning.

"Yes," thought Don, "they all dislike me, and I'm only a worry and trouble to my mother. I wish I was far away—anywhere."

He went on with his tea moodily and in silence, paying no heed to the reproachful glances of his mother's eyes, which seemed to him to say, and with some reason, "Don't be sullky, Don, my boy; try and behave as I could wish."

"It's of no use to try," he said to himself; and the meal passed off very silently, and with a cold chill on every one present.

"I'm very sorry, Laura," said her brother, as soon as Don had left the room; "and I don't know what to do for the best. I hate finding fault and scolding, but if the boy is in the wrong I must chide."

" Try and be patient with him, Josiah," said Mrs. Lavington pleadingly. " He is very young yet."

" Patient? I'm afraid I have been too patient. That scoundrel at the yard has unsettled him with his wild tales of the sea; and if I allowed it, Don would make him quite a companion."

" But, Josiah——"

"There, don't look like that, my dear. I promised you I would play a father's part to the boy, and I will; but you must not expect me to be a weak indulgent father, and spoil him with foolish lenity. There, enough for one day. I daresay we shall get all right in time."

" Oh, yes," cried Mrs. Lavington, earnestly. " He's a truehearted, brave boy; don't try to crush him down."

" Crush him, nonsense!" cried the merchant, angrily. " You really are too bad, Laura, and——"

He stopped, for just then Don re-entered the room to flush up angrily as he saw his mother in tears; and he had heard enough of his uncle's remark and its angry tone to make him writhe.

"Ill using her now," he said to himself, as he set his teeth and walked to the window.

The closing of the door made him start round quickly, to find that his mother was close behind him, and his uncle gone.

" What has Uncle Jos been saying to you, mother?" he cried angrily.

" Nothing—nothing particular, my boy," she faltered.

" He has," cried Don fiercely; "and I won't have it. He may scold and abuse me as much as he likes, but I will not have him ill use you."

"Ill use me, Don?" cried Mrs. Lavington. "Nonsense, my dear boy. Your uncle is all that is kind and good; and he loves you very dearly, Don, if you could only try—try a little more, my dear boy, to do what he likes, and please him."

" I do try, mother, but it's no good."

" Don't say that, Don. Try a little harder—for my sake, dear, as well as your own."

"I have tried, I am always trying, and it's of no use. Nothing pleases uncle, and the men in the yard know it."

"Don, my boy, what foolish obstinate fit is this which has come over you?" said Mrs. Lavington tenderly.

"I'm not obstinate," he said sullenly; "only unhappy."

"Is it not your own fault, my darling?" she whispered; "believe me, your uncle is one of the kindest and best of men."

Don shook his head.

"Are you going to prefer the opinion of the men of the yard to mine, dear?"

"No, mother, but uncle is your brother, and you believe in him and defend him. You know how harsh and unkind he is to me."

"Not unkind, Don, only firm and for your good. Now come, my boy, do, for my sake, try to drive away these clouds, and let us all be happy once more."

"It's of no use to try, mother; I shall never be happy here, tied down to a desk. It's like being uncle's slave."

"What am I to say to you, Don, if you talk like this?" said Mrs. Lavington. "Believe me you are wrong, and some day you will own it. You will see what a mistaken view you have taken of your uncle's treatment. There, I shall say no more now."

"You always treat me as if I were a child," said Don, bitterly. "I'm seventeen now, mother, and I ought to know something."

"Yes, my boy," said Mrs. Lavington gently; "at seventeen we think we know a good deal; and at forty we smile as we look back and see what a very little that 'good deal' was."

Don shook his head.

"There, we will have no more sad looks. Uncle is eager to do all he can to make us happy."

"I wish I could think so," cried Don, bitterly.

"You may, my dear. And now, come, try and throw aside all those fanciful notions about going abroad and meeting with adventures. There is no place like home, Don, and you will find out some day that is true."

"But I have no home till I make one," said the lad gloomily.

'You have an excellent home here, Don, the gift of one who has kindly taken the place toward you of your father. There, I will listen to no more from you, for this is all foolish fighting of your worse against your better self."

There was a quiet dignity in his mother's words which awed Don for the moment, but the gentle embrace given the next minute seemed to undo that which the firmness had achieved, and that night the cloud over the lad's life seemed darker than ever.

"She takes uncle's side and thinks he is everything," he said gloomily, as he went to bed. "She means right, but she is wrong. Oh, how I wish I could go right away somewhere and begin life all over again."

Then he lay down to sleep, but slumber did not come, so he went on thinking of many things, to fall into a state of unconsciousness at last, from which he awoke to the fact that it was day—a very eventful day for him, but he did not awaken to the fact that he was very blind.

CHAPTER III.

AN AWKWARD GUINEA.

IT was a busy day at the yard, for a part of the lading of a sugar ship was being stored away in Uncle Josiah's warehouses; but from the very commencement matters seemed to go wrong, and the state of affairs about ten o'clock was pretty ably expressed by Jem Wimble, who came up to Don as he was busy with pencil and book, keeping account of the deliveries, and said in a loud voice,—

"What did your uncle have for breakfast, Mas' Don?"

"Coffee—ham—I hardly know, Jem."

"Ho! Thought p'r'aps it had been cayenne pepper."

"Nonsense!"

"Ah, you may say that, but see how he is going it. 'Tarn't my fault that the dock men work so badly, and 'tarn't my fault that Mike isn't here, and——"

"Don't stand talking to Wimble, Lindon," said a voice sharply, and Uncle Josiah came up to the pair. "No, don't go away, Wimble. Did Bannock say he should stay away to-day?"

"Not to me, uncle."

"Nor to me, sir."

"It's very strange, just as we are so busy too. He has not drawn any money."

"P'r'aps press gang's got him, sir," suggested Jem.

"Humph! Hardly likely!" said Uncle Josiah; and he went on and entered the office, to come out at the end of a few minutes and beckon to Don.

"Lindon," he said, as the lad joined him, "I left nine guineas and a half in the little mahogany bowl in my desk yesterday. Whom have you paid?"

"Paid? No one, sir."

"But eight guineas are gone—missing."

"Eight guineas? Missing, sir?"

"Yes, do you know anything about them?"

"No, sir. I—that is—yes, I remember now: I picked up a guinea on the floor, and meant to give it to you. Here it is: I forgot all about it."

Don took a piece of gold from his flap waistcoat pocket, and handed it to his uncle, who looked at him so curiously that the boy grew confused.

"Picked this up on the floor, Lindon?" said Uncle Josiah.

"Yes, sir. It had rolled down by my desk."

"It is very strange," said Uncle Josiah, thoughtfully. "Well, that leaves seven missing. You had better look round and see if you can find them."

Don felt uncomfortable, he hardly knew why; but it seemed to him that his uncle looked at him doubtingly, and this brought a feeling of hot indignation into the boy's brain.

He turned quickly, however, entered the office, and with his uncle looking on, searched all over the floor.

"Well?"

"There's nothing here, sir. Of course not," cried Don eagerly; "Mrs. Wimble sweeps up every morning, and if there had been she would have found it."

Uncle Josiah lifted off his cocked hat, and put it on again wrong way first.

"This is a very unpleasant affair, Lindon," he said. "I can afford to lose seven guineas, or seven hundred if it came to that, but I can't afford to lose confidence in those whom I employ."

Don felt hot and cold as his uncle walked to the door and called Jem; and as he waited he looked at the map of an estate in the West Indies, all fly-specked and yellow, then at the portraits of three merchant vessels in full sail, all as yellow and fly-specked as the map, and showing the peculiarity emphasised by the ingenious artist, of their sails blown out one way and their house flags another.

"Surely uncle can't suspect me," he said to himself; and then the thought came again—"surely uncle can't suspect me."

"Come in here, Wimble," said Uncle Josiah, very sternly.

Jem took off his hat, and followed him into the office.

"Some money is missing from my desk, Wimble. Have you seen it?"

"Me, sir?" said Jem, stooping down and peering in all directions under the desks. "No, sir, I harn't seen it. Let's see, I don't think I've been here only when I locked up."

"By some mischance I left my desk unlocked when I went out in a hurry yesterday. Lindon here has found one piece on the floor."

"P'r'aps tothers is there, too," said Jem eagerly.

"No; we have looked. Call your wife. Perhaps she may have found them when sweeping."

"Not she, sir," said Jem. "If she had she'd ha' told me. 'Sides, how could they ha' got on the floor?"

"That remains to be proved, Wimble," said Uncle Josiah, drily. "Call your wife."

Jem went to the door, rubbing his ear, and as it happened, seeing his wife outside the cottage, telegraphed to her to come by working one arm about furiously.

Little Mrs. Wimble came up in a hurry, looking scared.

"Take off that there dirty apron," whispered Jem, making a dash at the offending garment, and snatching back his hand bleeding from the scratch of the pin by which it was fastened.

"Look at that," he began.

"Then you shouldn't——"

"Silence!" said Uncle Josiah. "Mrs. Wimble, did you sweep up this room to-day?"

"That I did, sir, and dusted too, and if there's any dust, it must be an——"

"Hush! don't talk so. Listen to me. Did you find any money on the floor?"

"Sakes alive, sir, no."

"You are quite sure?"

"Oh yes, sir, quite sure. Have you dropped anything?"

"Yes! no! That will do."

Mrs. Wimble stared.

"Don't you hear?" whispered Jem. "Be off!"

The little woman gave him an angry look, and then hurried from the office, looking put out and hurt.

"This money must be found," said Uncle Josiah sternly, as soon as they were alone. "You are sure that you have seen no more, Lindon?"

"Quite, uncle. I'm sorry I forgot about the guinea I found."

"Yes!" said Uncle Josiah, giving him a quick searching look. "You are quite certain, Wimble?"

"Me, sir? Oh, yes; I'm moral sartain."

"I should be sorry to suspect any one, and behave unjustly, but I must have this matter cleared up. Michael Bannock is away, and I cannot conceive his being absent without money, unless he is ill. Wimble, go and see."

"Yes, sir," said the yard man, with alacrity; and he went off shaking his head, as if all this was a puzzle beyond his capacity to comprehend.

"You had better go to your desk, Lindon," said Uncle Josiah, coldly.

Don started, and mounted his stool, but he could not write. His brain was confused; and from time to time he glanced at the stern-looking old merchant, and tried to grasp his thoughts. "Surely uncle can't suspect me—surely he can't suspect me!" he found himself saying again, and the trouble seemed to increase till he felt as if he must speak out and say how sorry he was that he had picked up the money and forgotten all about it, when Jem returned.

"He arn't ill, sir," said the man eagerly, "I found him close by, at the Little Half Moon, in the back street."

"Drinking?"

"Yes, sir, and treating a lot of his mates. He wanted me

to have some, and when I wouldn't, he said I should, and emptied half a glass over me. See here."

He held up one of his broad skirts which was liberally splashed.

Uncle Josiah frowned, and took a turn or two up and down the office. Then he stopped before Jem.

"Go round to Smithers the constable. You know: the man who came when the rum was broached."

"Yes, sir, I know."

"Ask Smithers to bring Michael Bannock round here. I must clear this matter up."

"Yes, sir," said Jem; and he hurried out, while Don drew a long breath.

"Uncle does not suspect me," he said to himself.

"The scoundrel! He must have taken advantage of your back being turned to come in here. You did not notice anything, Lindon?"

"No, uncle, and I hardly think he could have been left alone."

"But the money is missing; some of it was dropped; this man is always penniless; he has not drawn his wages, and yet he is half tipsy and treating his companions. I hope I am not suspecting him wrongfully, but it looks bad, Lindon, it looks bad."

The old merchant sat down and began to write. So did Don, who felt better now, and the time glided on till there were the sounds of feet heard in the yard, and directly after Mike, looking very red-eyed and flushed, entered the office, half pushed in by Jem Wimble and a hard-faced ugly man, who had a peculiar chip out of, or dent in, his nose.

"Morn', master," said Mike, boisterously. "Couldn't yer get on without yer best man i' th' yard?"

"Silence, sir!" cried Uncle Josiah, turning round, and glaring magisterially at the culprit.

"Take yer hat off, can't yer?" cried Jem, knocking it off for him, and then picking it up and handing it.

"Give man time, Jem Wimble," said Mike, with a grimace. "Want to pay me what you owes me, master?"

"Hold your tongue, sir! And listen. Constable, a sum of money has been abstracted from my desk, and this man, who I believe was penniless two days ago, is now staying away from his work treating his friends."

"Steady, master; on'y having a glass."

"He was paying for ale with a guinea when I fetched him out, sir," said the constable. "Now, Mike, you're wanted for another ugly job, so you may as well clear yourself of this if you can."

"What yer mean with your ugly job?" said the man, laughing.

"You'll know soon enough; you and four more are in trouble. Now then, what money have you got on you?"

"None 'tall."

"Out with it."

"Well, only two o' these. I did have three," grumbled the man, reluctantly taking out a couple of guineas from his pocket.

"Looks bad, sir," said the constable. "Now then, where did you get them?"

"What's that to you?"

"Enough for Mr. Christmas to charge you with robbing his desk, my lad; and this and what I've got against you will send you to Botany Bay."

"What, me? Rob a good master? Not a penny."

"What have you done with the rest?" continued the constable.

"Never had no more, and wouldn't have had that if I'd knowed."

"This will do, sir," said the constable. "You charge him here with stealing money from your desk?"

"I am afraid I must," said Uncle Josiah.

"What, me? charge me?" cried the man, angrily.

"Yes, Bannock, reluctantly; but it seems that you are the thief."

"No: not me!" cried the man, fiercely. "It warn't me. It was him."

Don started and turned pale, as the man stood pointing at him.

"What do you mean?" cried Uncle Josiah.

"Mean? Why, I ketched him a-helping hisself to the money, and he give me three guineas to hold my tongue."

"What?"

"And when I wouldn't take 'em he said if I didn't he'd say it was me; and that's the whole truth, and nothing else."

"Lindon, what have you to say to this?" cried Uncle Josiah.

Don thought of the guinea he had picked up, of his uncle's curious look when he gave it to him, and as he turned red and white with terror and dismay, mingled with confusion, he tried to speak, but try how he would, no words would come.

CHAPTER IV.

MIKE BANNOCK HAS A RIDE.

"YOU wretch!"

Those two words were a long time coming, but when they did escape from Lindon's lips, they made up in emphasis and force for their brevity.

"Steady, Master Don, steady," said Jem, throwing his arms round the boy's waist, and holding him back. "You arn't strong enough to fight him."

"Wretch? Oh! Well, I like that. Why, some men would ha' gone straight to your uncle here, and told him all about it; but I didn't, and I'd made up my mind to send him the money back, only I met two or three mates, and I had to change one of 'em to give the poor lads a drink o' ale."

"You own, then, that you had my money, sir?" cried the old merchant.

"Well—some on it, master. He give it me. S'pose I oughtn't to have took it, but I didn't like to come and tell you, and get the poor lad into trouble. He's so young, you see."

"Uncle, it is not true!" cried Lindon, excitedly.

"But you had one of the guineas in your pocket, sir."

"Yes, uncle, but——"

"Course he had," interrupted Mike sharply. "I told you it wouldn't do, Master Don. I begged you not to."

"You villain!" cried Don, grinding his teeth, while his uncle watched him with a sidelong look.

"Calling names won't mend it, my lad. I knowed it was wrong. I telled him not to, sir, but he would."

This was to the constable in a confidential tone, and that functionary responded with a solemn wink.

"It is not true, uncle!" cried Don again.

"Oh, come now," said Mike, shaking his head with half tipsy reproach, "I wouldn't make worse on it, my lad, by telling a lot o' lies. You did wrong, as I says to you at the time; but you was so orbst'nate you would. Says as you'd got such lots of money, master, as you'd never miss it."

Uncle Josiah gave vent to a sound resembling a disgusted grunt, and turned from the speaker, who continued reproachfully to Don,—

"What you've got to do, my lad, is to go down on your bended knees to your uncle, as is a good master as ever lived —and I will say that, come what may—and ask him to let you off this time, and you won't do so any more."

"Uncle, you won't believe what he says?" cried Don wildly.

Uncle Josiah did not reply, only looked at him searchingly.

"He can't help believing it, my lad," said Mike sadly. "It's werry shocking in one so young."

Don made a desperate struggle to free himself from Jem's encircling arms, but the man held fast.

"No, no, my lad; keep quiet," growled Jem. "I'm going to spoil the shape of his nose for him before he goes."

"Then you don't believe it, Jem?" cried Don, passionately.

"Believe it, my lad? Why, I couldn't believe it if he swore it 'fore a hundred million magistrits."

"No, that's allus the way with higgerant chaps like you, Jem Wimble," said Mike; "but it's all true, genelmen, and I'm sorry I didn't speak out afore like a man, for he don't deserve what I did for him."

"Hah!" ejaculated Uncle Josiah, and Don's face was full of despair.

"You charge Mike Bannock, then, with stealing this money, sir," said the constable.

"Yes, certainly."

"What?" roared Mike, savagely, "charge me?"

"That will do," said the constable, taking a little staff with a brass crown on the end from his pocket. "No nonsense, or I shall call in help. In the King's name, my lad. Do you give in?"

"Give in? What for? I arn't done nothing. Charge him; he's the thief."

Don started as if the word *thief* were a stinging lash.

Jem loosed his hold, and with double fists dashed at the scoundrel.

"You say Master Don's a thief!"

"Silence, Wimble! Stand back, sir," cried Uncle Josiah, sternly.

"But, sir——"

"Silence, man! Am I master here?"

Jem drew back muttering.

"Charge him, I say," continued Mike, boisterously; "and if you won't, I will. Look here, Mr. Smithers, I charge this 'ere boy with going to his uncle's desk and taking all the gold, and leaving all the silver in a little hogamee bowl."

"You seem to know all about it, Mike," said the constable, grimly.

"Course I do, my lad. I seed him. Caught him in the werry act, and he dropped one o' the guineas, and it run away under the desk, and he couldn't find it."

"You saw all that, eh?" said the constable.

"Every bit of it. I swears to it, sir."

"And how came you to be in the office to see it?"

"How come I in the office to see it?" said Mike, staring; "how come I in the office to see it?"

"Yes. Your work's in the yard, isn't it?"

"Course it is," said Mike, with plenty of effrontery; "but I heerd the money jingling like, and I went in to see."

"And very kind of you too, Mike," said the constable, jocularly. "Don't you forget to tell that to the magistrates."

"Magistrits? What magistrits? Master arn't going to give me in custody, I know."

"Indeed, but I am, you scoundrel," cried Uncle Josiah, wrathfully. "You are one of the worst kind of thieves——"

"Here, take that back, master."

"Worst kind of scoundrels—dogs who bite the hand that has fed them."

"I tell yer it was him," said Mike, with a ferocious glare at Don.

"All right, Mike, you tell the magistrates that," said the constable, "and don't forget."

"I arn't going 'fore no magistrits," grumbled Mike.

"Yes, you are," said the constable, taking a pair of handcuffs from his pocket. "Now then, is it to be quietly?"

Mike made a furious gesture.

"Just as you like," said the constable. "Jem Wimble, I call you in the King's name to help."

"Which I just will," cried Jem, with alacrity; and he made at Mike, while Don felt a strange desire tingling in his veins as he longed to help as well.

"I gives in," growled Mike. "I could chuck the whole lot on you outer winder, but I won't. It would only make it seem as if I was guilty, and it's not guilty, and so I tell you. Master says I took the money, and I says it was that young Don Lavington as is the thief. Come on, youngster. I'll talk to you when we're in the lock-up."

Don looked wildly from Mike to his uncle, whose eyes were fixed on the constable.

"Do you charge the boy too, sir?"

Uncle Josiah was silent for some moments.

"No! Not now!"

Lindon's heart leapt at that word "*no!*" But it sank again at the "*not now.*"

"But the case is awkward, sir," said the constable. "After what this man has said we shall be obliged to take some notice of the matter."

"'Bliged to? Course you will. Here, bring 'im along. Come on, mate. I can tell you stories all night now about my bygones. Keep up yer sperrits, and I daresay the magistrits 'll let you off pretty easy."

"If there is any charge made against my young clerk "—Don winced, for his uncle did not say, "against my nephew "—"I will be answerable for his appearance before the magistrates. That will be sufficient, I presume."

"Yes, sir, I suppose that will do," said the constable.

"But I s'pose it won't," said Mike. "He's the monkey and I'm only the cat. You've got to take him if you does your dooty, and master 'll be answerable for me."

"*Ex*actly," said the constable; "come along."

"Nay, but this arn't fair, master. Take one, take all. You bring us both."

"Come along."

"If you don't bring that there young un too, I won't go," exclaimed the scoundrel, fiercely.

Click!

A short struggle, and then *click* again, and Mike Bannock's hands were useless, but he threw himself down.

"Fair play, fair play," he cried, savagely; "take one, take all. Are you going to charge him, master?"

"Take the scoundrel away, Smithers, and once more I will be bail—before the magistrates, if necessary—for my clerk's appearance," cried Uncle Josiah, who was now out of patience. "Can I help?"

"Well, sir, you could," said the constable, grimly; "but if you'd have in three or four of your men, and a short step ladder, we could soon carry him off."

"No man sha'n't carry me off," roared Mike, as Jem ran out of the office with great alacrity, and returned in a very short time with three men and a stout ladder, about nine feet long.

"That's the sort, Wimble," said the constable. "Didn't think of a rope, did you?"

"Did I think of two ropes?" said Jem, grinning.

"Ah!" ejaculated the constable. "Now, Mike Bannock, I just warn you that any violence will make your case worse. Take my advice, get up and come quietly."

"Take young Don Lavington too, then, and I will."

"Get up, and walk quietly."

"Not 'less you takes him."

"Sorry to make a rumpus, sir," said the constable, apologetically; "but I must have him out."

"The sooner the better," said Uncle Josiah, grimly.

"I am ready to go, uncle," said Don, quietly. "I am not afraid."

"Hold your tongue, sir!" said the merchant, sternly; "and stand out of the way."

"Now, Mike," said the constable, "this is the third time of asking. Will you come quiet?"

"Take him too," cried Mike.

"Ready with those ropes, Wimble. You two, ready with that there. Now, Mike Bannock, you've been asked three times, and now you've got to mount that ladder."

"Any man comes a-nigh me," roared Mike, "I'll——"

He did not say what, for the constable dashed at him, and by an ingenious twist avoided a savage kick, threw the scoundrel over on his face, as he lay on the floor, and sat upon him, retaining his seat in spite of his struggles.

"Step the first," said the constable, coolly. "Now, Wimble, I want that ladder passed under me, so as to lie right along on his back. Do you see?"

"Yes, sir," cried Jem, eagerly; and taking the ladder as the constable sat astride the prostrate scoundrel, holding down his shoulders, and easing himself up, the ladder was passed between the officer's legs, and, in spite of a good deal of heaving, savage kicking, and one or two fierce attempts to bite, right along till it was upon Mike's back, projecting nearly two feet beyond his head and feet.

"Murder!" yelled Mike, hoarsely.

"What? does it hurt, my lad? Never mind; you'll soon get used to it."

The constable seated himself upon the ladder, whose sides and rounds thoroughly imprisoned the scoundrel in spite of his yells and struggles to get free.

"Now then, Wimble, I've got him. You tie his ankles, one each side, tightly to the ladder, and one of you bind his arms same way to the ladder sides. Cut the rope. Mr. Christmas will not mind."

The men grinned, and set to work so handily that in a few moments Mike was securely bound.

"Now then," said the constable, "I'll have one round his middle; give me a piece of rope; I'll soon do that."

He seized the rope, and, without rising, rapidly secured it to one side of the ladder.

"Now," he said, "raise that end."

This was done, the rope passed under Mike, drawn up on the other side, hauled upon till Mike yelled for mercy, and then knotted twice.

"There, my lads," said the constable, rising; "now turn him over."

The ladder was seized, turned, and there lay Mike on his back, safely secured.

"Here, undo these," he said, sullenly. "I'll walk."

"Too late, Mike, my boy. Now then, a couple of men head and tail. Let the ladder hang at arm's length. Best have given in quietly, and not have made yourself a show, Mike."

"Don't I tell you I'll walk?" growled the prisoner.

"And let us have all our trouble for nothing? No, my lad, it's too late. Ready there! Up with him. Good morning, sir. March!"

The men lent themselves eagerly to the task, for Mike was thoroughly disliked; and a few minutes later there was a crowd gathering and following Mike Bannock as he was borne off, spread-eagled and half tipsy, to ponder on the theft and his chances in the cold damp place known in Bristol as the lock-up.

Don Lavington stood in the office, waiting for his uncle to speak.

CHAPTER V.

A STUBBORN DISPOSITION.

"STOP!"

Don had taken his hat, and, seeing his uncle apparently immersed in a letter, was about to yield to his curiosity and follow the constable, when, as he reached the door, his uncle's word thundered out and made him turn and go on with his writing in response to a severe look and a pointing finger.

From time to time the boy looked up furtively as he sat, and wondered why his uncle did not say anything more about the money.

But the time glided on, and the struggle between his desire to speak out frankly and his indignant wounded pride continued.

A dozen times over he was on the point of crossing to the stern-looking old man, and begging him to listen and believe, but Uncle Josiah sat there with the most uncompromising of expressions on his face, and Don dared not speak. He dared not trust himself for very shame, as the incident had so upset him, that he felt sure that he must break down and cry like a child if he attempted to explain.

After a time there was the sound of voices talking and laughing, and the click of the heavy latch of the gate. Then through the open windows came the deep *burr burr* of Jem's bass, and the shrill inquiring tones of Sally Wimble, as she eagerly questioned her lord.

Then there were steps, some of which passed the office door;

and Don, as he sat with his head bent over a ledger, knew exactly whose steps those were, and where the makers of those steps were going to the different warehouses in the great yard.

Directly after Jem's foot was heard, and he tapped at the door, pushed it a little way, and waited.

"Come in," said Uncle Josiah, sharply.

Jem entered, doffing his cocked hat, and casting a sympathising look at Don, who raised his head. Then seeing that his employer was deeply immersed in the letter he was writing, Jem made a series of gesticulations with his hat, supplemented by some exceedingly queer grimaces, all meant as a kind of silent language, which was very expressive, but quite incomprehensible to Don.

"Well?" said Uncle Josiah, sharply.

"Beg pardon, sir! Thought you'd like to hear how we got on?"

"Well?"

"Went pretty quiet, sir, till we got about half-way there, and then he begun kicking like mad—leastways he didn't kick, because his legs was tied, but he let go all he could, and it was hard work to hold the ladder."

"And he is now safely locked up?"

"Yes, sir, and I've been thinking, sir, as he must have took that money when Master Don here was up in the warehouse along o' me."

"I daresay we shall find all out by-and-by, Wimble," said the old merchant, coldly. "That will do, now."

Jem looked uneasily at Don, as he turned his hat round to make sure which was the right way on, and moved slowly toward the door.

"Which, begging your pardon, sir, you don't think now as——"

"Well?" said the old merchant, sharply, for Jem had stopped.

"Think as Mrs. Wimble picked up any of the money, sir?"

"No, no, my man, of course not."

"Thankye, sir, I'm glad of that; and if I might make so bold, sir, about Master Don——"

"What do you wish to say, man?"

"Oh, nothing, sir, only I'm quite sure, sir, as it was all Mike Bannock's doing, and——"

"I think you had better go on with your work, Wimble, which you do understand, and not meddle with things that are beyond you."

"Certainly, sir, certainly," said Jem, quickly. "Just going, sir;" and giving Don a sympathetic look, he hurried out, but had hardly closed the door before he opened it again.

"Beg pardon, sir, Mrs. Lavington, sir, and Miss Kitty."

Don started from his stool, crimson with mortification. His mother! What would Uncle Josiah say?

Jem Wimble gave Don another look full of condolence before he closed the door, leaving Mrs. Lavington and her niece in the office.

Mrs. Lavington's face was full of anxiety and care, as she glanced from her son to her brother and back again, while Kitty's was as full of indignant reproof as she darted an angry look at Don, and then frowned and looked straight down at the floor.

"Well?" said the old merchant, coldly, "why have you come? You know I do not like you to bring Kitty here to the business place."

"I—I heard——" faltered Mrs. Lavington, who stood in great awe of her brother when he was in one of his stern moods.

"Heard? Well, what did you hear?"

"Such terrible news, Josiah."

"Well, well, what?"

"Oh, my brother!" she exclaimed, wildly, as she stepped forward and caught his hand, "tell me it is not true."

"How can I tell you what is not true when I don't know what you are talking about," cried the old man, impatiently. "My dear Laura, do you think I have not worries enough without your coming here?"

"Yes, yes; I know, dear."

"And you ought to know that I shall do what is just and right."

"I am sure of that, Josiah, but I felt obliged to come. Kitty and I were out shopping, and we met a crowd."

"Then you should have turned down a side street."

"But they were your men in the midst, and directly after I saw little Sally Wimble following."

"Oh, she was, was she?" cried the old man, glad of some one on whom to vent his spleen. "That woman goes. How dare she leave the gates when her husband is out? I shall be having the place robbed again."

"Yes, that is what she said, Josiah—that you had been robbed, and that Don—my boy—oh, no, no, no; say it is not true."

Mrs. Lavington looked wildly from one to the other, but there was a dead silence, and in a few minutes the poor woman's manner had entirely changed. When she first spoke it was as the timid, shrinking, affectionate woman; now it was as the mother speaking in defence of her child.

"I say it is not true," she cried. "You undertook to be a father to my poor boy, and now you charge him with having robbed you."

"Laura, be calm," said the old merchant, quietly; "and you had better take Kitty back home and wait."

"You have always been too stern and harsh with the poor boy," continued Mrs. Lavington, without heeding him. "I was foolish ever to come and trust to you. How dare you charge him with such a crime?"

"I did not charge him with any crime, my dear Laura" said the old merchant, gravely.

"Then it is not true?"

"It is true that I have been robbed, and that the man whom Lindon has persisted in making his companion, in spite of all I have said to the contrary, has charged him with the base, contemptible crime of robbing the master who trusted him."

"But it is not true, Josiah; and that is what you always do, treat my poor boy as if he were your servant instead of your nephew—your sister's boy."

"I treat Lindon as if he were my son when we are at home," said the old man, quietly. "When we are here at the office I treat him as my clerk, and I trust him to look after my interests, and to defend me from dishonest people."

Don looked up, and it was on his lips to say, "Indeed, uncle, I always have done so," when the old man's next words seemed to chill and harden him.

"But instead of doing his duty by me, I have constantly had to reprove him for making a companion of a man whom I weakly, and against my better judgment, allowed in the yard; and the result is I have been robbed, and this man accuses Lindon of committing the robbery, and bribing him to silence."

"But it is not true, Josiah. My son could not be guilty of such a crime."

"He will have every opportunity of disproving it before the magistrates," said Uncle Josiah, coldly.

"Magistrates!—my boy?" exclaimed Mrs. Lavington, wildly. "Oh, no, no, no, brother; you will not proceed to such extremities as these. My boy before the magistrates. Impossible!"

"The matter is out of my hands, now," said the old merchant, gravely. "I was bound to charge that scoundrel labourer with the theft. I could not tell that he would accuse your son of being the principal in the crime."

"But you will stop it now for my sake, dear. Don, my boy, why do you not speak, and beg your uncle's forgiveness?"

Don remained silent, with his brow wrinkled, his chin upon his breast, and a stubborn look of anger in his eyes, as he stood with his hands in his pockets, leaning back against his desk.

"Do you hear me, Don? Tell your uncle it is not true, and beg him to help you clear yourself from this disgrace."

The lad made no reply, merely crossing his legs, and made his shoe-buckles rasp together as he slowly moved his feet.

"Don!"

He looked up strangely, met his mother's earnest appealing gaze, and for the moment his better nature prevailed; but as he looked from her to his uncle, and saw the old man's grey eyes fixed upon him searchingly, a feeling of obstinate anger swept over him again, and made him set his teeth, as something seemed to whisper to him, "No; you told the truth, and he would not believe you. Let him prove you guilty if he can!"

It was not the first time in history that a boy had stubbornly fought against his better self, and allowed the worst part of his nature to prevail.

"Do you not hear me, Don?" cried his mother. "Why do you not speak?"

Don remained silent, and Kitty, as she looked at him, angrily uttered an impatient ejaculation.

"Don, my son, for my sake speak to your uncle. Do you not hear me?"

"Yes, mother."

"Then appeal to him to help you. Ask him to forgive you if you have done wrong."

"And she believes me guilty, too," thought Don, as he scowled at his feet.

"But you have not done wrong, my boy. I, your mother, will not believe it of you."

Don's better self began to force down that side of his mental scale.

"You may have been weak and foolish, Don, but nothing worse."

The evil scale went down now in turn, and with it the foolish, ignorant boy's heart sank low.

"Come, Don."

"I've nothing more to say, mother."

"Nothing more to say!" cried Mrs. Lavington, wildly. "Oh, yes, yes, you have much to say, my boy. Come, throw away this wilful pride and obstinacy."

"I wish I could," thought Don one moment. "It is as cruel

as it is unjust," he thought the next; and he felt more obstinately full of pride than ever.

"Don, I command you to speak," said Mrs. Lavington, whose manner now began to change; but unfortunately the stern tone she adopted had the wrong effect, and the wrinkles in the boy's face grew deeper, and the position more strained.

If Uncle Josiah, who had never had boys of his own, had come down from the lofty perch he had assumed, taken the boy's hand, and said in kindly and frank tones, "Come, Don, my boy, there are troubles enough in life, clouds sufficient to obscure too much sunshine; speak out, let's have all this over, and clear the storm away,"—if he had said something like that, Don would have melted, and all would have been well; but accustomed to manage men with an iron rule, Uncle Josiah had somehow, in spite of his straightforward, manly, and just character, seemed to repel the boy whose charge he had taken, and instead now of making the slightest advance, he said to himself, "It is not my duty to eat humble pie before the obstinate young cub. It will be a severe lesson for him, and will do him good."

So the breach widened. Don seemed to grow sulky and sullen, when he was longing to cast himself upon his mother's neck. The poor woman felt indignant at her son's conduct, and the last straw which broke the camel's back was laid on the top of the load by Kitty, who, moved by a desire to do good, made matters far worse by running across to Don, and in an impetuous way catching his hands and kissing him.

"Don, dear!" she cried.

The boy's face lit up. Here was some one who would believe him after all, and he responded to her advances by grasping her hands tightly in his.

"Do, do speak, Don dear, and beg father to forgive you," she cried. "Tell him it was a mistake, and that you will never do so again."

Don let fall her hands, the deep scowl came over his brow again, and he half turned away.

"No, no, Don, dear," she whispered; "pray don't be

obstinate. Confess that you did it, and promise father to do better in the future. He will forgive you; I know he will."

Don turned his back with an impatient gesture, and Kitty burst into tears, and went slowly to her aunt, to whose hands she clung.

"Laura, dear," said Uncle Josiah, gravely, "I think we had better bring this painful interview to an end. You may rest assured that I shall do what is just and right by Don. He shall have every opportunity for clearing himself."

"I am not guilty," cried Don, fiercely throwing back his head.

"I thought so this morning, my boy," said the old merchant, gravely. "Your conduct now is making me think very differently. Laura, I will walk home with you, if you please."

"Josiah! Don, my boy, pray, pray speak," cried Mrs. Lavington, piteously.

Don heard her appeal, and it thrilled him, but his uncle's words had raised up an obstinacy that was stronger than ever, and while longing to throw himself in his mother's arms—passionately longing so to do—his indignant pride held him back, and he stood with his head bent, as in obedience to her brother Mrs. Lavington took his arm, and allowed him to lead her out of the office, weeping bitterly the while.

Don did not look up to meet his mother's yearning gaze, but for months and years after he seemed to see that look when far away in the midst of peril, and too late he bitterly upbraided himself for his want of frankness and power to subdue his obstinate pride.

"He thinks me guilty!" he said to himself, as he stood with his head bent, listening, and unaware of the fact that some one was still in the room, till a light step came towards him, his hand was caught, and his cheek rapidly kissed.

"Kitty!"

"Coming, father."

Then there was a rapid step, the door closed, and Don stood

in the same attitude, listening to the steps on the gravel, and then to the bang of the wicket-gate.

Alone with his thoughts, and they were many and strange.

What should he do? Go right away, and—and——

"Mas' Don."

He looked up, and Jem stood at the door.

CHAPTER VI.

JEM WIMBLE TALKS SENSE.

"MAY I come in?"

Don nodded.

"The master's gone, and took the ladies 'long with him. Why, don't look like that, my lad. Your uncle don't think you took the money?"

Don nodded.

"But your mother don't, sir?"

"Yes, Jem, she believes me guilty too."

"I never did!" cried Jem, excitedly. "But sure-*lie* Miss Kitty don't?"

"Yes, Jem, they all think I'm a thief. Everybody does," cried Don, passionately.

"No, everybody don't," said Jem, fiercely; "so don't talk like that, Mas' Don. Why, even I couldn't ha' stole that money—me, as is only yard-man, and nothing o' no consequence t'other day. So if I couldn't ha' done it, I'm quite sure as you, as is a young gentleman born and bred, couldn't."

"But they think I did. Everybody thinks so."

"Tell yer everybody don't think so," cried Jem, sharply. "I don't, and as for them, they've all got dust in their eyes, that's what's the matter with them, and they can't see clear. But didn't you tell 'em as you didn't?"

"Yes, Jem," said Don, despondently; "at first."

"Then why didn't you at last, too? Here, cheer up, my lad; it'll all blow over and be forgotten, same as the row was about that sugar hogshead as I let them take away. I don't say shake hands 'cause you're like master and me only man, but I shakes hands with you in my 'art, my lad, and I says, don't be down over it."

"You couldn't shake hands with a thief, you mean, Jem," said Don, bitterly.

"Look here, Mas' Don, I can't punch your head because, as aforesaid, you're young master, and I'm only man; but for that there same what you said just now I hits you in my 'art. Thief indeed! But ah, my lad, it was a pity as you ever let Mike come into the office to tell you his lies about furren parts."

"Yes, Jem, it was."

"When you might ha' got all he told you out o' books, and the stories wouldn't ha' been quite so black."

"Ah, well, it's all over now."

"What's all over?"

"My life here, Jem. I shall go right away."

"Go? What?"

"Right away. Abroad, I think."

"And what'll your mother do?"

"Forget me, I hope. I always was an unlucky fellow Jem."

"What d'yer mean? Run away?"

"Yes, I shall go away."

"Well, that's clever, that is. Why, that's just the way to make 'em think you did it. Tshah! You stop like a man and face it out."

"When everybody believes me guilty?"

"Don't be so precious aggrawatin', my lad," cried Jem, plaintively. "Don't I keep on a-telling you that I don't believe you guilty. Why, I'd just as soon believe that I stole our sugar and sold bundles of tobacco leaves to the marine store shops."

Don shook his head.

"Well, of all the aggrawatin' chaps I ever did see, you're 'bout the worst, Mas' Don. Don't I tell you it'll be all right?"

"No, Jem, it will not be all right. I shall have to go before the magistrates."

"Well, what of that?"

"What of that?" cried Don, passionately. "Why, that scoundrel Mike will keep to his story."

"Let him!" cried Jem, contemptuously. "Why, who d ever believe him i' preference to you?"

"My uncle—my mother—my cousin."

"Not they, my boy. They don't believe it. They only think they do. They're sore just now, while it's all fresh. To-morrow by this time they will be a-hanging o' themselves round about your neck, and a-askin' of your pardon, and kissin' of you."

"No, Jem, no."

"Well, I don't mean as your uncle will be kissin' of you, of course; but he'll be sorry too, and a-shaking of your hand."

Don shook his head.

"There, don't get wagging your head like a Chinee figger, my lad. Take it like a man."

"It seems that the only thing for me to do, Jem, is to tie up a bundle and take a stick, and go and try my luck somewhere else."

"And you free and independent! Why, what would you say if you was me, tied up and married, and allus getting into trouble at home."

"Not such trouble as this, Jem."

"Not such trouble as this, my lad? Worser ever so much, for you don't deserve it, and I do, leastwise, my Sally says I do, and I suppose I do for being such a fool as to marry her."

"You ought to be ashamed to talk like that, Jem."

"So ought you, Mas' Don. I've often felt as if I should like to do as you say and run right off, but I don't do it."

"You have felt like that, Jem?" cried Don, eagerly.

"Yes, often, my lad."

"Then let's go, Jem. Nobody cares for us here. Let's go

right away to one of the beautiful foreign countries Mike told me about, and begin a new life."

"Shall us, Mas' Don?"

"Yes; why not? Get a passage in some ship, and stop where we like. He has told me of dozens of places that must be glorious."

"Then we won't go," said Jem, decidedly. "If Mike Bannock says they're fine spots, don't you believe him; they're bad uns."

"Then let's go and select a place for ourselves," cried Don.

"Lor! I do wonder at you, Mas' Don, wantin' to leave such a mother as you've got, and asking me to leave my wife. Why, what would they do?"

"I don't know," said Don, sadly. "They care very little for us now. You can do as you like; I shall go."

"Nay, nay, you won't, my lad."

"Yes, Jem, I think I shall."

"Ah, that's better! Think about it."

"I should have thought that you'd be glad to come with me, Jem."

"So I should, my lad; but there's a some'at as they calls dooty as allus seems to have hold on me tight. You wait a bit, and see how things turn out."

"But I shall have to appear before the magistrates, and be called a thief."

"Ah, well, that won't be pleasan. my lad, of course; but wait."

"Then you wouldn't go with me, Jem?"

"Don't tempt a man, Mas' Don, because I should like to go with you, and course I shouldn't like to go with you, because I shouldn't like you to go. There, I must get on with my work."

At that very moment came the call of a shrill voice—

"Jem!"

"There I told you so. She see me come in here, and she's after me because I haven't got on with my casks. Oh, how sharp she is!"

Jem gave Don an intelligent nod of the head, and moved out, while the lad stood gazing at the opposite window and listened to the sharp voice addressing the foreman of the yard.

"Poor Jem! He isn't happy either!" said Don, sadly, as the voices died away. "We might go right off abroad, and they'd be sorry then and think better of us. I wish I was ten thousand miles away."

He seated himself slowly on his stool, and rested his arms upon the desk, folding them across his chest; and then, looking straight before him at the door, his mental gaze went right through the panels, and he saw silver rivers flowing over golden sands, while trees of the most glorious foliage drooped their branches, and dipped the ends in the glancing water. The bright sun shone overhead; the tendrils and waving grass were gay with blossoms; birds of lovely plumage sang sweetly; and in the distance, on the one hand, fading away into nothingness, were the glorious blue mountains, and away to his right a shimmering sea.

Don Lavington had a fertile brain, and on the canvas of his imagination he painted panorama after panorama, all bright and beautiful. There were no clouds, no storms, no noxious creatures, no trials and dangers. All was as he thought it ought to be, and about as different from the reality as could be supposed. But Don did not know that in his youthful ignorance, and as he sat and gazed before him, he asked himself whether he had not better make up his mind to go right away.

"Yes, I will go!" he said, excitedly, as he started up in his seat.

"No," he said directly after, as in imagination now he seemed to be gazing into his mother's reproachful eyes, "it would be too cowardly; I could not go."

CHAPTER VII.

DON AND JEM GO HOME TO TEA.

IT required no little effort on Don's part to go home that afternoon to the customary meat tea which was the main meal of the day at his uncle's home.

He felt how it would be—that his uncle would not speak to him beyond saying a few distant words, such as were absolutely necessary. Kitty would avert her eyes, and his mother keep giving him reproachful looks, every one of which was a silent prayer to him to speak.

The afternoon had worn away, and he had done little work for thinking. His uncle had not been back, and at last Jem's footstep was heard outside, and he passed the window to tap lightly on the door and then open it.

"Come, Mas' Don," he said, cheerily, "going to work all night?"

"No, Jem, no. I was just thinking of going."

"That's right, my lad, because it's past shutting-up time. Feel better now, don't you?"

"No, Jem, I feel worse."

"Are you going to keep the yard open all the evening, Jem?" cried a shrill voice. "Why don't you lock up and come in to tea?"

"There! hear that!" said Jem, anxiously. "Do go, Mas' Don, or I sha'n't get to the end on it. 'Nuff to make a man talk as you do."

"Jem!"

"Here, I'm a-coming, arn't I?" he cried, giving the door a thump with his fist. "Don't shout the ware'us down!"

"Jem!"

"Now did you ever hear such a aggrawatin' woman?" cried Jem. "She's such a little un that I could pick her up, same as you do a kitten, Mas' Don—nothing on her as you may say; but the works as is inside her is that strong that I'm 'fraid of her."

"Jem!"

He opened the door with a rush.

"Ya-a-a-as!" he roared; "don't you know as Mas' Don arn't gone?"

Little Mrs. Wimble, who was coming fiercely up, flounced round, and the wind of her skirts whirled up a dust of scraps of matting and cooper's chips as she went back to the cottage.

"See that, Mas' Don? Now you think you've all the trouble in the world on your shoulders, but look at me. Talk about a woman's temper turning the milk sour in a house. Why, just now there's about three hundred hogsheads o' sugar in our ware'us—two hundred and ninety-three, and four damages not quite full, which is as good as saying three hundred—see the books whether I arn't right. Well, Mas' Don, I tell you for the truth that I quite frights it—I do, indeed—as she'll turn all that there sweetness into sour varjus 'fore she's done. Going, sir?"

"Yes, Jem, I'm going—home," said Don; and then to himself, "Ah, I wish I had a home."

"Poor Mas' Don!" said Jem, as he watched the lad go out through the gate; "he's down in the dumps now, and no mistake; and dumps is the lot o' all on us, more or less."

Then Jem went in to his tea, and Don went slowly home to his, and matters were exactly as he had foreseen. His uncle was scarcely polite; Kitty gave him sharp, indignant glances when their eyes met, and then averted hers; and from time to time his mother looked at him in so pitiful and imploring a manner that one moment he felt as if he were an utter scoundrel, and the next that he would do anything to take her in his arms and try and convince her that he was not so bad as she thought.

It was a curious mental encounter between pride, obstinacy, and the better feelings of his nature; and unfortunately the former won, for soon after the meal was over he hurried out of the room.

"I can't bear it," he cried to himself, as he went up to his own little chamber,—" I can't bear it, and I will not. Every one's against me. If I stop I shall be punished, and I can't face all that to-morrow. Good-bye, mother. Some day you'll think differently, and be sorry for all this injustice, and then——"

A tear moistened Don's eye as he thought of his mother and her tender, loving ways, and of what a pity it was that they ever came there to his uncle's, and it was not the tear that made Don see so blindly.

"I can't stand it, and I will not," he cried, passionately. "Uncle hates me, and Mike Bannock's right, scoundrel as he is. Uncle has robbed me, and I'll go and fight for myself in the world, and when I get well off I'll come back and seize him by the throat and make him give up all he has taken."

Don talked to himself a good deal more of this nonsense, and then, with his mind fully made up, he went to the chest of drawers, took out a handkerchief, spread it open upon the bed, and placed in it a couple of clean shirts and three or four pairs of stockings.

"There," he said, as he tied them up tightly as small as he could, "I won't have any more. I'll go and start fair, so that I can be independent and be beholden to nobody."

Tucking the bundle under his arm, he could not help feeling that it was a very prominent-looking package—the great checked blue and white handkerchief seeming to say, "This boy's going to seek his fortune!" and he wished that he was not obliged to take it.

But, setting his teeth, he left the room with the drawers open, and his best suit, which he had felt disposed to take, tossed on a chair, and then began to descend

It was a glorious summer evening, and though he was in dirty, smoky Bristol, everything seemed to look bright and attractive, and to produce a sensation of low-spiritedness such as he had never felt before.

He descended and passed his mother's room, and then went down more slowly, for he could hear the murmur of voices in the dining-room, which he had to pass to reach the front door, outside which he did not care what happened ; but now he had to pass that dining-room, and go along the passage and by the stand upon which his cocked hat hung.

It was nervous work, but he went on down the first flight, running his hand slowly along the hand-balustrade, all down which he had so often slid while Kitty looked on laughing, and yet alarmed lest he should fall. And what a long time ago that seemed !

He had just reached the bottom flight, and was wondering what to say if the door should open and his uncle meet him with the blue bundle under his arm, when the dining-room door did open, and he dashed back to the landing and stood in the doorway of his mother's room, listening as a step was heard upon the stairs.

"Kitty !" he said to himself, as he thrust against the door, which yielded to his pressure, and he backed in softly till he could push the door to, and stand inside, watching through the crack.

There was the light, soft step coming up and up, and his heart began to beat, he knew not why, till something seemed to rise in his throat, and made his breath come short and painfully.

His mother !

She was coming to her room, and in another moment she would be there, and would find him with the bundle under his arm, about to run away.

Quick as thought he looked sharply round, bundle in hand, when, obeying the first impulse, he was about to push it beneath the bedclothes, but cast aside the plan because he felt that it would be noticed, and quick as thought he tossed the light bundle up on the top of the great canopy of the old-fashioned bedstead, to lie among the gathering of flue and dust.

By that time the footsteps were at the door.

"What shall I say?" Don asked himself; "she will want to know why I am here."

He felt confused, and rack his brains as he would, no excuse would come.

But it was not wanted, for the light footstep with the rustle of silk passed on upstairs, and Don opened the door slightly to listen. His breath came thickly with emotion as he realised where his mother had gone. It was to his bedroom door, and as he listened he heard her tap lightly.

"Don! Don, my boy!" came in low, gentle tones.

For one moment the boy's heart prompted him to rush up and fling himself in her arms, but again his worse half suggested that he was to be scolded and disbelieved, and mentally thrusting his fingers into his ears, he stepped out, glided down the staircase in the old boyish fashion of sliding down the banister, snatched his hat from the stand, and softly stole out to hurry down the street as hard as he could go.

He had been walking swiftly some five minutes, moved by only one desire—that of getting away from the house—when he awoke to the fact that he was going straight towards the constable's quarters and the old-fashioned lock-up where Mike must be lying, getting rid of the consequences of his holiday-making that morning.

Don turned sharply round in another direction, one which led him towards the wharves where the shipping lay.

While this was taking place, Jem Wimble had been banging the doors and rattling his keys as he locked up the various stores, feeling particularly proud and self-satisfied with the confidence placed in him.

After this was done he had a wash at the pump, fetching a piece of soap from a ledge inside the workshop where the cooper's tools were kept, and when he had duly rubbed and scrubbed and dried his face and hands, he went indoors to stare with astonishment, for his little wife was making the most of her size by sitting very upright as she finished her tea.

Jem plumped himself indignantly down, and began his. This was a new annoyance. Sally had scolded times out of number, and found fault with him for being so late, but this was the first time that she had ever begun a meal without his being present, and he felt bitterly hurt.

"As if I could help it," he said, half aloud. "A man has his work to do, and he must do it."

"Five o'clock's tea-time, and you ought to have been here."

"And if I wasn't here, it was your dooty to wait for me, marm."

"Was it?" cried Sally; "then I wasn't going to. I'm not going to be ordered about and ill-treated, Jem; you always said you liked your tea ready at five o'clock. I had it ready at five o'clock, and I waited till half-past, and it's now five-and-twenty to six."

"I don't care if it's five-and-twenty to nineteen!" cried Jem angrily. "It's your dooty to wait, same as it's mine to shut up."

"You might have shut up after tea."

"Then I wasn't going to, marm."

"Then you may have your tea by yourself, for I've done, and I'm not going to be trampled upon by you."

Sally had risen in the loudness of her voice, in her temper, and in her person, for she had got up from her chair; but neither elevation was great; in fact, the personal height was very small, and there was something very kittenish and comic in her appearance, as she crossed the bright little kitchen to the door at the flight of stairs, and passing through, banged it behind her, and went up to her room.

"Very well," said Jem, as he sat staring at the door; "very well, marm. So this is being married. My father used to say that if two people as is married can't agree, they ought to divide the house between 'em, but one ought to take the outside and t'other the in. That's what I'm a-going to do,

"'HULLO, JEM, YOU HERE?'" (*p.* 63).

only, seeing what a bit of a doll of a thing you are, and being above it, I'm going to take the outside myself. There's coffee bags enough to make a man a good bed up in the ware'us, and it won't be the first time I've shifted for myself, so I shall stop away till you fetches me back. Do you hear?"

"Oh, yes, I can hear," replied Sally from the top of the stairs, Jem having shouted his last speech.

"All right, then," said Jem: "so now we understands each other and can go ahead."

Tightening up his lips, Jem rinsed out the slop-basin, shovelled in a good heap of sugar, and then proceeded to empty the teapot, holding the lid in its place with one fat finger the while.

This done, he emptied the little milk jug also, stirred all well up together, and left it for a few minutes to cool, what time he took the cottage loaf from the white, well-scrubbed trencher, pulled it in two, took a handful of bread out of one half, and raising the lump of fresh Somersetshire butter on the point of a knife, he dabbed it into the hole he had made in the centre, shut it up by replacing the other half of the bread, and then taking out his handkerchief spread it upon his knee and tied the loaf tightly therein. Then for a moment or two he hesitated about taking the knife, but finally concluding that the clasp knife in his pocket would do, he laid the blade on the table, gave his tea a final stir, gulped down the basinful, tucked the loaf in the handkerchief under his left arm, his hat very much on one side, and then walked out and through the gate, which he closed with a loud bang.

"Oh!" ejaculated Sally, who had run to the bedroom window, "he has gone!"

Sally was quite right, Jem, her husband, was gone away to his favourite place for smoking a pipe, down on the West Main wharf, where he seated himself on a stone mooring post, placed the bundle containing the loaf beside him, and then— began to eat heartily? Nothing of the kind. Jem was thinking very hard about home and his little petulant, girlish wife.

Then he started and stared.

"Hullo, Jem, you here?"

"Why, Mas' Don, I thought you was at home having your tea."

"I thought you were having yours, Jem."

"No, Mas' Don," said Jem sadly; "there's my tea"—and he pointed to the bundle handkerchief; "there's my tea; leastwise I will tell the truth, o' course—there's part on it; t'other part's inside, for I couldn't tie that up, or I'd ha' brought it same ways to have down here and look at the ships."

"Then why don't you eat it, man?"

"'Cause I can't, sir. I've had so much o' my Sally that I don't want no wittals."

Don said nothing, but sat down by Jem Wimble to look at the ships.

CHAPTER VIII.

KITTY CHRISTMAS SITS UP.

"MY dear Laura," said Uncle Josiah that same evening, "you misjudge me; Lindon's welfare is as dear to me as that of my little Kitty."

"But you seemed to be so hard and stern with him."

"That is your weak womanly way of looking at it, my dear I may have been stern, but no more so than the matter warranted. No, my dear sister, can you not see that I mean all this as a lesson for Lindon? You know how discontented he has been with his lot, like many more boys at his time of life, when they do not judge very well as to whether they are well off."

"Yes, he has been unsettled lately."

"Exactly, and this is due to his connection with that ne'er-do-weel scoundrel, for whom the boy has displayed an unconquerable liking. Lindon has begged the man on again four times after he had been discharged from the yard for drunkenness and neglect."

"I did not know this," said Mrs. Lavington.

"No, I do not bring all my business troubles home. I consented because I wished Lindon to realise for himself the kind of man whose cause he advocated; but I never expected that it would be brought home to him so severely as this."

"Then indeed, Josiah, you do not think Lindon guilty?"

"Bah! Of course not, you foolish little woman. The boy is too frank and manly, too much of a gentleman to degrade himself in such a way. Guilty? Nonsense! Guilty of being proud and obstinate and stubborn. Guilty of neglecting his work to listen to that idle scoundrel's romancing about places he has never seen."

"He is so young."

"Young? Old enough to know better."

"But if you could bring it home to him more gently."

"I think the present way is an admirable one for showing the boy his folly. The bird who kept company with the jackdaws had his neck wrung, innocent as he was. I want Lindon to see how very near he has been to having his neck wrung through keeping company with a jackdaw. Now, my dear Laura, leave it to me. The magistrates will grasp the case at once, and Master Lindon will receive a severe admonition from some one else, which will bring him to his senses, and then we shall go on quite smoothly again."

"You cannot tell how happy you have made me feel," said Mrs. Lavington, as she wept silently.

"Well," said Uncle Josiah, "I want to make you happy, you poor timid little bird. Now, then, try to believe that I am acting for the best."

"And you will not be so stern with him?"

"As far as my lights will illumine me, I will do what is right by my sister's boy, Laura—the lad I want to see grow up into a straightforward Englishman, proud of his name. There, can I say more fairly than that?"

"No. I only beg that you will think of Lindon as a high-spirited boy, who, though he does not always do as you wish, is still extremely sensitive."

"Proud and stubborn, eh, Laura?"

"I will say no more, my own brother, only leave myself in your hands."

"Yes, you may well look at the clock," said Uncle Josiah, laughing, as he put his arm round his sister, and kissed her very tenderly; "the young dog is unconscionably late."

"You do not think—after what I said?"

"Think? Nonsense. No, no. Lindon is *too* manly for that. Here, I am sure that you have a terrible headache, and you are worn out. Go to bed, and I'll sit up for the young rascal, and have a talk to him when he comes in."

"No, no!" exclaimed Mrs. Lavington excitedly; "I do not like you to sit up for him. I will."

"Not you. Too tired out as it is. No, my dear, you shall go to bed, and I will sit up for him."

"Then let neither of us sit up."

"Afraid I shall scold him, eh?"

"I cannot help being afraid of something of the kind, dear."

"Very well, then we will both go, and let Jessie sit up."

The maid was rung for, and entered.

"We are going to bed, Jessie. Master Lindon has not returned yet. You will sit up until he comes in."

"Yes, sir."

The maid left the room, and brother and sister sat looking at each other.

"Did you speak, Josiah?" said Mrs. Lavington.

"No; I was only thinking that I do not trust you and you don't trust me."

"What do you mean?" faltered the poor woman, who looked more agitated now.

"You were not going to bed, but to listen for Lindon's return, and were then going to watch whether I left my room to talk to him."

Mrs. Lavington was silent.

"Guilty," said Uncle Josiah, smiling. "Come now, fair play. Will you go to your room and promise to stay there till breakfast time to-morrow morning, if I give you my word to do the same?"

"Yes," said the shrinking woman eagerly.

"That's agreed to, then. Good-night, Laura, my dear."

"Good-night, Josiah."

Ten minutes after all was still in the house, but matters did not turn out quite as Uncle Josiah intended. For before he was undressed, a bedroom door was opened very gently, and the creak it gave produced a low ejaculation of dismay.

Then there was five minutes' interval before a slight little figure stole gently downstairs and glided into the kitchen, where round red-faced Jessie was seated in a window, her chair being opposite to what looked like a lady's back, making the most careful bows from time to time, to which the lady made no response, for it was only Jessie's cloak hanging on a peg with her old bonnet just above.

The slight little figure stood in the kitchen doorway listening, and then Jessie seemed to be bowing her head to the fresh comer, who did take some notice of the courtesy, for, crossing the kitchen rapidly, there was a quick sharp whisper.

"Jessie, Jessie!"

No reply.

"Jessie, Jessie!"

"Two new and one stale," said the maid.

"Oh, how tiresome! Jessie, Jessie!"

"Slack baked."

"Jessie!" and this time there was a shake of the maid's shoulder, and she jumped up, looking startled.

"Lor, Miss Kitty, how you frightened me!"

"You were asleep."

"Sleep? Me, miss? That I'm sure I wasn't."

"You were, Jessie, and I heard father tell you to sit up till Cousin Lindon came home."

"Well, that's what I'm adoin' of, miss, as plain as I can," said Jessie.

She spoke in an ill-used tone, for it had been a busy day consequent upon a certain amount of extra cleaning, but Kitty did not notice it.

"I shall stay till I hear my cousin's knock," she said; "and then run upstairs. I hope he will not be long."

"So do I, Miss Kitty," said the woman with a yawn. "What's made him so late? Is it because of the trouble at the yard?"

"Yes, Jessie; but you must not talk about it."

"But I heerd as Master Don took some money."

"He did not, Jessie!" cried Kitty indignantly. "There isn't a word of truth in it. My Cousin Lindon couldn't have done such a thing. It's all a mistake, and I want to see him come in, poor boy, and tell him that I don't believe it. I'll whisper it to him just as he's going up to bed, and it will make him happy, for I know he thinks I have gone against him, and I only made believe that I did."

Snurrrg!

The sound was very gentle, and Kitty did not hear it, for she was looking intently toward the door in the belief that she had heard Don's footstep.

But it was only that of some passer on his way home, and Kitty went on,—

"You mustn't talk about it, Jessie, for it is a great trouble, and aunt is nearly heart-broken, and——"

Snurg-urg!

This time there was so loud and gurgling a sound that Kitty turned sharply upon the maid, who, after emitting a painful snore, made her young mistress the most polite of bows.

"Jessie! you're asleep."

Snurrg! and a bow.

"Oh, Jessie, you're asleep again. How can you be so tiresome?"

Snurrg! gurgled Jessie again, and Kitty gave an impatient stamp of her little foot.

"How can any one sleep at a time like this?" she half sobbed. "It's too bad, that it is."

Jessie bowed to her politely, and her head went up and down as if it were fixed at the end of a very easy moving spring, but when Kitty reproached her the words had not the slightest effect, and a dull stupid stare was given, of so irritating a nature that some people would have felt disposed to awaken the sleeper by administering a sound slap upon the hard round cheek.

One hour, two hours, three hours passed away, and still no Don; and at last, unable to bear the company of the snoring woman longer, Kitty left her and went into the drawing-room, where, kneeling down at the end of the couch under the window, she remained watching the dark street, waiting for him who did not come.

Kitty watched till the street began to look less dark and gloomy, and by degrees the other side became so plain that she could make out the bricks on the opposite walls.

Then they grew plainer and plainer, and there was a bright light in the sky, for the sun was near to its rising.

Then they grew less plain, then quite indistinct, for Kitty was crying bitterly, and she found herself wondering whether Don could have come in and gone to bed.

A little thought told her that this was impossible, and the tears fell faster still.

Where could he be? What could he be doing? Ought she to awaken her aunt?

Kitty could not answer these self-imposed questions, and as her misery and despair grew greater it seemed as if the morning was growing very cold and the bricks of the houses opposite more and more obscure, and then soon after they were quite invisible, for she saw them not.

CHAPTER IX.

A SOCIAL THUNDERBOLT.

"MORNING!" said Uncle Josiah, as, after a turn up and down the dining-room, he saw the door open and his sister enter, looking very pale and red-eyed. "Why, Laura, you have not been to bed."

"Yes," she said sadly. "I kept my word, and now I feel sorry that I did, for I fell into a heavy sleep from which I did not wake till half an hour ago.'

"Glad of it," said her brother bluffly. "That's right, my dear, make the tea; I want my breakfast, for I have plenty of work to-day."

Mrs. Lavington hastily made the tea, for the urn was hissing on the table when she came down, Uncle Josiah's orders being that it was always to be ready at eight o'clock, and woe betide Jessie if it was not there.

"Have—have you seen Don this morning?"

"No. And when he comes down I shall not say a word. There, try and put a better face on the matter, my dear. He will have to appear at the magistrate's office, and there will be a few admonitions. That's all. Isn't Kitty late?"

"Yes. Shall I send up for her?"

"No; she will be down in a few minutes, I daresay, and Lindon too."

The few minutes passed, and Uncle Josiah looked stern. Then he rang for the servants, and his brow grew more heavy. Neither Kitty nor Lindon down to prayers.

"Shall I send up, Josiah?"

"No; they know what time we have prayers," said the old man sternly; and upon the servants entering he read his customary chapter and the prayers, but no one stole in while the service was in progress, and when it was over the old merchant looked more severe than ever.

Mrs. Lavington looked more troubled as her brother grew more severe, but she did not speak, feeling that she might make matters worse.

Just then Jessie brought in the ham and eggs, and as she took off the cover, and Mrs. Lavington began to pour out tea, the old man said roughly,—

"Go and tell Miss Kitty to come down to breakfast directly."

The maid left the room.

"You did not send a message to Don, Josiah."

"No. I suppose his lordship was very late. No business to have gone out."

Uncle Josiah began his breakfast. Mrs. Lavington could not taste hers.

Then Jessie entered, looking startled.

"If you please, sir——"

"Well, if you please what?"

"Miss Kitty, sir."

"Yes?"

"She's not in her room."

"Eh?" ejaculated the old merchant. "Humph! come down and gone for a walk, I suppose. Back soon."

The breakfast went on, but there was no Kitty, no Don, and Uncle Josiah began to eat his food ferociously.

At last he got up and rang the bell sharply, and Jessie responded.

"What time did Master Lindon come home?" he said.

"Come home, sir?"

"Yes; did I not speak plainly? I said what time did Master Lindon come home?"

"Please, sir, he didn't come home at all."

"What!" roared Uncle Josiah, and Mrs. Lavington nearly let her cup fall.

"Please, sir, I sat in my chair waiting all the night."

"And he has not been back?"

"No, sir."

"Nonsense! Go and knock at his door. Tell him to come at once."

"Excuse me, Josiah," said Mrs. Lavington excitedly; "let me go."

Uncle Josiah grunted his consent, and Mrs. Lavington hurried out into the hall, and then upstairs.

"Slipped in while you were half asleep," said the old man to Jessie.

"No, sir, indeed. I've been watching carefully all night."

"Humph! There's half a crown for you to buy a hat ribbon, Jessie. Well," he continued as his sister entered hastily, "what does he say?"

"Josiah!" cried the trembling woman, "what does this mean? Don was out when I went up yesterday evening, and he has not been to his room all night."

"What?"

"Neither has Kitty been to hers."

Uncle Josiah thrust back his chair, and left his half-eaten breakfast.

"Look here," he exclaimed in a hoarse voice; "what nonsense is this?"

"No nonsense, Josiah," cried Mrs. Lavington. "I felt a presentiment."

"Felt a stuff and nonsense!" he said angrily. "Kitty not in her room? Kitty not been to bed? Here, Jessie!"

"Yes, sir."

"You did go to sleep, didn't you?"

"Ye—e—e—s, sir!"

"I thought as much, and"—here tut-tut-tut—"that would not explain it. Hullo, what do you want?"

This was to the cook, who tapped, opened the door, and then held up her hand as if to command silence.

"Please, 'm, would you mind coming here?" she said softly.

Mrs. Lavington ran to the door, followed the woman across

the hall, unaware of the fact that the old merchant was close at her heels.

They paused as soon as they were inside the drawing-room, impressed by the scene before them, for there, half sitting, half lying, and fast asleep, with the tears on her cheeks still wet, as if she had wept as she lay there unconscious, was Kitty, for the bricks on the opposite wall had been too indistinct for her to see.

"Don't wake her," said Uncle Josiah softly, and he signed to them to go back into the hall, where he turned to Jessie.

"Did you see Miss Kitty last night?"

"Ye—es, sir."

"Where?"

"She comed into the kitchen, sir."

"After we had gone to bed?"

"Yes, sir."

"And you said nothing just now?"

"No, sir, I didn't like to."

"That will do. Be off," said the old man sternly. "Laura. Here!"

Mrs. Lavington followed her brother back into the dining-room.

"The poor child must have been sitting up to watch for Lindon's return."

"And he has not returned, Josiah," sobbed Mrs. Lavington.

"Here, stop! What are you going to do?"

"I am going up to his room to see," said the sobbing woman.

Uncle Josiah made no opposition, for he read the mother's thought, and followed her upstairs, where a half-open drawer told tales, and in a few moments Mrs. Lavington had satisfied herself.

"I cannot say exactly," she said piteously; "but he has made up a bundle of his things."

"The coward!" cried Uncle Josiah fiercely.

"Gone! gone! My poor boy!"

"Hush!" cried the old man sternly. "He has sneaked off

like a contemptible cur. No, I will not believe it of him," he added impetuously. "Lindon has too much stuff in him to play such a despicable part. You are wrong, Laura. Come down and finish breakfast. I will not believe it of the boy."

"But he has gone, Josiah, he has gone," sobbed his sister.

"Then if he has, it is the yielding to a sudden impulse, and as soon as he comes to his senses he will return. Lindon will not be such a coward, Laura. Mark my words."

"You are saying this to comfort me," said Mrs. Lavington sadly.

"I am saying what I think," cried her brother. "If I thought he had gone right off, I would say so, but I do not think anything of the kind. He may have thought of doing so last night, but this morning he will repent and come back."

He took his sister's hand gently, and led her downstairs, making her resume her place at the table, and taking his own again, as he made a pretence of going on with his breakfast; but before he had eaten his second mouthful there was a dull heavy thump at the front door.

"There!" cried the old man; "what did I say? Here he is."

Before the front door could be opened, Kitty, who had been awakened by the knock, came in looking scared and strange.

"Don," she said; "I have been asleep. Has he come back?"

"Yes I think this is he," said the old man gently. "Come here, my pet; don't shrink like that. I'm not angry."

"If you please, sir," said Jessie, "here's a woman from the yard."

"Mrs. Wimble?"

"Yes, sir; and can she speak to you a minute?"

"Yes, I'll come—no, show her in here. News. An ambassador, Laura," said the old man with a grim smile, as Jessie went out. "There, Kitty, my dear, don't cry. It will be all right soon."

At that moment little Mrs. Wimble entered, white cheeked,

red eyed, limp and miserable looking, the very opposite of the trim little Sally who lorded it over her patient husband.

"Mrs. Wimble!" cried Mrs. Lavington, catching the little woman's arm excitedly; "you have brought some news about my son."

"No," moaned Sally, with a passionate burst of sobs. "Went out tea-time, and never come back all night."

"Yes, yes, we know that," said Uncle Josiah sternly; "but how did you know?"

"Know, sir? I've been sitting up for him all this dreadful night."

"What, for my nephew?"

"No, sir, for my Jem."

"Lindon—James Wimble!" said Uncle Josiah, as he sank back in his seat. "Impossible! It can't be true."

CHAPTER X.

GONE!

"SPEAK, woman!" cried Mrs. Lavington hoarsely; and she shook little Sally by the arm. "What do you mean?"

"I don't know, ma'am. I'm in such trouble," sobbed Sally. "I've been a very, very wicked girl—I mean woman. I was always finding fault, and scolding him."

"Why?" asked Uncle Josiah sternly.

"I don't know, sir."

"But he is a quiet industrious man, and I'm sure he is a good husband."

"Yes, he's the best of husbands," sobbed Sally.

"Then why did you scold him?"

"Because I was so wicked, I suppose. I couldn't help it, sir."

"But you think he has run away?"

"Yes, sir; I'm sure of it. He said he would some day if I was so cruel, and that seemed to make me more cruel, and—and—he has gone."

"It is impossible!" said Uncle Josiah. "He must have met with some accident."

"No, sir, he has run away and left me. He said he would. I saw him go—out of the window, and he took a bundle with him, and—and—what shall I do? what shall I do?"

"Took a bundle?" said Uncle Josiah, starting.

"Yes, sir, and—and I wish I was dead."

"Silence, you foolish little woman! How dare you wish

such a thing? Stop; listen to what I say. Did my nephew Lindon come to the yard last night?"

"No, sir; but him and my Jem were talking together for ever so long in the office, and I couldn't get Jem away."

Uncle Josiah gave vent to a low whistle.

"Please ask Master Don what my Jem said."

"Do you not understand, my good woman, that my son has not been home all night?" said Mrs. Lavington, piteously.

"What? not been home?" cried Sally, sharply. "Then they're gone off together."

Uncle Josiah drew a long breath.

"That Master Don was always talking to my poor Jem, and he has persuaded him, and they're gone."

"It is not true!" cried Kitty in a sharp voice as she stood by the table, quivering with anger. "If Cousin Don has gone away, it is your wicked husband who has persuaded him. Father, dear, don't let them go; pray, pray fetch them back."

Uncle Josiah's brow grew more rugged, and there were hard lines about his lips, till his sister laid her hand upon his arm, when he started, and took her hand, looking sadly down in her face.

"You hear what Kitty says," whispered Mrs. Lavington; "pray—pray fetch them back."

Little Mrs. Wimble heard her words, and gave the old merchant an imploring look.

But the old man's face only grew more hard.

"I am afraid it must be true," he said. "Foolish boy! Woman, your husband has behaved like an idiot."

"But you will send and fetch them back, Josiah."

"Don't talk nonsense, Laura," said the old man angrily. "How can I fetch them back? Foolish boy! At a time like this. Is he afraid to face the truth?"

"No, no, Josiah," cried Mrs. Lavington; "it is only that he was hurt."

"Hurt? He has hurt himself. That man will be before the magistrates to-day, and I passed my word to the constable that Lindon should be present to answer the charge made against him."

"Yes, dear, and he has been thoughtless. But you will forgive him, and have him brought back."

"Have him brought back!" cried Uncle Josiah fiercely. "What can I do? The law will have him brought back now."

"What? Oh, brother, don't say that!"

"I must tell you the truth," said Uncle Josiah sternly. "It is the same as breaking faith, and he has given strength to that scoundrel's charge."

"But what shall I do?" sobbed little Sally Wimble. "My Jem hadn't done anything. Oh, please, sir, fetch him back."

"Your husband has taken his own road, my good woman," said Uncle Josiah coldly, "and he must suffer for it."

"But what's to become of me, sir? What shall I do without a husband?"

"Go back home and wait."

"But I have no home, sir, now," sobbed Sally. "You'll want the cottage for some other man."

"Go back home and wait."

"But you'll try and fetch him back, sir?"

"I don't know what I shall do yet," said the old man sternly. "I'm afraid I do not know the worst. There, go away now. Who's that?"

There was a general excitement, for a loud knock was heard at the door.

Jessie came in directly after, looking round eyed and staring.

"Well, what is it?" said Uncle Josiah.

"If you please, sir, Mr. Smithers the constable came, and I was to tell you that you're to be at the magistrate's office at eleven, and bring Master Don with you."

"Yes," said Uncle Josiah bitterly; "at the magistrate's office at eleven, and take Lindon with me. Well, Laura, what have you to say to that?"

Mrs. Lavington gave him an imploring look.

"Try and find him," she whispered, "for my sake."

"Try and find him!" he replied angrily. "I was willing to

look over everything—to try and fight his battle and prove to the world that the accusation was false."

"Yes, yes, and you will do so now—Josiah—brother."

"I cannot," said the old man sternly. "He has disgraced me, and openly declared to the world that the accusation of that scoundrel is true."

CHAPTER XI.

THINKING BETTER OF IT.

DON stood looking at Jem Wimble for some few minutes in silence, as if the sight of some one else in trouble did him good. Then he sat down on the stock of an old anchor, to begin picking at the red rust scales as he too stared at the ships moored here and there.

The tall masts and rigging had a certain fascination for Don, and each vessel seemed to offer a way out of his difficulties. For once on board a ship with the sails spread, and the open sea before him, he might cross right away to one of those beautiful lands of which Mike had spoken, and then——

The thought of Mike altered the case directly, and he sat staring straight before him at the ships.

Jem was the next to break the silence.

"Thinking you'd like to go right away, Master Don?"

"Yes, Jem."

"So was I, sir. Only think how nice it would be somewhere abroad, where there was no Sally."

"And no Uncle Josiah, Jem."

"Ay, and no Mike to get you into trouble. Be fine, wouldn't it?"

"Glorious, Jem."

"Mean to go, Master Don?"

"What, and be a miserable coward? No."

"But you was a-thinking something of the kind, sir."

"Yes, I was, Jem. Everybody is stupid sometimes, and I was stupid then. No. I've thought better of it."

"And you won't go, sir?"

"Go? No. Why, it would be like saying what Mike accused me of was true."

"So it would, sir. Now that's just how I felt. I says to myself, 'Jem,' I says, 'don't you stand it. What you've got to do is to go right away and let Sally shift for herself; then she'd find out your vally,' I says, 'and be sorry for what she's said and done;' but I knew if I did she'd begin to crow and think she'd beat me, and besides, it would be such a miserable cowardly trick. No, Mas' Don, I'm going to grin and bear it, and some day she'll come round and be as nice as she's nasty now."

"Yes, that's the way to look at it, Jem; but it's a miserable world, isn't it?"

"Well, I arn't seen much on it, Mas' Don. I once went for a holiday as far as Bath, and that part on it was miserable enough. My word, how it did rain! In half an hour I hadn't got a dry thread on me. Deal worse than Bristol, which isn't the most cheersome o' places when you're dull."

"No, Jem, it isn't. Of course you'll be at the court tomorrow?"

"I suppose so, Mas' Don. And I say they'd better ask me if I think you took that money. My! but I would give it to some on 'em straight. Can you fight, Mas' Don?"

"I don't know, Jem. I never tried."

"I can. You don't know what a crack I could give a man. It's my arms is so strong with moving sugar hogsheads, I suppose. I shouldn't wish to be the man I hit if I did my best."

"You mean your worst, Jem."

"Course I do, Mas' Don. Well, as I was going to say, I should just like to settle that there matter with Mr. Mike without the magistrates. You give him to me on a clear field for about ten minutes, and I'd make Master Mike down hisself on his knees, and say just whatever I pleased."

"And what good would that do, Jem?"

"Not much to him, Mas' Don, because he'd be so precious

6

sore afterwards, but it would do me good, and I would feel afterwards what I don't feel now, and that's cheerful. Never mind, sir, it'll all come right in the end. Nothing like coming out and sitting all alone when you're crabby. Wind seems to blow it away. When you've been sitting here a bit you'll feel like a new man. Mind me smoking a pipe?"

"No, Jem; smoke away."

"Won't have one too, Mas' Don?"

"No, Jem; you know I can't smoke."

"Then here goes for mine," said Jem, taking a little dumpy clay pipe from one pocket and a canvas bag from another, in which were some rough pieces of tobacco leaf. These he crumbled up and thrust into the bowl, after which he took advantage of the shelter afforded by an empty cask to get in, strike a light, and start a pipe.

Once lit up, Jem returned to his old seat, and the pair remained in the same place till it was getting dusk, and lights were twinkling among the shipping, when Jem rose and stretched himself.

"That's your sort, Mas' Don," he said. "Now I feels better, and I can smile at my little woman when I get home. You aren't no worse?"

"No, Jem, I am no worse."

"Nothing like coming out when you're red hot, and cooling down. I'm cooled down, and so are you. Come along."

Don felt a sensation of reluctance to return home, but it was getting late, and telling himself that he had nothing to do now but act a straightforward manly part, and glad that he had cast aside his foolish notions about going away, he trudged slowly back with his companion, till turning into one of the dark and narrow lanes leading from the water side, they suddenly became aware that they were not alone, for a stoutly built sailor stepped in front of them.

"Got a light, mate?" he said.

"Light? Yes," said Jem readily; and he prepared to get out his flint and steel, when Don whispered something in his ear.

"Ay, to be sure," he said; "why don't you take a light from him?"

"Eh? Ah, to be sure," said the sailor. "I forgot. Here, Joe, mate, open the lanthorn and give us a light."

Another sailor, a couple of yards away, opened a horn lanthorn, and the first man bent down to light his pipe, the dull rays of the coarse candle showing something which startled Don.

"Come on, Jem," he whispered; "make haste."

"Ay? To be sure, my lad. There's nothing to mind though. Only sailors."

As he spoke there were other steps behind, and more from the front, and Don realised that they were hemmed in that narrow lane between two little parties of armed men.

Just then the door of the lanthorn was closed, and the man who bore it held it close to Jem's face.

"Well?" said that worthy, good-temperedly, "what d'yer think of me, eh? Lost some one? 'cause I arn't him."

"I don't know so much about that," said a voice; and a young-looking man in a heavy pea jacket whispered a few words to one of the sailors.

Don felt more uneasy, for he saw that the point of a scabbard hung down below the last speaker's jacket, which bulged out as if there were pistols beneath, all of which he could dimly make out in the faint glow of the lanthorn.

"Come away, Jem, quick!" whispered Don.

"Here, what's your hurry, my lads?" said the youngish man in rather an authoritative way. "Come and have a glass of grog."

"No, thank ye," said Jem; "I've got to be home."

"So have we, mate," said the hoarse-voiced man who had asked for a light; "and when a horficer asks you to drink you shouldn't say no."

"I knew it, Jem," whispered Don excitedly. "Officer! do you hear?"

"What are you whispering about, youngster?" said the man in the pea jacket. "You let him be."

"Good-night," said Jem shortly. "Come on, Mas' Don."

He stepped forward, but the young man hurried on the men, who had now closed in round them; and as Jem gave one of them a sturdy push to get off, the thrust was returned with interest.

"Where are you shovin' to, mate?" growled the man. "Arn't the road wide enough for you?"

"Quiet, my lad," said the officer sharply. "Here, you come below here and have a glass of grog,"

"I don't want no grog," said Jem; "and I should thank you to tell your men to let me pass."

"Yes, by-and-by," said the officer. "Now then, my lads, sharp."

A couple of men crowded on Jem, one of them forcing himself between the sturdy fellow and Don, whose cheeks flushed with anger as he felt himself rudely thrust up against the wall of one of the houses.

"Here, what are you doing of?" cried Jem sharply.

"Being civil," said one of the men with a laugh. "There, no nonsense. Come quiet."

He might just as well have said that to an angry bull, for as he and his companion seized Jem by the arms, they found for themselves how strong those arms were, one being sent staggering against Don, and the other being lifted off his legs and dropped upon his back.

"Now, Mas' Don, run!" shouted Jem.

But before the words were well out of his lips, the party closed in upon him, paying no heed to Don, who in accordance with Jem's command had rushed off in retreat.

A few moments later he stopped, for Jem was not with him, but struggling with all his might in the midst of the knot of men who were trying to hold him.

"Mas' Don! Help, help!" roared Jem; and Don dashed at the gang, his fists clenched, teeth set, and a curious singing noise in his ears. But as he reached the spot where his companion was making a desperate struggle for his liberty, Jem shouted again,—

"No, no! Mas' Don; run for it, my lad, and get help if you can."

Like a flash it occurred to Don that long before he could get help Jem would be overpowered and carried off, and with the natural fighting instinct fully raised, he struck out with all his might as he strove to get to the poor fellow, who was writhing and heaving, and giving his captors a tremendous task to hold him.

"Here, give him something to keep him quiet," growled a voice.

"No, no; get hold of his hands; that's right. Serve this cockerel the same. Down with him, quick!" cried the officer sharply; and in obedience to his words the men hung on to poor Jem so tenaciously that he was dragged down on the rough pavement, and a couple of men sat panting upon him while his wrists were secured, and his voice silenced by a great bandage right over his mouth.

"You cowards!" Jem tried to roar, as, breathless with exertion, bleeding from a sharp back-handed blow across the mouth, and giddy with excitement and the effects of a rough encounter between his head and the wall, Don made one more attempt to drag himself free, and then stood panting and mastered by two strong men.

"Show the light," said the officer, and the lanthorn was held close to Don's face.

"Well, if the boy can fight like that," said the officer, "he shall."

"Let us go," cried Don. "Help! he——"

A jacket was thrown over his head, as the officer said mockingly,—

"He shall fight for his Majesty the king. Now, my lads, quick. Some one coming, and the wrong sort."

Don felt himself lifted off his feet, and half smothered by the hot jacket which seemed to keep him from breathing, he was hurried along two or three of the lanes, growing more faint and dizzy every moment, till in the midst of a curious nightmare-like sensation, lights began suddenly to dance before his eyes; then all was darkness, and he knew no more till he seemed to wake up from a curious sensation of sickness, and to be listening to Jem Wimble, who would keep on saying in a stupid, aggravating manner,—

"Mas' Don, are you there?"

The question must have been repeated many times before Don could get rid of the dizzy feeling of confusion and reply,—

"Yes; what do you want?"

"Oh, my poor lad!" groaned Jem. "Here, can you come to me and untie this?"

"Jem!"

"Yes."

"What does it mean? Why is it so dark? Where are we?"

"Don't ask everything at once, my lad, and I'll try to tell you."

"Has the candle gone out, Jem? Are we in the big cellar?"

"Yes, my lad," groaned Jem, "we're in a big cellar."

"Can't you find the candle?" said Don, with his head humming and the mental confusion on the increase. "There's a flint and steel on the ledge over the door."

"Is there, my lad? I didn't know it," muttered Jem.

"Jem, are you there?"

"Yes, yes, my lad, I'm here."

"Get a light, quick. I must have fallen and hurt myself; my face bleeds."

"Oh, my poor dear lad!"

"Eh? What do you mean? You're playing tricks, Jem, and it's too bad. Get a light."

"My hands is tied fast behind me, Mas' Don," groaned Jem, "and we're pitched down here in a cellar."

"What?"

"Oh, dear! oh, dear! I don't mind for myself," groaned Jem, in his despair, "but what will she do?"

"Jem!"

"I often said I wished I could be took away, but I didn't

mean it, Mas' Don; I didn't mean it. What will my Sally do?"

"Jem, are you mad?" shouted Don. "This darkness—this cellar. It's all black, and I can't think; my head aches, and it's all strange. Don't play tricks. Try and open the door and let's go."

"What, don't you know what it all means, Mas' Don?" groaned Jem.

"No, I don't seem as if I could think. What does it mean?"

"Mean, my lad? Why, the press-gang's got us, and unless we can let 'em know at home, we shall be took aboard ship and sent off to sea."

"What?"

The light had come—the mental light which drove away the cloud of darkness which had obscured Don Lavington's brain. He could think now, and he saw once more the dark lane, the swinging lanthorn, and felt, as it were, the struggle going on; and then, sitting up with his hands to his throbbing head, he listened to a low moaning sound close at hand.

"Jem," he said. "Jem! Why don't you speak?"

There was no answer, for it was poor Jem's turn now; the injuries he had received in his desperate struggle for liberty had had their effect, and he lay there insensible to the great trouble which had come upon him, while it grew more terrible to Don, in the darkness of that cellar, with every breath he drew.

CHAPTER XII.

PRISONERS.

"WHAT'S the matter?" cried Don, starting up, as there was the sound of bolts being shot back, and a light shone in upon the darkness.

Don could hardly believe it possible, but it was quite true. In spite of pain and anxiety, weariness had mastered him, and he had been asleep.

As the light shone in, Don could see Jem lying, apparently asleep, but in a very uncomfortable position, and that they were in a low, arched cellar, one which at some time had been used for storing casks; for in one corner there were some mouldy staves, and, close by, a barrel, whose hoops seemed to have slipped down, so that it was in a state of collapse.

He had no time to see more, for half a dozen well-armed sailors came in after a bluff-looking man, who crossed at once to the prisoners.

"Hold the lanthorn here," he said sharply. "Now let's have a look at you."

He examined their injuries in an experienced way, roughly, but not unkindly.

"All right, my lad," he said to Don; "you will not die this time. Now you."

He spent longer over Jem, who roused up and looked at him curiously, as if he did not quite understand.

"Been rather rough with this one, my lads."

"Couldn't help it," said one of the sailors; "he fote so hard. So did this young chap too."

"Nothing wrong with him, I daresay," said the bluff man. "No bones broken. All right in a day or two."

Don had been silent while Jem was examined, for he felt that this man was either a doctor, or one who knew something about surgery; but as soon as he had finished, the boy, whose indignation had been growing, turned to him haughtily.

"Now, sir!" he exclaimed, "have the goodness to explain the meaning of this outrage."

"Cock-a-doodle-doo!" cried the bluff man.

"It is nothing to laugh at, sir. I insist upon knowing why we have been ill-used and dragged here by your men."

"Well crowed, my young cockerel," said the bluff man, laughing. "They said you fought well with your fists, so you can with your tongue."

"Insulting us now you have us down will not save you," cried Don fiercely.

"No, my lord," said the bluff man, as Jem rose up, shook his head, and stood by Don.

The men laughed.

"You coward!" cried Don in hot anger; "but you shall all suffer for it. My uncle will set the law to work, and have you all punished."

"Really, this is growing serious," said the bluff man in mock alarm.

"You will find it no laughing matter. You have made a mistake this time; so now let us go at once."

"Well, I would with pleasure, my noble captain," said the bluff man, with mock solemnity; "but his Majesty is in sore need just now of some dashing young fellows who can fight; and he said to our first lieutenant, 'Short of men, Mr. Morrison? Dear me, are you? Well then, the best thing you can do is to send round Bristol city, and persuade a few of the brave and daring young fellows there to come on board my good ship *Great Briton*, and help me till I've settled my quarrel with my enemies;' so we have persuaded you."

"You are adding insult to what you have done, sir. Now

let us pass. You and your miserable press-gang shall smart for this. Stand aside, sir."

"What, after taking all this trouble? Hardly."

"Here, I'm all right again now, Mas' Don. Press-gang, eh?" cried Jem. "Here, let me get at him."

Jem made a dash at the bluff man, but his arms were seized, and he was held back, struggling hard.

"Ah, I wish we had fifty of you," said the bluff man. "Don't hurt him, my lads. There, there, steady; you can't do anything. That will do. Save your strength to fight for the king."

"You cowards!" cried Jem, who suddenly turned so faint that the men easily mastered him, laid him on his back, and one held him down, while another held Don till the rest had passed out, the bluff man only standing at the entrance with another holding up the light.

"Come along," he shouted; and the man who held Jem left him, and ran out.

"Do you hear?" cried the bluff man again. "Come along!"

"How can I, when he's sticking on like a rat?" growled the man who held Don. "Did you ever see such a young ruffian?"

The bluff man took a stride or two forward, gripped Don by the shoulder, and forced him from his hold.

"Don't be a young fool," he said firmly, but not unkindly. "It's plucky, but it's no good. Can't you see we're seven to one?"

"I don't care if you're a hundred," raged Don, struggling hard, but vainly.

"Bravo, boy! That's right; but we're English, and going to be your messmates. Wait till you get at the French; then you may talk like that."

He caught Don by the hips, and with a dexterous Cornish wrestling trick, raised him from the ground, and then threw him lightly beside Jem.

"You'll do," he said. "I thought we'd let you go, because

you're such a boy, but you've got the pluck of a man, and you'll soon grow."

He stepped quickly to the entrance, and Don struggled to his feet, and dashed at him again, but only flung himself against the door, which was banged in his face, and locked.

"The cowards!" panted Don, as he stood there in the darkness. "Why, Jem!"

"Yes, Mas' Don."

"They won't let us go."

"No, Mas' Don, that they won't."

"I never thought the press-gang would dare to do such a thing as this."

"I did, sir. They'd press the monkeys out of a wild beast show if they got the chance."

"But what are we to do?"

"I d' know, sir."

"We must let my uncle know at once."

"Yes, sir, I would," said Jem grimly; "I'd holloa."

"Don't be stupid. What's the good?"

"Not a bit, sir."

"But my uncle—my mother, what will they think?"

"I'll tell yer, sir."

"Yes?"

"They'll think you've run away, so as not to have to go 'fore the magistrates."

"Jem, what are you saying? Think I'm a thief?"

"I didn't say that, sir; but so sure as you don't go home, they'll think you've cut away."

"Jem!" cried Don in a despairing voice, as he recalled the bundle he had made up, and the drawer left open.

"Well, sir, you was allus a-wanting to go abroad, and get away from the desk," said Jem ill-naturedly—"oh, how my head do ache!—and now you've got your chance."

"But that was all nonsense, Jem. I was only thinking then like a stupid, discontented boy. I don't want to go. What will they say?"

"Dunno what they'll say," said Jem dolefully, "but I know

what my Sally will say. I used to talk about going and leaving her, but that was because I too was a hidyut. I didn't want to go and leave her, poor little lass. Too fond on her, Mas' Don. She only shows a bit o' temper."

"Jem, she'll think you've run away and deserted her."

"Safe, Mas' Don. You see, I made up a bundle o' witties as if I was a-going, and she saw me take it out under my arm, and she called to me to stop, but I wouldn't, because I was so waxy."

"And I made up a bundle too, Jem. I—I did half think of going away."

"Then you've done it now, my lad. My Sally will think I've forsook her."

"And they at home will think of me as a thief. Oh, fool—fool—fool!"

"What's the use o' calling yourself a fool, Mas' Don, when you means me all the time? Oh, my head, my head!

"Jem, we must escape."

"Escape? I on'y wish we could. Oh, my head: how it do ache."

"They will take us off to the tender, and then away in some ship, and they will not know at home where we are gone Jem, get up."

"What's the good, sir? My head feels like feet, and if I tried to stand up I should go down flop!"

"Let me help you, Jem. Here, give me your hand. How dark it is? Where's your hand?"

"Gently, my lad; that's my hye. Arn't much use here in the dark, but may want 'em by-and-by. That's better. Thank ye, sir. Here, hold tight."

"Can't you stand, Jem?"

"Stand, sir? yes: but what's the matter? It's like being in a round-about at the fair."

"You'll be better soon."

"Better, sir? Well, I can't be worse. Oh, my head, my head! I wish I'd got him as did it headed up in one of our barrels, I d give him such a roll up and down the ware'us floor as 'ud make him as giddy as me."

"Now try and think, Jem," said Don excitedly. "They must not believe at home that we are such cowards as to run away."

"No, sir; my Sally mustn't think that."

"Then what shall we do?"

"Try to get out, sir, of course."

"Can you walk?"

"Well, sir, if I can't, I'll crawl. What yer going to do?"

"Try the door. Perhaps they have left it unlocked."

"Not likely," said Jem. "Wish I'd got a candle. It's like being a rat in a box trap. It *is* dark."

"This way, Jem. Your hand."

"All right, sir. Frontards: my hands don't grow out o' my back."

"That's it. Now together. Let's get to the wall."

There was a rustling noise and then a rattle.

"Phew! shins!" cried Jem. "Oh, dear me. That's barrel staves, I know the feel on 'em. Such sharp edges, Mas' Don. Mind you don't tread on the edge of a hoop, or it'll fly up and hit you right in the middle.'

Flip!

"There, I told you so. Hurt you much, my lad?"

"Not very much, Jem. Now then; feel your way with me. Let's go all round the place, perhaps there's another way out."

"All right, sir. Well, it might be, but I say as it couldn't be darker than this if you was brown sugar, and shut up in a barrel in the middle o' the night."

"Now I am touching the wall, Jem," said Don. "I'm going to feel all round. Can you hear anything?"

"Only you speaking, my lad."

"Come along then."

"All right, Mas' Don. My head aches as if it was a tub with the cooper at work hammering of it."

Don went slowly along the side of the great cellar, guiding himself in the intense darkness by running his hands over the damp bricks; but there was nothing but bare wall till he had passed down two sides, and was half way along the third, when he uttered a hasty ejaculation.

"It's all right, Jem. Here is a way into another cellar."

"Mind how you go, sir. Steady."

"Yes, but make haste."

"There's a door," whispered Don. "Loose my hand."

He hastily felt all over the door, but it was perfectly blank, not so much as a keyhole to be found, and though he pressed and strained at it, he could make no impression.

"It's no use, Jem. Let's try the other door."

"I don't believe there are no other door," said Jem. "That's the way out."

"No, no; the way out is on the other side."

"This here is t'other side," said Jem, "only we arn't over there now."

"I'm sure it can't be."

"And I'm sure it can be, my lad. Nothing arn't more puzzling than being shut up in the dark. You loses yourself directly, and then you can't find yourself again."

"But the door where the men went out is over there."

"Yah! that it arn't," cried Jem. "Don't throw your fisties about that how. That's my nose."

"I'm very sorry, Jem. I did not mean——"

"Course you didn't, but that's what I said. When you're in the dark you don't know where you are, nor where any one else is."

"Let's try down that other side, and I'll show you that you are wrong."

"Can't show me, my lad. You may make me feel, but you did that just now when you hit me on the nose. Well? fun' it?"

"No, not yet," said Don, as he crept slowly along from the doorway; and then carefully on and on, till he must have come to the place from which they started.

"No, not yet," grumbled Jem. "Nor more you won't *if* you go on for ever."

"I'm afraid you're right, Jem."

"I'm right, and I arn't afraid," said Jem; "leastwise, save that my head's going on aching for ever."

Don felt all round the cellar again, and then heaved a sigh.

"Yes; there's only one door, Jem. Could we break it down?"

"I could if I'd some of the cooper's tools," said Jem, quietly; "but you can't break strong doors with your fisties, and you can't get out of brick cellars with your teeth."

"Of course, we're underground."

"Ay! no doubt about that, Mas' Don."

"Let's knock and ask for a pencil and paper to send a message."

Jem uttered a loud chuckle as he seated himself on the floor.

"I like that, Mas' Don. 'Pon my word I do. Might just as well hit your head again the wall."

"Better use yours for a battering ram, Jem," said Don, angrily. "It's thicker than mine."

There was silence after this.

"He's sulky because of what I've said," thought Don.

"Oh, my poor head!" thought Jem. "How it do ache!"

Then he began to think about Sally, and what she would say or do when she found that he did not come back.

Just at the same time Don was reflecting upon his life of late, and how discontented he had been, and how he had longed to go away, while now he felt as if he would give anything to be back on his old stool in the office, writing hard, and trying his best to be satisfied with what seemed to be a peaceful, happy life.

A terrible sensation of despair came over him, and the idea of being dragged off to a ship, and carried right away, was unbearable. What were glorious foreign lands with their wonders to one who would be thought of as a cowardly thief?

As he leaned against a wall there in the darkness his busy brain pictured his stern-looking uncle telling his weeping mother that it was a disgrace to her to mourn over the loss of a son who could be guilty of such a crime, and then run away to avoid his punishment.

"Oh! if I had only been a little wiser," thought Don, "how much happier I might have been."

Then he forced himself to think out a way of escape, a little further conversation with Jem making him feel that he must depend upon himself, for poor Jem's injury seemed to make him at times confused; in fact, he quite startled his fellow prisoner by exclaiming suddenly,—

"Now where did I put them keys?"

"Jem!"

"Eh? All right, Sally. 'Tarn't daylight yet."

"Jem, my lad, don't you know where you are?"

"Don't I tell you? Phew! my head. You there, Mas' Don?"

"Yes, Jem. How are you?"

"Oh, lively, sir, lively; been asleep, I think. Keep a good heart, Mas' Don, and——"

"Hist! Here they come," cried Don, as he saw the gleam of a light through the cracks of the door. "Jem, do you think you could make a dash of it as soon as they open the door?"

"No, Mas' Don, not now. My head's all of a boom-whooz, and I seem to have no use in my legs."

"Oh!" ejaculated Don despairingly.

"But never you mind me, my lad. You make a run for it, dive down low as soon as the door's open. That's how to get away."

Cling! clang!

Two bolts were shot back and a flood—or after the intense darkness what seemed to be a flood—of light flashed into the cellar, as the bluff man entered with another bearing the lanthorn. Then there was a great deal of shuffling of feet as if heavy loads were being borne down some stone steps; and as Don looked eagerly at the party, it was to see four sailors, apparently wounded, perhaps dead, carried in and laid upon the floor.

A thrill of horror ran through Don. He had heard of the

acts of the press-gangs as he might have heard of any legend, and then they had passed from his mind; but now all this was being brought before him and exemplified in a way that was terribly real. These four men just carried in were the last victims of outrage, and his indignation seemed to be boiling up within him when the bluff-looking man said good-humouredly,—

"That's the way to get them, my lad. Those four fellows made themselves tipsy and went to sleep, merchant sailors; they'll wake up to-morrow morning with bad headaches and in His Majesty's Service. Fine lesson for them to keep sober."

Don looked at the men with disgust. A few moments before he felt indignant, and full of commiseration for them; but the bluff man's words had swept all that away.

Then, crossing to where the man stood by the lanthorn-bearer, Don laid his hand upon his arm.

"You are not going to keep us, sir?" he said quietly. "My mother and my uncle will be very uneasy at my absence, and Jem—our man, has a young wife."

"No, no; can't listen to you, my lad," said the bluff man; "it's very hard, I know, but the king's ships must be manned—and boyed," he added with a laugh.

"But my mother?"

"Yes, I'm sorry for your mother, but you're too old to fret about her. We shall make a man of you, and that chap's young wife will have to wait till he comes back."

"But you will let me send a message to them at home?"

"To come and fetch you away, my lad? Well, hardly. We don't give that facility to pressed men to get away. There, be patient; we will not keep you in this hole long."

He glanced at the four sleeping men, and turned slowly to go, giving Don a nod of the head, but, as he neared the door he paused.

"Not very nice for a lad like you," he said, not unkindly. "Here, bring these two out, my lads; we'll stow them in the warehouse. Rather hard on the lad to shut him up with these swine. Here, come along."

A couple of the press-gang seized Don by the arms, and a couple more paid Jem Wimble the same attention, after which they were led up a flight of steps, the door was banged to and bolted, and directly after they were all standing on the floor of what had evidently been used as a tobacco warehouse, where the lanthorn light showed a rough step ladder leading up to another floor.

"Where shall we put 'em, sir?" said a sailor.

"Top floor and make fast," said the bluff man.

"But you will let me send word home?" began Don.

"I shall send you back into that lock-up place below, and perhaps put you in irons," said the man sternly. "Be content with what I am doing for you. Now then, up with you, quick!"

There was nothing for it but to obey, and with a heavy heart Don followed the man with the lanthorn as he led the way to the next floor, Jem coming next, and a guard of two well-armed men and their bluff superior closing up the rear.

The floor they reached was exactly like the one they had left, and they ascended another step ladder to the next, and then to the next.

"There's a heap of bags and wrappers over yonder to lie down on, my lads," said the bluff man. "There, go to sleep and forget your troubles. You shall have some prog in the morning. Now, my men, sharp's the word."

They had ascended from floor to floor through trap-doors, and as Don looked anxiously at his captors, the man who carried the lanthorn stooped and raised a heavy door from the floor and held it and the light as his companions descended, following last and drawing down the heavy trap over his head.

The door closed with a loud clap, a rusty bolt was shot, and then, as the two prisoners stood in the darkness listening, there was a rasping noise, and then a crash, which Don interpreted to mean that the heavy step ladder had been dragged away and half laid, half thrown upon the floor below

Then the sounds died away.

"This is a happy sort o' life, Mas' Don," said Jem, breaking the silence. "What's to be done next? Oh! my head, my head!"

"I don't know, Jem," said Don despondently. "It's enough to make one wish one was dead."

"Dead! Wish one was dead, sir? Oh, come. It's bad enough to be knocked down and have the headache. Dead! No, no. Where did he say them bags was?"

"I don't know, Jem."

"Well, let's look. I want to lie down and have a sleep."

"Sleep? At a time like this!"

"Why not, sir? I'm half asleep now. Can't do anything better as I see."

"Jem," said Don passionately, "we're being punished for all our discontent and folly, and it seems more than I can bear."

"But we must bear it, sir. That's what you've got to do when you're punished. Don't take on, sir. P'r'aps, it won't seem so bad when it gets light. Here, help me find them bags he talked about."

Don was too deep in thought, for the face of his mother was before him, and he seemed to see the agony she suffered on his account.

"Justly punished," he kept muttering; "justly punished, and now it is too late—too late."

"Here y'are, Mas' Don," cried Jem; "lots of 'em, and I can't help it, I must lie down, for my head feels as if it was going to tumble off."

Don heard him make a scuffling noise, as if he were very busy moving some sacks.

"There!" Jem cried at last; "that's about it. Now, Mas' Don, I've made you up a tidy bed; come and lie down."

"No, Jem, no; I'm not sleepy."

"Then I must," muttered Jem; and after a little more scuffling noise all was still for a few minutes, after which there was a regular heavy breathing, which told that the great trouble he was in had not been sufficient to keep Jem Wimble awake.

Don stood for some time in the darkness, but by degrees a

wretched feeling of weariness came over him, and he sat down painfully upon the floor, drawing his knees up to his chin, embracing them, and laying his head upon them.

He wanted to think of his position, of his folly, and of the trouble which it had brought upon him. Jem's heavy breathing came regularly from somewhere to his left, and he found himself, as he crouched together there in the darkness, envying the poor fellow, much as he was injured.

"But then he has not so much on his mind as I have," thought Don. "Once let me get clear away from here, how different I will be."

CHAPTER XIII.

HOW TO ESCAPE?

*R*UMBLE! *Bump!*

Don started and stared, for something had shaken him as if a sudden blow had been given against the floor.

What did it all mean? Where was he? What window was that through which the sun shone brightly, and why was he in that rough loft, in company with a man lying asleep on some sacks?

Memory filled up the vacuum directly, and he knew that his head was aching, and that he had been fast asleep.

Crash!

That was a bolt shot back, and the noise which awakened him must have been the big step ladder placed against the beam beneath the trap-door.

As Don watched he saw the trap, like a square piece of the floor, rise up slowly, and a rough, red face appear, framed in hair.

"Ship ahoy!" shouted the owner of the face. "What cheer, messmates? Want your hot water?"

Just then the man, whose hands were out of sight, and who had kept on pushing up the trap door with his head, gave it a final thrust, and the door fell over with a loud *flap*, which made Jem Wimble sit up, with his face so swollen and bruised that his eyes were half closed; and this and his dirty face gave him an aspect that was more ludicrous than strange.

"What's the matter?" he said sharply. "Who are you?

I—where—was—to me. Have I been a-dreaming? No: we're pressed!"

"Pressed you are, my lads; and Bosun Jones has sent you up some hot slops and soft tack. There you are. Find your own tablecloth and silliver spoons."

He placed a large blue jug before them, in which was some steaming compound, covered by a large breakfast cup, stuck in the mouth of the jug, while on a plate was a fair-sized pile of bread and butter.

"There you are, messmates; say your grace and fall to."

"Look here," said Don quickly. "You know we were taken by the press-gang last night?"

"Do I know? Why, didn't I help?"

"Oh!" ejaculated Don, with a look of revulsion, which he tried to conceal. "Look here," he said; "if you will take a message for me to my mother, in Jamaica Street, you shall have a guinea."

"Well, that's handsome, anyhow," said the man, laughing. "What am I to say to the old lady?"

"That we have been seized by the press-gang, and my uncle is to try and get us away."

"That all?"

"Yes, that's all. Will you go?"

"Hadn't you better have your breakfuss?"

"Breakfast? No," said Don. "I can't eat."

"Better. Keep you going, my lad."

"Will you take my message?"

"No, I won't."

"You shall have two guineas."

"Where are they?"

"My mother will gladly give them to you."

"Dessay she will."

"And you will go?"

"Do you know what a bosun's mate is, my lad?"

"I? No. I know nothing about the sea."

"You will afore long. Well, I'll tell you; bosun's mate's a gentleman kep' aboard ship to scratch the crew's backs."

"You are laughing at me," cried Don angrily.

"Not a bit of it, my lad. If I was to do what you want, I should be tied up to-morrow, and have my back scratched."

"Flogged?"

"That's it."

"For doing a kind act? For saving my poor mother from trouble and anxiety?"

"For not doing my dooty, my lad. There, a voyage or two won't hurt you. Why, I was a pressed man, and look at me."

"Maintop ahoy! Are you coming down?" came from below.

"Ay, ay, sir!" shouted the sailor.

"Wasn't that the man who had us shut up here?" cried Don.

"To be sure: Bosun Jones," said the man, running to the trap and beginning to descend.

"You'll take my message?"

"Nay, not I," said the man, shaking his head. "There, eat your breakfuss, and keep your head to the wind, my lads."

Bang!

The door was shut heavily and the rusty bolt shot. Then the two prisoners listened to the descending footsteps and to the murmur of voices from below, after which Don looked across the steaming jug at Jem, and Jem returned the stare.

"Mornin', Mas' Don," he said. "Rum game, arn't it?"

"Do you think he'll take my message, Jem?"

"Not a bit on it, sir. You may take your oath o' that."

"Will they take us aboard ship?"

"Yes, sir, and make sailors on us, and your uncle's yard 'll go to rack and ruin; and there was two screws out o' one o' the shutter hinges as I were going to put in to-day."

"Jem, we must escape them."

"All right, Mas' Don, sir. 'Arter breakfast."

"Breakfast? Who is to eat breakfast?"

"I am, sir. Feels as if it would do me good."

"But we must escape, Jem—escape."

"Yes, sir; that's right," said Jem, taking off the cup, and sniffing at the jug. "Coffee, sir. Got pretty well knocked about last night, and I'm as sore this morning as if they'd been rolling casks all over me. But a man must eat."

"Eat then, and drink then, for goodness' sake," cried Don impatiently.

"Thankye, sir," said Jem; and he poured out a cup of steaming coffee, sipped it, sipped again, took three or four mouthfuls of bread and butter, and then drained the cup.

"Mas' Don!" he cried, "it's lovely. Do have a cup. Make you see clear."

As he spoke he refilled the mug and handed it to Don, who took it mechanically, and placed it to his lips, one drop suggesting another till he had finished the cup.

"Now a bit o' bread and butter, Mas' Don?"

Don shook his head, but took the top piece, and began mechanically to eat, while Jem partook of another cup, there being a liberal allowance of some three pints.

"That's the way, sir. Wonderful what a difference breakfuss makes in a man. Eat away, sir; and if they don't look out we'll give them press-gang."

"Yes, but how, Jem? how?"

"Lots o' ways, sir. We'll get away, for one thing, or fasten that there trap-door down; and then they'll be the prisoners, not us. 'Nother cup, sir? Go on with the bread and butter. I say, sir, do I look lively?"

"Lively?"

"I mean much knocked about? My face feels as if the skin was too tight, and as if I couldn't get on my hat."

"It does not matter, Jem," said Don, quietly. "You have no hat."

"More I haven't. I remember feeling it come off, and it wasn't half wore out. Have some more coffee, Mas' Don. 'Tarnt so good as my Sally makes. I'd forgot all about her just then. Wonder whether she's eating her breakfast?"

Don sighed and went on eating. He was horribly low-spirited, but his youthful appetite once started, he felt the need of food, and kept on in silence, passing and receiving the cup till all was gone.

"That job's done," said Jem, placing the jug on the plate, and the cup in the mouth of the jug. "Now then, I'm ready, Mas' Don. You said escape, didn't you, sir?"

"Yes. What shall we do?"

"Well, we can't go down that way, sir, because the trap door's bolted."

"There is the window, Jem."

"Skylights, you mean, sir," said Jem, looking up at the sloping panes in the roof. "Well, let's have a look. Will you get a-top o' my shoulders, or shall I get a-top o' yourn?"

"I couldn't bear you, Jem."

"Then up you gets, my lad, like the tumblers do at the fair."

It seemed easy enough to get up and stand on the sturdy fellow's shoulders, but upon putting it to the test, Don found it very hard, and after a couple of failures he gave up, and they stood together looking up at the sloping window, which was far beyond their reach.

"Dessay it's fastened, so that we couldn't open it," said Jem.

"The fox said the grapes were sour when he could not get at them, Jem."

"That's true, Mas' Don. Well, how are we to get up?"

They looked round the loft, but, with the exception of the old sacking lying at one end, the place was bare.

"Here, come to the end, Jem, and let me have another try," said Don.

"Right, sir; come on," cried Jem; and going right to the end of the loft, he bent his body a little and leaned his hands against the wall.

This simplified matters.

"Stand fast, Jem," cried Don, and taking a spring, he landed upon his companion's broad back, leap-frog fashion, but only to jump off again.

"What's the matter, Mas' Don?"

"Only going to take off my shoes."

"Ah, 'twill be better. I didn't grumble before, but you did hurt, sir."

Don slipped off his shoes, uttered a word or two of warning, and once more mounted on Jem's back. It was easy then to get into a kneeling, and then to a standing, position, the wall being at hand to steady him.

"That's your sort, Mas' Don. Now hold fast, and step up on to my shoulders as I rise myself up; that's the way," he continued, slowly straightening himself, and placing his hands behind Don's legs, as he stood up, steadily, facing the wall.

"What next, Jem?"

"Next, sir? Why, I'm going to walk slowly back under the window, for you to try and open it, and look out and see where we are. Ready?"

"Yes."

"Hold tight, sir."

"But there's nothing to hold by, Jem, when you move away."

"Then you must stand fast, sir, and I'll balance you like. I can do it."

Don drew a long breath, and felt no faith, for as soon as Jem moved steadily from the wall, his ability in balancing was not great.

"Stand firm, sir. I've got you," he said.

"Am I too heavy, Jem?"

"Heavy? no, sir; I could carry two on you. Stand fast; 'tarn't far. Stand fast. That's your sort. Stand—oh!"

Everything depended upon him, and poor Jem did his best; but after three or four steps Don felt that he was going, and to save himself from a fall he tried to jump lightly down.

This would have been easy enough had not Jem been so earnest. He, too, felt that it was all wrong, and to save his companion, he tightened his hold of the calves of Don's legs as the lad stood erect on his shoulders.

The consequence was that he gave Don sufficient check as he leaped to throw him off his balance; and in his effort to save him, Jem lost his own, and both came down with a crash and sat up and rubbed and looked at each other.

"Arn't hurt, are you, Mas' Don?"

"Not hurt?" grumbled Don. "I am hurt horribly."

"I'm very sorry, sir; so am I. But I arn't broke nowhere! Are you?"

"Broken? no!" said Don rising. "There, let's try again."

"To be sure, sir. Come, I like that."

"Look here, Jem. When you straighten up, let me steady myself with my hands on the sloping ceiling there; now try."

The former process was gone through, after listening to find all silent below; and Don stood erect once more, supporting himself by the wall.

"Now edge round gently, Jem. That's right."

Jem obeyed, and by progressing very slowly, they got to within about ten feet of the window, which Don saw that he could reach easily, when the balance was lost once more.

"Don't hold, Jem!" cried Don; and he leaped backwards, to come down all right this time.

By no means discouraged, they went back to the end; and this time, by progressing more slowly, the window was reached, and, to their great delight, Don found that it was fastened inside, opening outwards by means of a couple of hinges at the highest end, and provided with a ratchet, to keep it open to any distance required.

"Can you bear me if I try to open it, Jem?"

"Can I? Ah!"

Jem was a true bearer, standing as fast as a small elephant as Don opened the window, and then supporting himself by a beam which ran across the opening, thrust out his head and surveyed the exterior.

He was not long in making out their position—in the top floor of a warehouse, the roof sloping, so that escape along it was impossible, while facing him was the blank wall of a higher building, evidently on the other side of a narrow alley. Don looked to right, but there was no means of making their position known so as to ask for help. To the left he was no better off, and seeing that the place had been well chosen as a temporary lock-up for the impressed men, Don prepared to descend.

"Better shut the window fust, Mas' Don."

The suggestion was taken, and then Don leaped down and faced his fellow-prisoner, repeating the information he had roughly communicated before.

"Faces a alley, eh?" said Jem. "Can't we go along the roof."

"I don't believe a cat could go in safety, Jem."

"Well, we aren't cats, Mas' Don, are we? Faces a alley, eh? Wasn't there no windows opposit'?"

"Nothing but a blank wall."

"Well, it's all right, Mas' Don. We'd better set to work. Only wants a rope with one end fastened in here, and then we could slide down."

"Yes," said Don gloomily; "the window is unfastened, and the way clear, but where's the rope?"

"There," said Jem, and he pointed to the end of the loft.

CHAPTER XIV.

WORKING UNDER DIFFICULTIES.

"THERE? Those sacks?"

"That's it, Mas' Don. I've got my knife. You got yourn?"

"Yes."

"Then here goes, then, to unravel them sacks till we've got enough to make a rope. This loft's a capital place to twist him. It's all right, sir, only help me work away, and to-night we'll be safe home."

"To-night, Jem? Not before?"

"Why, we sha'n't have the rope ready; and if we had, it would be no use to try by daylight. No, sir; we must wait till it's dark, and work away. If we hear any one coming we can hide the rope under the other sacks; so come on."

They seated themselves at the end of the loft, and worked away rapidly unravelling the sacking and rolling the yarn up into balls, each of which was hidden as soon as it became of any size.

As the hours went on, and they were not interrupted, the dread increased that they might be summoned to descend as prisoners before they had completed their work; but Jem's rough common sense soon suggested that this was not likely to be the case.

"Not afore night, Mas' Don," he said. "They won't take us aboard in the day. We're smuggled goods, we are; and if they don't mind, we shall be too many for them. 'Nother hour, and I shall begin to twist up our rope."

About midday the same sailor came up and brought them some bread and meat.

"That's right, my lads," he said. "You're taking it sensible, and that's the best way. If we've any luck to-night, you'll go aboard afore morning. There, I mustn't stop."

He hurried down, closing and fastening the trap, and Jem pointed to the food.

"Eat away, Mas' Don, and work same time. Strikes me we sha'n't go aboard afore close upon daylight, for they've got us all shut up here snug, so as no one shall know, and they don't dare take us away while people can see. Strikes me they won't get all the men aboard this time, eh, Mas' Don?"

"Not if we can prevent it," said Don, with his hand upon the rough piece of sacking which covered his share of the work. "Think it's safe to begin again?"

"Ay! go on. Little at a time, my lad, and be ready to hide it as soon as you hears a step."

In spite of their trouble, they ate with a fair appetite, sharpened perhaps by the hope of escape, and the knowledge that they must not be faint and weak at the last moment.

The meal was finished, and all remaining silent, they worked on unravelling the sacking, and rolling up the yarn, Don thinking of home, and Jem whistling softly a doleful air.

"If we don't get away, Mas' Don," he said, after a pause, "and they take us aboard ship and make sailors of us——"

"Don't talk like that, Jem! We must—we will get away."

"Oh, yes, it's all very well to talk, Mas' Don, but it's as well to be prepared for the worst. Like as not we sha'n't get away, and then we shall go aboard, be made sailors, and have to fight the French."

"I shall not believe that, Jem, till it takes place."

"I shall, my lad, and I hope when I'm far away as your mother, as is a reg'lar angel, will do what's right by my Sally, as is a married woman, but only a silly girl after all, as says and does things without thinking what they mean. I was horrid stupid to take so much notice of all she said, and all through that I'm here."

"Haven't we got enough ready, Jem?" said Don, impatiently, for his companion's words troubled him. They seemed to fit his own case.

"Yes, I should think that will do now, sir, so let's begin and twist up a rope. We sha'n't want it very thick."

"But we shall want it very strong, Jem."

"Here goes, then, to make it," said Jem, taking the balls of yarn, knotting the ends together, and then taking a large piece of sack and placing it beside him.

"To cover up the stuff if we hear any one coming, my lad. Now then, you pay out, and I'll twist. Mustn't get the yarn tangled."

Don set to work earnestly, and watched his companion, who cleverly twisted away at the gathered-up yarn, and then rolled his work up into a ball.

The work was clumsy, but effective, and in a short time he had laid up a few yards of a very respectable line, which seemed quite capable of bearing them singly.

Foot by foot the line lengthened, and the balls of yarn grew less, when just in the middle of their task Don made a dash at Jem, and threw down the yarn.

"Here, what yer doing? You'll get everything in a tangle, sir."

"Hush! Some one coming."

"I can't hear him."

"There is, I tell you. Listen!"

Jem held his head on one side like a magpie, and then shook it.

"Nobody," he said; but hardly had he said the words than he dabbed the rope under him, and seized upon the yarn, threw some of the old sacks upon it, and then laid his hand on Don's shoulder, just as the trap-door was raised softly a few inches, and a pair of eyes appeared at the broad crack.

Then the trap made a creaking noise, and a strange sailor came up, to find Jem seated on the floor tailor-fashion, and Don lying upon his face, with his arms crossed beneath his forehead, and some of the old sacking beneath him.

"AHOY!" SHOUTED THE SAILOR, BENDING OVER THE TRAP-DOOR" (p. 114).

The man came up slowly, and laid the trap back in a careful way, as if to avoid making a noise, and then, after a furtive look at Jem, who gave him a sturdy stare in return, he stood leaning over the opening and listening.

Footsteps were heard directly after, and a familiar voice gave some order. Directly after the bluff-looking man with whom they had had so much dealing stepped up into the loft.

"Well, my lads," he said, "how are the sore places?"

Jem did not answer.

"Sulky, eh? Ah, you'll soon get over that. Now, my boy, let's have a look at you."

He gave Don a clap on the shoulder, and the lad started up as if from sleep, and stared at the fresh comer.

"Won't do," said the bluff man, laughing. "Men don't wake up from sleep like that. Ah! of course: now you are turning red in the face. Didn't want to speak to me, eh? Well, you are all right, I see."

Don did not attempt to rise from where he half sat, half lay, and the man gave a sharp look round, letting his eyes rest for a few moments upon the window, and then turning them curiously upon the old sacking.

To Don's horror he approached and picked up a piece close to that which served for a couch.

"How came all this here?" he said sharply.

"Old stuff, sir. Been used for the bales o' bacco, I s'pose," said the furtive-looking man.

"Humph. And so you have made a bed of it, eh? Let's have a look."

The perspiration stood on Don's forehead.

"Well," said the bluff man, "why don't you get up? Quick!"

He took a step nearer Don, and was in the act of stooping to take him by the arm, when there was a hail from below.

"Ahoy!" shouted the sailor, bending over the trap-door.

"Wants Mr. Jones," came up.

"Luff wants you, sir," said the man.

"Right. There, cheer up, my lads; you might be worse

off than you are," said the bluff visitor pleasantly. Then, clapping Don on the shoulder, "Don't sulk, my lad. Make the best of things. You're in the king's service now, so take your fate like a man."

He nodded and crossed to the trap.

"Ahoy, there! Below there! I'm coming.—Can't expect a bosun to break his neck."

He said these last words as his head and shoulders were above the floor, and gave the prisoners a friendly nod just as his eyes were disappearing.

"Come along, my lad," he said, when he was out of sight.

"Ay! ay!" growled the furtive-looking man, slowly following, and giving those he left behind a very peculiar smile, which he lengthened out in time and form, till he was right down the ladder, with the trap-door drawn over and resting upon his head. This he slowly lowered, till only his eyes and brow were seen, and he stayed like that watching for a minute, then let the lid close with a *flap*, and shut him, as it were, in a box.

"Gone!" said Jem. "Lor', how I should ha' liked to go and jump on that there trap just while he was holding it up with his head. I'd ha' made it ache for him worse than they made mine."

"Hist! Don't talk so loud," whispered Don. "He listens."

"I hope he's a-listening now," said Jem, loudly; "a lively smiling sort of a man. That's what he is, Mas' Don. Sort o' man always on the blue sneak."

Don held up his hand.

"Think they suspect anything, Jem?" he whispered.

"Sometimes I do, and sometimes I don't, Mas' Don. That stoutish chap seemed to smell a rat, and that smiling doorknocker fellow was all on the spy; but I don't think he heared anything, and I'm sure he didn't see. Now, then, can you tell me whether they're coming back?"

Don shook his head, and they remained thinking and watching for nearly an hour before Jem declared that they must risk it.

"One minute," said Don; and he went on tiptoe as far as the trap-door, and lying down, listened and applied his eyes to various cracks, before feeling convinced that no one was listening.

"Why, you didn't try if it was fastened," cried Jem; and taking out his knife, he inserted it opposite to the hinges, and tried to lever up the door.

It was labour in vain, for the bolt had been shot.

"They don't mean to let us go, Mas' Don," said Jem. "Come on, and let's get the rope done."

They returned to the sacking, lifted it up, and taking out the unfinished rope, worked away rapidly, but with the action of sparrows feeding in a road—one peck and two looks out for danger.

Half-a-dozen times at least the work was hidden, some sound below suggesting danger, while over and over again, in spite of their efforts, the rope advanced so slowly, and the result was so poor, that Don felt in despair of its being done by the time they wanted it, and doubtful whether if done it would bear their weight.

He envied Jem's stolid patience and the brave way in which he worked, twisting, and knotting about every three feet, while every time their eyes met Jem gave him an encouraging nod.

Whether to be successful or not, the making of the rope did one thing—it relieved them of a great deal of mental strain.

In fact, Don stared wonderingly at the skylight, as it seemed to him to have suddenly turned dark.

"Going to be a storm, Jem," he said. "Will the rain hurt the rope?"

"Storm, Mas' Don? Why, it's as clear as clear. Getting late, and us not done."

"But the rope must be long enough now."

"Think so, sir?"

"Yes; and if it is not, we can easily drop the rest of the way."

"What! and break our legs, or sprain our ankles, and be caught? No let's make it another yard or two."

"Hist! quick!"

They were only just in time, for almost before they had thrown the old sacking over the rope, the bolt of the trap-door was thrust back, and the sinister-looking sailor entered with four more, to give a sharp look round the place, and then roughly seize the prisoners.

"Now, then,!" cried Jem sharply, "what yer about? Arn't going to tie us up, are you?"

"Yes, if you cut up rough again," said the leader of the little party. "Come on."

"Here, what yer going to do?" cried Jem.

"Do? You'll see. Not going to spoil your beauty, mate."

Don's heart sank low. All that hopeful labour over the rope thrown away! and he cast a despairing look at Jem.

"Never mind, my lad," whispered the latter. "More chances than one."

"Now then! No whispering. Come along!" shouted the sinister-looking man, fiercely. "Come on down. Bring 'em along."

Don cast another despairing look at Jem, and then marched slowly toward the opening in the floor.

CHAPTER XV.

A DESPERATE ATTEMPT.

JUST as the prisoners reached the trap-door a voice came from below.

"Hold hard there, my lads. Bosun Jones has been down to the others, and he says these here may stop where they are."

"What for?"

"Oh, one o' the four chaps we brought in last night's half wild, and been running amuck. Come on down."

"Yah!" growled the sinister sailor, scowling at Jem, as if there were some old enmity between them.

"I say, don't," said Jem mockingly. "You'll spoil your good looks. Say, does he always look as handsome as that?"

The man doubled his fist, and made a sharp blow at Jem, and seemed surprised at the result; for Jem dodged, and retorted, planting his fist in the fellow's chest, and sending him staggering back.

The man's eyes blazed as he recovered himself, and rushed at Jem like a bull-dog.

Obeying his first impulse, Don, who had never struck a blow in anger since he left school, forgot fair play for the moment, and doubled his fists to help Jem.

"No, no, Mas' Don; I can tackle him," cried Jem; "and I feel as if I should like to now."

But there was to be no encounter, for a couple of the other sailors seized their messmate, and forced him to the trap-door, growling and threatening all manner of evil to the sturdy little prisoner, who was standing on his defence.

"No, no, mate," said the biggest and strongest of the party "it's like hitting a man as is down. Come on."

There was another struggle, but the brute was half thrust to the ladder, and directly after the trap was closed again, and the bolt shot.

"Well, I never felt so much like fighting before—leastwise not since I thrashed old Mike behind the barrel stack in the yard," said Jem, resuming his coat, which he had thrown off.

"Did you fight Mike in the yard one day?" said Don wonderingly. "Why, Jem, I remember; that's when you had such a dreadful black eye."

"That's right, my lad."

"And pretended you fell down the ladder out of floor number six."

"That's right again, Mas' Don," said Jem, grinning.

"Then that was a lie?"

"Well, I don't know 'bout it's being a lie, my lad. P'r'aps you might call it a kind of a sort of a fib."

"Fib? It was an untruth."

"Well, but don't you see, it would have looked so bad to say, 'I got that eye a-fighting?' and it was only a little while 'fore I was married. What would my Sally ha' said if she know'd I fought our Mike?"

"Why, of course; I remember now, Mike was ill in bed for a week at the same time."

"That's so, Mas' Don," said Jem, chuckling; "and he was werry ill. You see, he come to the yard to work, after you'd begged him on, and he was drunk as a fiddler—not as ever I see a fiddler that way. And then, i'stead o' doing his work, he was nasty, and began cussing. He cussed everything, from the barrow and truck right up to your uncle, whose money he took, and then he began cussing o' you, Mas' Don; and I told him he ought to be ashamed of hisself for cussing the young gent as got him work; and no sooner had I said that than I found myself sitting in a puddle, with my nose bleeding."

"Well?" said Don, who was deeply interested.

"Well, Mas' Don, that's all."

"No, it isn't, Jem; you say yon fought Mike."

"Well, I s'pose I did, Mas' Don."

"'Suppose you did'?"

"Yes; I only recklect feeling wild because my clean shirt and necktie was all in a mess. I don't recklect any more—only washing my sore knuckles at the pump, and holding a half hun'erd weight up again my eye."

"But Mike stopped away from work for a week."

'Yes, Mas' Don. He got hisself a good deal hurt somehow."

"You mean you hurt him?"

"Dunno, Mas' Don. S'pose I did, but I don't 'member nothing about it. And now look here, sir; seems to me that in half-hour's time it'll be quite dark enough to start; and if I'd got five guineas, I'd give 'em for five big screws, and the use of a gimlet and driver."

What for?"

"To fasten down that there trap."

"It would be no good, Jem; because if they found the trap fast, they'd be on the watch for us outside."

"Dessay you're right, sir. Well, what do you say? Shall we begin now, or wait?"

Don looked up at the fast darkening skylight, and then, after a moment's hesitation,—

"Let's begin now, Jem. It will take some time."

"That's right, Mas' Don; so here goes, and good luck to us. It means home, and your mother, and my Sally; or going to fight the French."

"And we don't want to be obliged to fight without we like, Jem."

"That's true," said Jem; and going quickly to the trap, he laid his ear to the crack and listened.

"All right, my lad. Have it out," he said; and the sacks were cast aside, and the rope withdrawn.

"Will it bear us, Jem?"

"I'm going to try first, and if it'll bear me it'll bear you."

"But you can't get up there."

"No, but you can, my lad; and when you're there you can fasten the rope to that cross-bar, and then I can soon be with you. Ready?"

"Wait till I've got off my shoes."

"That's right; stick 'em in your pockets, my lad. Now then, ready?"

Don signified his readiness. Jem laid him a back up at the end wall. Don mounted, and then jumped down again.

"What's the matter?"

"I haven't got the rope."

"My: what a head I have!" cried Jem, as Don tightly knotted the rope about his waist; and then, mounting on his companion's back once more, was borne very slowly, steadying himself by the sloping roof, till the window was reached.

"Hold fast, Jem."

"Right it is, my lad."

There was a clicking of the iron fastening, the window was thrust up higher and higher, till it was to the full extent of the ratchet support, and then by passing one arm over the light cross-beam, which divided the opening in two, Don was able to raise himself, and throw his leg over the front of the opening, so that the next minute he was sitting on the edge with one leg down the sloping roof, and the other hanging inside, but in a very awkward position, on account of the broad sky-light.

"Can't you open it more?" said Jem.

"No; that's as far as the fastening will hold it up."

"Push it right over, Mas' Don, so as it may lie back against the roof. Mind what you're doing, so as you don't slip. But you'll be all right. I've got the rope, and won't let it go."

Don did as he was told, taking tightly hold of the long cross central bar, and placing his knees, and then his feet, against the front of the opening, so that he was in the position of a four-footed animal. Then his back raised up the hinged skylight higher and higher, till, holding on to the cross-bar with one hand, and the ratchet fastening with the other, he thrust up and up, till the skylight was perpendicular, and he paused, panting with the exertion.

"All right, Mas' Don; I've got the rope. Now lower it down gently, till it lies flat on the slope. That's the way; steady! steady!"

Bang! crash! jingle!

"Oh, Mas' Don!"

"I couldn't help it, Jem; the iron fastening came out. The wood's rotten."

For the skylight had fallen back with a crash, and some of the broken glass came musically jingling down, some of it sliding along the tiles, and dropping into the alley below.

There was a dead silence, neither of the would-be evaders of the enforced king's service moving, but listening intently for the slightest sound.

"Think they heared it, Mas' Don?" said Jem, at last, in a hoarse whisper.

"I can't hear anything," replied Don, softly.

They listened again, but all was wonderfully quiet. A distant murmur came from the busy streets, and a clock struck nine.

"Why, that's Old Church," said Jem in a whisper. "We must be close down to the water side, Mas' Don."

"Yes, Jem. Shall we give it up, or risk it?"

"I'll show you d'reckly," said Jem. "You make that there end fast round the bar. It isn't rotten, is it?"

"No," said Don, after an examination; "it seems very solid." And untying the rope from his waist, he knotted it to the little beam.

The next minute Jem gave a heavy drag at the rope, then a jerk, and next swung to it, going to and fro for a few seconds.

"Hold a ton," whispered Jem; and reaching up as high as he could, he gripped the rope between his legs and over his ankle and foot, and apparently with the greatest ease drew himself up to the bar, threw a leg over and sat astride with his face beaming.

"They sha'n't have us this time, Mas' Don," he said, running the rope rapidly through his hands until he had reached the end, when he gathered it up in rings, till he had enough to throw beyond the sloping roof.

"Here goes!" he whispered; and he tossed it from him into the gathering gloom.

The falling rope made a dull sound, and then there was a sharp gliding noise.

One of the broken fragments of glass had been started from where it had lodged, and slid rapidly down the tiles.

They held their breath as they waited to hear it fall tinkling beyond on the pavement; but they listened in vain, for the simple reason that it had fallen into the gutter.

"All right, Mas' Don! here goes!" said Jem, and he lowered the rope to its full extent.

"Hadn't I better go first, and try the rope, Jem?"

"What's the good o' your going first? It might break, and then what would your mother say to me? I'll go; and, as I said afore, if it bears me, it'll bear you."

"But, if it breaks, what shall I say to little Sally?"

"Well, I wouldn't go near her if I was you, Mas' Don. She might take on, and then it wouldn't be nice; or she mightn't take on, and that wouldn't be nice. Hist! what's that?"

"Can't hear anything, Jem."

"More can I. Here, shake hands, lad, case I has a tumble."

"Don't, don't risk it, Jem," whispered Don, clinging to his hand.

"What! after making the rope! Oh, come, Mas' Don, where's your pluck? Now then, I'm off; and when I'm down safe, I'll give three jerks at the line, and then hold it steady. Here goes—once to be ready, twice to be steady, three times to be—off!"

Don's heart felt in his mouth as his companion grasped the

rope tightly, and let himself glide down the steep tiled slope, till he reached the edge over the gutter; and then, as he disappeared, dissolving—so it seemed—into the gloom, Don's breath was held, and he felt a singular pain at the chest.

He grasped the rope, though, as he sat astride at the lower edge of the opening; and the loosely twisted hemp seemed to palpitate and quiver as if it were one of Jem's muscles reaching to his hands.

Then all at once the rope became slack, as if the tension had been removed, and Don turned faint with horror.

"It's broken!" he panted; and he strained over as far as he could without falling to hear the dull thud of his companion's fall.

Thoughts fly fast, and in a moment of time Don had seen poor Jem lying crushed below, picked up, and had borne the news to his little wife. But before he had gone any further, the rope was drawn tight once more, and as he held it, there came to thrill his nerves three distinct jerks.

"It's all right!" he panted; and grasped the rope with both hands. "Now then," he thought, "it only wants a little courage, and I can slide down and join him, and then we're free."

Yes; but it required a good deal of resolution to make the venture. "Suppose Jem's weight had unwound the rope; suppose it should break; suppose——"

"Oh, what a coward I am!" he muttered; and swinging his leg free, he lay upon his face for a moment, right upon the sloping tiles and then let the rope glide through his hands.

It was very easy work down that slope, only that elbows and hands suffered, and sundry sounds suggested that waistcoat buttons were being torn off. But that was no moment for studying trifles; and what were waistcoat buttons to liberty?

Another moment, and his legs were over the edge, and he was about to attempt the most difficult part of the descent, grasping beforehand, that as soon as he hung clear of the eaves, he should begin to turn slowly round.

"Now for it!" he said; and he was about to descend perpendicularly, when the rope was suddenly jerked violently. There was a loud ejaculation, and Jem's voice rose to where he hung.

"No, no, Mas' Don. Back! back! Don't come down."

Then, as he hung, there came the panting and noise of a terrible struggle far below.

CHAPTER XVI.

PRISONERS AGAIN

DON'S grasp tightened on the rope, and as he lay there, half on, half off the slope, listening, with the beads of perspiration gathering on his forehead, he heard from below shouts, the trampling of feet and struggling.

"They've attacked Jem," he thought. "What shall I do? Go to his help?"

Before he could come to a decision the noise ceased and all was perfectly still.

Don hung there thinking.

What should he do—slide down and try to escape, or climb back?

Jem was evidently retaken, and to escape would be cowardly, he thought; and in this spirit he began to draw himself slowly back till, after a great deal of exertion, he had contrived to get his legs beyond the eaves, and there he rested, hesitating once more.

Just then he heard voices below, and holding on by one hand, he rapidly drew up a few yards of the rope, making his leg take the place of another hand.

There was a good deal of talking, and he caught the word "rope," but that was all. So he continued his toilsome ascent till he was able to grasp the edge of the skylight opening, up to which he dragged himself, and sat listening, astride, as he had been before the attempt was made.

All was so still that he was tempted to slide down and escape for no sound suggested that any one was on the watch. But Jem! poor Jem! It was like leaving him in the lurch.

Still, he thought, if he did get away, he might give the alarm, and find help to save Jem from being taken away.

"And if they came up and found me gone," he muttered, "they would take Jem off aboard ship directly, and it would be labour in vain."

"Oh! Let go!"

The words escaped him involuntarily, for whilst he was pondering, some one had crept into the great loft floor, made a leap, and caught him by the leg, and, in spite of all his efforts to free himself, the man hung on till, unable to kick free, Don was literally dragged in and fell, after clinging for a moment to the cross-beam, heavily upon the floor.

"I've got him!" cried a hoarse voice, which he recognised. "Look sharp with the light."

Don was on his back half stunned and hurt, and his captor, the sinister-looking man, was sitting upon his chest, half suffocating him, and evidently taking no little pleasure in inflicting pain.

Footsteps were hurriedly ascending; then there was the glow of a lanthorn, and directly after the bluff-looking man appeared, followed by a couple of sailors, one of whom bore the light.

"Got him?"

"Ay, ay! I've got him, sir."

"That's right! But do you want to break the poor boy's ribs? Get off!"

Don's friend, the sinister-looking man, rose grumblingly from his captive's chest, and the bluff man laughed.

"Pretty well done, my lad," he said. "I might have known you two weren't so quiet for nothing. There, cast off that rope, and bring him down."

The sinister man gripped Don's arm savagely, causing him intense pain, but the lad uttered no cry, and suffered himself to be led down in silence to floor after floor, till they were once more in the basement.

"Might have broken your neck, you foolish boy," said the bluff man, as a rough door was opened. "You can stop here for a bit. Don't try any more games."

He gave Don a friendly push, and the boy stepped forward once more into a dark cellar, where he remained despairing and motionless as the door was banged behind him, and locked; and then, as the steps died away, he heard a groan.

"Any one there" said a faint voice, followed by the muttered words,—"Poor Mas' Don. What will my Sally do? What will she do?"

"Jem, I'm here," said Don huskily; and there was a rustling sound in the far part of the dark place.

"Oh! you there, Mas' Don? I thought you'd got away."

"How could I get away when they had caught you?" said Don, reproachfully.

"Slid down and run. There was no one there to stop you. Why, I says to myself when they pounced on me, if I gives 'em all their work to do, they'll be so busy that they won't see Mas' Don, and he'll be able to get right away. Why didn't you slither and go?"

"Because I should have been leaving you in the lurch, Jem; and I didn't want to do that."

"Well, I—well, of all—there!—why, Mas' Don, did you feel that way?"

"Of course I did."

"And you wouldn't get away because I couldn't?"

"That's what I thought, Jem."

"Well, of all the things I ever heared! Now I wonder whether I should have done like that if you and me had been twisted round; I mean, if you had gone down first and been caught."

"Of course you would, Jem."

"Well, that's what I don't know, Mas' Don. I'm afraid I should have waited till they'd got off with you, and slipped down and run off."

"I don't think you'd have left me, Jem."

"DON'S CAPTOR WAS SITTING UPON HIS CHEST" (p. 127).

"I dunno, my lad. I should have said to myself, I can bring them as 'd help get Mas' Don out; and gone."

Don thought of his own feelings, and remained silent.

"I say, Mas' Don, though, it's a bad job being caught; but the rope was made strong enough, warn't it?"

"Yes, but it was labour in vain."

"Well, p'r'aps it was, sir; but I'm proud of that rope all the same. Oh!"

Jem uttered a dismal groan.

"Are you hurt, Jem?"

"Hurt, sir! I just am hurt—horrible. 'Member when I fell down and the tub went over me?"

"And broke your ribs, and we thought you were dead? Yes, I remember."

"Well, I feel just the same as I did then. I went down and a lot of 'em fell on me, and I was kicked and jumped on till I'm just as if all the hoops was off my staves, Mas' Don; but that arn't the worst of it, because it won't hurt me. I'm a reg'lar wunner to mend again. You never knew any one who got cut as could heal up as fast as me. See how strong my ribs grew together, and so did my leg when I got kicked by that horse."

"But are you in much pain now?"

"I should just think I am, Mas' Don; I feel as if I was being cut up with blunt saws as had been made red hot first."

"Jem, my poor fellow!" groaned Don.

"Now don't go on like that, Mas' Don, and make it worse."

"Would they give us a candle, Jem, do you think, if I was to knock?"

"Not they, my lad; and I don't want one. You'd be seeing how queer I looked if you got a light. There, sit down and let's talk."

Don groped along by the damp wall till he reached the place where his companion lay, and then went down on his knees beside him.

"It seems to be all over, Jem," he said.

"Over? Not it, my lad. Seems to me as if it's all just going to begin."

"Then we shall be made sailors."

"S'pose so, Mas' Don. Well, I don't know as I should so much mind if it warn't for my Sally. A man might just as well be pulling ropes as pushing casks and winding cranes."

"But we shall have to fight, Jem."

"Well, so long as it's fisties I don't know as I much mind, but if they expect me to chop or shoot anybody, they're mistook."

Jem became silent, and for a long time his fellow prisoner felt not the slightest inclination to speak. His thoughts were busy over their attempted escape, and the risky task of descending by the rope. Then he thought again of home, and wondered what they would think of him, feeling sure that they would believe him to have behaved badly.

His heart ached as he recalled all the past, and how much his present position was due to his own folly and discontent, while, at the end of every scene he evoked, came the thought that no matter how he repented, it was too late— too late!

"How are you now, Jem?" he asked once or twice, as he tried to pierce the utter darkness; but there was no answer, and at last he relieved the weariness of his position by moving close up to the wall, so as to lean his back against it, and in this position, despite all his trouble, his head drooped forward till his chin rested upon his chest, and he fell fast asleep for what seemed to him only a few minutes, when he started into wakefulness on feeling himself roughly shaken.

"Rouse up, my lad, sharp!"

And looking wonderingly about him, he clapped one hand over his eyes to keep off the glare of an open lanthorn.

CHAPTER XVII.

ON BOARD.

IT was a strange experience, and half asleep and confused, Don could hardly make out whether he was one of the captives of the press-gang, or a prisoner being conveyed to gaol in consequence of Mike Bannock's charge.

All seemed to be darkness, and the busy gang of armed men about him worked in a silent, furtive way, hurrying their prisoners, of whom, as they all stood together in a kind of yard behind some great gates, there seemed to be about a dozen, some injured, some angry and scowling, and full of complaints and threats now that they were about to be conveyed away; but every angry remonstrance was met by one more severe, and sometimes accompanied by a tap from the butt of a pistol, or a blow given with the hilt or flat of a cutlass.

"This here's lively, Mas' Don," said Jem, as he stood beside his companion in misfortune.

"I want to speak to the principal officer," said Don, excitedly. "We must not let them drive us off as if we were sheep."

"Will you take a bit of good advice, my lad?" said a familiar voice at his ear.

"If it is good advice," said Don, sharply.

"Then hold your tongue, and go quietly. I'll speak to the lieutenant when we get aboard."

Don glanced sharply at the bluff-looking boatswain who had spoken, and he seemed to mean well; but in Don's excitement ne could not be sure, and one moment he felt disposed to make a bold dash for liberty, as soon as the gates were opened, and then to shout for help; the next to appeal to his fellow-prisoners to make a bold fight for liberty; and while these thoughts were running one over another in his mind, a sharp order was given, the gates were thrown open, and they were all marched down a narrow lane, dimly lit by one miserable oil lamp at the end.

Almost as they reached the end the familiar odour, damp and seaweedy, of the tide reached Don's nostrils; and directly after he found himself being hurried down a flight of wet and slippery stone steps to where a lanthorn showed a large boat, into which he was hurried along with the rest. Then there was the sensation of movement, as the boat rose and fell. Fresh orders. The splash of oars. A faint creaking sound where they rubbed on the tholes, and then the regular measured dip, dip, and splash, splash.

"Tide runs sharp," said a deep voice. "Give way, my lads, or we shall be swept by her; that's it."

Don listened to all this as if it were part of a dream, while he gazed wildly about at the dimly-seen moving lights and the black, shadowy-looking shapes of the various vessels which kept on looming up, till after gradually nearing a light away to his left, the boat was suddenly run up close to a great black mass, which seemed to stand up out of the water that was lapping her sides.

Ten minutes later the boat in which he had come off was hanging to the davits, and he, in company with his fellows, was being hurried down into a long low portion of the 'tween decks, with a couple of lanthorns swinging their yellow light to and fro, and trying to make halos, while an armed marine stood sentry at the foot of the steps leading up on deck.

Every one appeared too desolate and despondent to say much; in fact, as Don sat upon the deck and looked at those who surrounded him, they all looked like so many wounded men in hospital, or prisoners of war, in place of being Englishmen— whose duty henceforth was to be the defence of their country.

"Seems rum, don't it?" said Jem in a whisper. "Makes a man feel wild to be laid hold on like this."

"It's cruel! it's outrageous!" cried Don, angrily.

"But here we are, and—what's that there noise?" said Jem, as a good deal of shouting and trampling was heard on deck. Then there was a series of thumps and more trampling and loud orders.

"Are they bringing some more poor wretches on board, Jem?"

"Dunno. Don't think so. Say, Mas' Don, I often heared tell of the press-gang, and men being took; but I didn't know it was so bad as this."

"Wait till morning, Jem, and I hope we shall get justice done to us."

"Then they'll have to do it sharp, for it's morning now, though it's so dark down here, and I thought we were moving; can't you feel?"

Jem was quite right; the sloop was under weigh. Morning had broken some time; and at noon that day, the hope of being set at liberty was growing extremely small, for the ship was in full sail, and going due west.

CHAPTER XVIII.

JEM IS HUNGRY.

THE first time the pressed men were mustered Don was well prepared.

"You leave it to me, Jem," he whispered. "I'll wait till our turn comes, and then I shall speak out to the officer and tell him how we've been treated."

"You'd better make haste, then, Mas' Don, for if the thing keeps on moving like this, I sha'n't be able to stand and hear what you have to say."

For a good breeze was blowing from the south coast, sufficient to make the waves curl over, and the sloop behave in rather a lively way; the more so that she had a good deal of canvas spread, and heeled over and dipped her nose sufficiently to admit a great wave from time to time to well splash the forward part of the deck.

Don made no reply, for he felt white, but he attributed it to the mental excitement from which he suffered.

There were thirty pressed men on deck, for the most part old sailors from the mercantile marine, and these men were drafted off into various watches, the trouble to the officers being that of arranging the fate of the landsmen, who looked wretched in the extreme.

"'Pon my word, Jones," said a smart-looking, middle-aged man in uniform, whom Don took to be the first lieutenant, "about as sorry a lot of Bristol sweepings as ever I saw."

"Not bad men, sir," said the petty officer addressed. "Wait till they've shaken down into their places."

"Now's your time, Mas' Don," whispered Jem. "Now or never."

Don was on the alert, but just as the officer neared them the vessel gave a sudden pitch, and of the men standing in a row the minute before, not one remained upon his feet. For it seemed as if the deck had suddenly dropped down; and as Don and Jem rolled over into the lee scuppers, they were pretty well doused by the water that came splashing over the bows, and when, amidst a shout of laughter from the sailors, the order was given for them to get up and form in line again, Jem clung tightly to Don, and said, dolefully,—

"It's of no use, Mas' Don; I can't. It's like trying to stand on running barrels; and—oh, dear me!—I do feel so precious bad."

Don made no reply, but caught at the side of the vessel, for everything around seemed to be swimming, and a peculiarly faint sensation had attacked him, such as he had never experienced before.

"There, send 'em all below," said the officer, who seemed half angry, half amused. "Pretty way this is, of manning His Majesty's ships. There, down with you. Get 'em all below."

Don did not know how he got below. He had some recollection of knocking the skin off his elbows, and being half dragged into a corner of the lower deck, where, for three days, he lay in the most abjectly miserable state, listening to the sighs and groans of his equally unfortunate companions, and the remarks of Jem, who kept up in his waking moments a running commentary on the miseries of going to sea.

"It's wuss than anything I ever felt or saw," he muttered. "I've been ill, and I've been in hospital, but this here's about the most terrible. I say, Mas' Don, how do you feel now?"

"As if I'd give anything to have the ship stopped, for us to be set ashore."

"No, no, you can't feel like that, Mas' Don, because that's exactly how I feel. I am so ill. Well, all I can say is that it serves the captain and the lieutenant and all the rest of em jolly well right for press-ganging me."

"What do you mean?" said Don, dolefully.

"Why, that they took all that trouble to bring me aboard to make a sailor of me, and they'll never do it. I'm fit to go into a hospital, and that's about all I'm fit for. Sailor? Why, I can't even stand upright on the precious deck."

"Well, my lads," said a hearty voice just then; "how long are you going to play at being old women? Come, rouse a bit."

"No, thankye, sir," said Jem, in a miserable tone. "Bit? I haven't bit anything since I've been aboard."

"Then rouse up, and bite something now," cried the boatswain. "Come, my lad," he continued, turning to Don, "you've got too much stuff in you to lie about like this. Jump up, and come on deck in the fresh air."

"I feel so weak, sir; I don't think I could stand."

"Oh, yes, you can," said the boatswain. "That's better If you give way to it, you'll be here for a week."

"Are we nearly there, sir?" said Jem, with a groan.

"Nearly there? you yellow-faced lubber. What do you mean?"

"Where we're going to," groaned Jem.

"Nearly there? No. Why?"

"Because I want to go ashore again. I'm no use here."

"We'll soon make you of some use. There, get up."

"But aren't we soon going ashore?"

"If you behave yourself you may get a run ashore at the Cape or at Singapore; but most likely you won't leave the ship till we get to China."

"China?" said Jem, sitting up sharply. "China?"

"Yes, China. What of that?"

"China!" cried Jem. "Why, I thought we were sailing round to Plymouth or Portsmouth, or some place like that. China?"

"We're going straight away or China, my lad, to be on that station for some time."

"And when are we coming back, sir?"

"In about three years."

"Mas' Don," said Jem, dolefully; "let's get up on deck, sir, and jump overboard, so as to make an end of it."

"You'd better not," said the boatswain, laughing at Jem's miserable face. "You're in the king's service now, and you've got to work. There, rouse up, and act like a man."

"But can't we send a letter home, sir?" asked Don.

"Oh, yes, if you like, at the first port we touch at, or by any ship we speak. But come, my lad, you've been sea-sick for days; don't begin to be home sick. You've been pressed as many a better fellow has been before you. The king wants men, and he must have them. Now, young as you are, show that you can act like a man."

Don gave him an agonised look, but the bluff boatswain did not see it.

"Here, you fellows," he cried to the rest of the sick men; "we've given you time enough now. You must get up and shake all this off. You'll all be on deck in a quarter of an hour, so look sharp."

"This here's a nice game, Mas' Don. Do you know how I feel?"

"No, Jem; but I know how I feel."

"How's that, sir?"

"That if I had been asked to serve the king I might have joined a ship; but I've been dragged here in a cruel way, and the very first time I can get ashore, I mean to stay."

"Well, I felt something like that, Mas' Don; but they'd call it desertion."

"Let them call it what they like, Jem. They treated us like dogs, and I will not stand it. I shall leave the ship first chance. You can do as you like, but that's what I mean to do."

"Oh, I shall do as you do, Mas' Don. I was never meant for a sailor, and I shall get away as soon as I can."

"Shall you?" said a voice that seemed familiar; and they both turned in the direction from which it came, to see a dark figure rise from beside the bulk head, where it had lain unnoticed by the invalids, though if they had noted its presence, they would have taken it for one of their fellow-sufferers.

JEM IS HUNGRY.

"What's it got to do with you?" said Jem, shortly, as he scowled at the man, who now came forward sufficiently near the dim light for them to recognise the grim, sinister-looking sailor, who had played so unpleasant a part at the *rendezvous* where they were taken after being seized.

"What's it got to do with me? Everything. So you're goin' to desert, both of you, are you? Do you know what that means?"

"No; nor don't want," growled Jem.

"Then I'll tell you. Flogging, for sartain, and p'r'aps stringing up at the yard-arm, as an example to others."

"Ho!" said Jem; "do it? Well, you look the sort o' man as is best suited for that; and just you look here. Nex' time I ketches you spying and listening to what I say, I shall give you a worse dressing down than I give you last time, so be off."

"Mutinous, threatening, and talking about deserting," said the sinister-looking sailor, with a harsh laugh, which sounded as if he had a young watchman's rattle somewhere in his chest. "Nice thing to report. I think this will do."

He went off rubbing his hands softly, and mounted the ladder, Jem watching him till his legs had disappeared, when he turned sharply to Don.

"Him and me's going to have a regular set-to some day, Mas' Don. He makes me feel warm, and somehow that bit of a row has done me no end o' good. Here, come on deck, and let's see if he's telling tales. Come on, lad. P'r'aps I've got a word or two to say as well."

Don had not realised it before, but as he followed Jem, he suddenly woke to the fact that he did not feel so weak and giddy, while, by the time he was on deck, it as suddenly occurred to him that he could eat some breakfast.

"I thought as much," said Jem. "Lookye there, Mas' Don. Did you ever see such a miserable sneak?"

For there, not half-a-dozen yards away, was the sinister-looking sailor talking to the bluff boatswain.

"Oh, yes, of course," said the latter, as he caught sight of the recruits. "So does every man who is pressed, and if he does not say it, he thinks it. There, be off."

The ill-looking sailor gave Jem an ugly look and went aft, while the boatswain turned to Don.

"That's right," he said. "Make a bit of an effort, and you're all the better for it. You'll get your sea legs directly."

"I wish he'd tell us where to get a sea leg o' mutton, Mas' Don," whispered Jem. "I *am* hungry."

"What's that?" said the boatswain.

"Only said I was hungry," growled Jem.

"Better and better. And, now, look here, you two may as well set to work without grumbling. And take my advice; don't let such men as that hear either of you talk about desertion again. It doesn't matter this time, but, by-and-by, it may mean punishment."

CHAPTER XIX.

A CONVERSATION.

THE gale was left behind, and the weather proved glorious as they sped on towards the tropics, both going through all the drudgery to be learned by Government men, in company with the naval drill.

There was so much to see and learn that Don found it impossible to be moody; and, for the most part, his home-sickness and regrets were felt merely when he went to his hammock at nights; while the time spent unhappily there was very short, for fatigue soon sent him to sleep.

The boatswain was always bluff, manly, and kind, and following out his advice, both Jem and Don picked up the routine of their life so rapidly as to gain many an encouraging word from their officers—words which, in spite of the hidden determination to escape at the first opportunity, set them striving harder and harder to master that which they had to do.

"Yes," Jem used to say, "they may be civil, but soft words butters no parsnips, Mas' Don; and being told you'll some day be rated A.B. don't bring a man back to his wife, nor a boy—I mean another man—back to his mother."

"You might have said boy, Jem; I'm only a boy."

"So 'm I, Mas' Don—sailor boy. You seem getting your head pretty well now, Mas' Don, when we're up aloft."

"That's what I was thinking of you, Jem."

"Well, yes, sir, tidy—tidy like, and I s'pose it arn't much worse than coming down that there rope when we tried to get away; but I often feel when I'm lying out on the yard, with my feet in the stirrup, that there's a precious little bit between being up there and lying down on the deck, never to get up again."

"You shouldn't think of it, Jem. I try not to."

"So do I, but you can't help it sometimes. How long have we been at sea now?"

"Six months, Jem."

"Is it now? Don't seem so long. I used to think I should get away before we'd been aboard a week, and it's six months, and we arn't gone. You do mean to go if you get a chance?"

"Yes, Jem," said Don, frowning. "I said I would, and I will."

"Arn't it being a bit obstinate like, Mas' Don?"

"Obstinate? What, to do what I said I'd do?"

"Well, p'r'aps not, sir; but it do sound obstinate all the same."

"You like being a sailor then, Jem?"

"Like it? Being ordered about, and drilled, and sent aloft in rough weather, and all the time my Sally thousands o' miles away? Well, I do wonder at you, Mas' Don, talking like that."

"It was your own fault, Jem. I can't help feeling as I did. It was such a cruel, cowardly way of kidnapping us, and dragging us away, and never a letter yet to tell us what they think at home, after those I sent. No, Jem, as I've said before, I'd have served the king as a volunteer, but I will not serve a day longer than I can help after being pressed."

"T'others seem to have settled down."

"So do we seem to, Jem; but perhaps they're like us, and only waiting for a chance to go."

"Don't talk out loud, Mas' Don. I want to go home: but somehow I sha'n't quite like going when the time does come."

"Why not?"

"Well, some of the lads make very good messmates, and the

officers arn't bad when they're in a good temper; and I've took to that there hammock, Mas' Don. You can't think of how I shall miss that there hammock."

"You'll soon get over that, Jem."

"Yes, sir, dessay I shall; and it will be a treat to sit down at a decent table with a white cloth on, and eat bread and butter like a Christian."

"Instead of tough salt junk, Jem, and bad, hard biscuits."

"And what a waste o' time it do seem learning all this sailoring work, to be no use after all. Holy-stoning might come in. I could holy-stone our floor at home, and save my Sally the trouble, and——" Jem gave a gulp, then sniffed very loudly. "Wish you wouldn't talk about home."

Don smiled sadly, and they were separated directly after.

The time went swiftly on in their busy life, and though his absence from home could only be counted in months, Don had shot up and altered wonderfully. They had touched at the Cape, at Ceylon, and then made a short stay at Singapore before going on to their station farther east, and cruising to and fro.

During that period Don's experience had been varied, but the opportunity he was always looking for did not seem to come.

Then a year had passed away, and they were back at Singapore, where letters reached both, and made them go about the deck looking depressed for the rest of the week.

Then came one morning when there was no little excitement on board, the news having oozed out that the sloop was bound for New Zealand, a place in those days little known, save as a wonderful country of tree-fern, pine, and volcano, where the natives were a fierce fighting race, and did not scruple to eat those whom they took captive in war.

"Noo Zealand, eh?" said Jem.

"Port Jackson and Botany Bay, I hear, Jem, and then on to New Zealand. We shall see something of the world."

"Ay, so we shall, Mas' Don. Bot'ny Bay! That's where they sends the chaps they transports, arn't it?"

"Yes, I believe so."

"Then we shall be like transported ones when we get there. You're right, after all, Mas' Don. First chance there is, let me and you give up sailoring, and go ashore."

"I mean to, Jem; and somehow, come what may, we will."

CHAPTER XX.

A NATURALIZED NEW ZEALANDER.

THREE months had passed since the conversation in the last chapter, when after an adverse voyage from Port Jackson, His Majesty's sloop-of-war under shortened sail made her way slowly towards what was in those days a land of mystery.

A stiff breeze was blowing, and the watch were on deck, ready for reducing sail or any emergency. More were ready in the tops, and all on board watching the glorious scene unfolding before them.

"I say, Mas' Don, look ye there," whispered Jem, as they sat together in the foretop. "If this don't beat Bristol, I'm a Dutchman."

"Beat Bristol!" said Don contemptuously; "why, it's as different as can be."

"Well, I dunno so much about that," said Jem. "There's that mountain yonder smoking puts one in mind of a factory chimney. And look yonder too!—there's another one smoking ever so far off. I say, are those burning mountains?"

"I suppose so, unless it's steam. But what a lovely place!"

There were orders for shortening sail given just then, and they had no more opportunity for talking during the next quarter of an hour, when, much closer in, they lay in the top once more, gazing eagerly at the glorious prospect of sea and sky, and verdant land and mountain. The vessel slowly rounded what appeared to be a headland, and in a short time the wind seemed to have dropped, and the sea to have grown calm. It was like entering a lovely lake; and as they went slowly on and on, it was to find that they were forging ahead in a perfect archipelago, with fresh beauties opening up each minute.

The land was deliciously green, and cut up into valley, hill, and mountain. One island they were passing sent forth into the clear sunny air a cloud of silvery steam, which floated slowly away, like a white ensign spread to welcome the newcomers from a civilised land. At their distance from the shore it was impossible to make out the individual trees, but there seemed to be clumps of noble pines some distance in, and the valleys were made ornamental with some kind of feathery growth.

"Well, all I've got to say, Mas' Don, is this here—Singpore arn't to be grumbled at, and China's all very well, only hot; but if you and me's going to say good-bye to sailoring, let's do it here."

"That's exactly what I was thinking, Jem," replied Don.

"Say, Mas' Don, p'r'aps it arn't for me, being a servant and you a young master, to make remarks."

"Don't talk nonsense, Jem; we are both common sailors."

"Well then, sir, as one sailor to another sailor, I says I wish you wouldn't get into bad habits."

"I wish so too, Jem."

"There you are again!" said Jem testily.

"What do you mean?"

"Why, so sure as I thinks something sensible and good, you always ketches me up and says you had thought it before."

"Nonsense, Jem! Well, have it your way. I quite agree with you."

"No, I won't, sir; you're master. Have it your way. I quite agree with you. Let's go ashore here."

"If you can get the chance, Jem.—How lovely it looks!'

"Lovely s nothing to it, sir. Mike used to brag about what he'd seen in foreign countries, but he never see anything to come up to this."

"I don't think any one could see a more beautiful place, Jem."

"But I don't like the look o' that, sir."

"Of what?"

"That there yonder. That smoke."

"What, on that little island? No, Jem; it's steam."

"Well, don't you know what that means?"

"No."

"Then I've got something at last as you arn't got first!" cried Jem excitedly, as he sheltered his eyes from the glare of the sun. "Yes; that's it's, sure. Cooking!"

"Cooking? What's cooking?"

"That place where the steam is, Mas' Don. I say, you know what they do here? That's the place where they do it."

"Do what?"

"Cook people. That's the spot, safe."

"Nonsense!" said Don laughing.

"Ah! you may call it nonsense, Mas' Don; but if them sort o' things is done here, I think we'd better stop on board."

Just at that moment the captain, who was busy with his spy-glass examining the place and looking for a snug anchorage, suddenly gave an order, which was passed on, and with the rapidity customary on board a man-of-war, the stout boarding nettings, ready for use on an emergency, were triced up to the lower rigging, so that before long the vessel, from its bulwarks high up toward the lower yards, presented the appearance of a cage.

While this was going on, others of the men stood to their arms, guns were cast loose and loaded, and every precaution taken against a surprise.

The reason for all this was that quite a fleet of long canoes, propelled by paddles, suddenly began to glide out from behind one of the islands, each canoe seeming to contain from eighty to a hundred men.

The effect was beautiful, for the long, dark vessels, with their grotesque, quaintly carved prows and sterns, seemed to be like some strange living creatures working along paths of silver, so regularly went the paddles, turning the sea into lines of dazzling light.

The men were armed with spears and tomahawks, and as they came nearer, some could be seen wearing black feathers tipped with white stuck in their hair, while their dark, nearly naked bodies glistened in the sun like bronze.

"Are they coming to attack us, Jem?" said Don, who began to feel a strange thrill of excitement.

"Dessay they'd like to, Mas' Don; but it strikes me they'd think twice about it. Why, we could sail right over those long thin boats of theirs, and send 'em all to the bottom."

Just then there was an order from the deck, and more sail was taken in, till the ship hardly moved, as the canoes came dashing up, the men of the foremost singing a mournful kind of chorus as they paddled on.

"Ship ahoy!" suddenly came from the first canoe. "What ship's that?"

"His Majesty's sloop-of-war *Golden Danaë*," shouted back the first lieutenant from the chains. "Tell your other boats to keep back, or we shall fire."

"No, no, no: don't do that, sir! They don't mean fighting," came back from the boat; and a big savage, whose face was blue with tattooing, stood up in the canoe, and then turned and spoke to one of his companions, who rose and shouted to the occupants of the other canoes to cease paddling.

"Speaks good English, sir," said the lieutenant to the captain.

"Yes. Ask them what they want, and if it's peace."

The lieutenant shouted this communication to the savage in the canoe.

"Want, sir?" came back; "to trade with you for guns and powder, and to come aboard."

'How is it you speak good English?"

"Why, what should an Englishman speak?"

"Then you are not a savage?"

"Now do I look like one?" cried the man indignantly.

"Of course; I forgot—I'm an Englishman on a visit to the country, and I've adopted their customs, sir—that's all."

"Oh, I see," said the lieutenant, laughing; "ornaments and all."

"May they come aboard, sir?"

"Oh, yes; if they leave their arms."

The man communicated this to the occupants of the boat, and there was a good deal of excited conversation for a time.

"That fellow's a runaway convict for certain, sir," said the lieutenant. "Shall we get him aboard, and keep him?"

"No. Let him be. Perhaps he will prove very useful."

'The chiefs say it isn't fair to ask them to come without their arms," said the tattooed Englishman. "How are they to know that you will not be treacherous?"

'Tell them this is a king's ship, and if they behave themselves they have nothing to fear," said the captain. "Stop! Six of them can come aboard armed if they like. You can lead them and interpret."

"I'll tell them, sir; but I won't come aboard, thank you. I'm a bit of a savage now, and the crew might make remarks, and we should quarrel."

He turned to the savages, and the captain and lieutenant exchanged glances, while directly after the canoe was run along-side, and half-a-dozen of the people sprang up the side, and were admitted through the boarding netting to begin striding about the deck in the most fearless way.

They were fine, herculean-looking fellows, broad-shouldered and handsome, and every man had his face tattooed in a curious scroll-like pattern, which ended on the sides of his nose.

Their arms were spears and tomahawks, and two carried by a stout thong to the wrist a curiously carved object, which looked like a model of a paddle in pale green stone, carefully polished, but which on closer inspection seemed to be a weapon for using at close quarters.

As they paraded the deck, with their quick eyes grasping everything, they made no scruple about placing their faces close to those of the sailors, and then drawing themselves up with a conscious look of satisfaction and self-esteem, as they compared their physique with that of their visitors.

One of them, a great fellow of about six feet three, and stout and muscular in proportion, stopped suddenly in front of Jem, at whom he seemed to frown, and turned to Don, upon whose chest he laid the back of his hand.

"Pakeha," he said in a deep voice; "Ngati pakeha."

"Tell him he's another, Mas' Don," said Jem.

The savage turned fiercely upon Jem, gripping Don's arm the while.

"Pakeha," he said; "Ngati pakeha. Maori pakeha. My pakeha!"

Then to Don—"You my pakeha. Give me powder—gun."

"Don't you wish you may get it, old chap?" said Jem. "Wants you to give him powder and gun."

The savage nodded approval.

"Yes," he said; "powder gun—you give."

A call from one of his companions summoned the savage away, and he joined them to partake of some rum and water, which the captain had had prepared on their behalf.

"Won't you come up and have some rum?" said the lieutenant to the tattooed Englishman in the boat.

"No, thank you; but you may send me down the bottle if you like, sir. Look here! shall I show you where you can anchor?"

The lieutenant glanced at his superior officer, and in answer to his nod turned to the man again.

"Can you show us a safe anchorage?"

"I can show you half-a-dozen, all safe," said the man. "When you like, I'll lead the way."

"A boat shall follow you, and take soundings."

The first cutter was manned with a well-armed crew, and the lieutenant stepped in—Don and Jem being two of the number.

The tattooed Englishman shouted something to the men busy on the ship, and they unwillingly left the deck, slipped down into their canoe, and this led off, followed by the first cutter.

"Give way, my lads!" said the lieutenant; "and mind this: there must be no straying off in any shape whatever—that is, if we land. These fellows seem friendly, but we are only a few among hundreds, and I suppose you know what your fate would be if they got the upper hand."

"'YOU MY PAKEHA. GIVE ME POWDER—GUN.'"

"Make tattooed chiefs of us seemingly, sir," said Jem.

"Or hot joints," said the officer laconically. "Ready there with that lead."

The men rowed steadily on after the first canoe, and the man with the lead kept on making casts, but getting no bottom except at an excessive depth, as they went on, the scene growing more beautiful as each point was passed. The other canoes followed, and a curious thrill ran through Don, as he felt how helpless they would be if the savages proved treacherous, for the boat and her crew could have been overpowered at once; and the lieutenant was evidently uneasy, as he saw that they were taken right round to the back of a small island, gradually losing sight of the ship.

But he had his duty to do, and keeping a strict watch, after passing the word to his men to have their arms ready, he made them row on, with the lead going all the time.

It was a curious experience, and Don's heart beat as he thought of the possibility of escaping from the boat, and taking to the shore, wondering the while what would be the consequences. The man in the leading canoe was evidently well treated, and quite one in authority; and if they landed and joined these people, why should not he and Jem become so too?

These were a few of the passing thoughts suggested by the novelty and beauty of the place, which seemed ten times more attractive to those who had been for months cooped up on shipboard; but the toil in which he was engaged kept Don from taking more than a casual glance ashore.

Bosun Jones sat at the tiller side by side with the lieutenant, and scraps of their conversation reached Don's ears.

"Well, sir," said the former, "as you say, we're out of the reach of the sloop's guns; but if anything happens to us, we may be sure that the captain will take pretty good revenge."

"And a deal of good that will do us, Jones," said the lieutenant. "I believe that scoundrel is leading us into a trap."

"If he is, sir, I hope for one chance at him," said the boatswain; "I don't think I should miss my man."

The leading canoe went on for quite a quarter of a mile after they had passed out of sight of the ship, the cutter following and taking soundings all the way, till they seemed to be quite shut in by high land, and the water was as smooth as a lake.

There, about five hundred yards from the shore, the canoe stopped, and almost at the same moment the water shallowed, so that the man in the bows got soundings in ten fathoms; directly after, nine; then eight; and eight again, at which depth the water seemed to remain.

"Come, that's honest leading!" said the lieutenant, brightening; "as snug a berth as a ship could be in. Why, Jones, what a position for a port!"

"This do, sir?" shouted the tattooed Englishman. "You'll be quite in shelter here, and the water keeps the same right up to the shore."

A few more soundings were taken, and then the boat returned to the ship, which made her way in and anchored before night, with the canoes hanging about, and some of the chiefs eagerly besieging the gangway to be allowed on deck. But special precautions were taken; sentries were doubled; and, as if feeling that the fate of all on board depended upon his stringent regulations, the captain only allowed about half-a-dozen of the savage-looking people to come on board at a time.

By a little management Don had contrived that Jem should have the hammock next to his; and that night, with the soft air playing in through the open port-hole, they listened to the faint sounds on shore, where the savages were evidently feasting, and discussed in a whisper the possibility of getting away.

CHAPTER XXI.

AN INVITATION.

IT seemed to Don that the object of the captain in coming to New Zealand was to select and survey portions of the coast for a new settlement; and for the next few days well-armed boat parties were out in all directions sounding, and in two cases making short journeys inland.

"I say," said Jem one morning, as he and Don stood gazing over the side of the ship at the verdant shores.

"Well, Jem, what do you say?"

"Has that ugly-looking chap Ramsden been telling tales about us?"

"I don't know; why?"

"Because here's a fortnight we've been at anchor, and since the first day neither of us has been out in a boat."

"Hasn't been our turn, Jem."

"Well, p'r'aps not, sir; but it do seem strange. Just as if they thought we should slip away."

"And I suppose we've given up all such thoughts as that now."

"Oh, have we?" said Jem sarcastically; and then there was silence for a time, till Jem, who had been watching the steam rise from the little island about a quarter of a mile away, exclaimed, "Wonder what's being cooked over yonder, Mas' Don. I know; no, I don't. Thought it was washing day, but it can't be, for they don't hardly wear any clothes."

"It's volcanic steam, Jem. Comes out of the earth."

"Get along with you, Mas' Don. Don't get spinning yarns."

"I'm telling you the truth, Jem."

"Are you, sir? Well, p'r'aps it's what you think is the truth, I say, arn't it lovely out here? How I should like to have a cottage just on that there point, and my Sally to keep it tidy. Hullo! what's up?"

The boatswain's shrill pipe was heard just then, and a boat's crew was summoned to take an exploring party ashore.

To Don's great delight, he and Jem formed part of the boat's crew; and at last he felt that he was to see something of the beautiful place, which grew more attractive every time he scanned the coast.

This time the captain was going to land; and, as the men were provided with axes, it seemed that they were about to make their way into the woods.

The natives had been most friendly, bringing off and receiving presents; but, all the same, no precautions were omitted to provide for the safety of the ship and crew.

It was a glorious morning, with hardly a breath of wind stirring, and the savages were lolling about on the shore. Their canoes were run up on the sands, and there was an aspect of calm and repose everywhere that seemed delightful.

But the boat's crew had little time given them for thinking. The captain and a midshipman of about Don's age took their places in the stern sheets, Bosun Jones seized the tiller, the word was given, the oars splashed the water simultaneously, and the boat sped over the calm surface of the transparent sea, sending the shoals of fish darting away.

The boat's head was set in quite a fresh direction, and she was run ashore a little way from the mouth of a rushing river, whose waters came foaming down through blocks of pumice and black masses of volcanic stone.

As the boat's head touched the shore, the men leaped over right and left, and dragged her a short distance up the black glistening heavy sand, so that the captain could land dryshod.

Then preparations were made, arms charged, and Bosun Jones gave Don a friendly nod before turning to the captain.

"Will you have this lad, sir, to carry a spare gun for you?"

"Yes," said the captain; "a good plan;" and Don's eyes sparkled. "No," said the captain the next moment; "he is only a boy, and the walking will be too hard for him. Let him and another stay with the boat."

Don's brow clouded over with disappointment, but it cleared a little directly after as he found that Jem was to be his companion; and as the party marched off toward where the forest came down nearly to the sea, they, in obedience to their orders, thrust the boat off again, climbed in, and cast out her grapnel a few fathoms from the shore.

"I am disappointed," said Don, after they had sat in the boat some time, watching their companions till they had disappeared.

"Oh, I dunno, Mas' Don; we've got some beef and biscuit, and somewhere to sit down, and nothing to do. They, poor fellows, will come back hot and tired out."

"Yes; but's it's so dull here."

"Well, I dunno 'bout that," said Jem, looking lazily round at the glorious prospect of glistening sea, island and shore, backed up by mountains; "I call it just lovely."

"Oh, it's lovely enough, Jem; but I want to go ashore."

"Now if you call my cottage dull inside the yard gates at Bristol, I'm with you, Mas' Don; but after all there's no place like home."

There was a dead silence, during which Don sat gazing at a group of the savages half-a-mile away, as they landed from a long canoe, and ran it up the beach in front of one of the native *whares* or dwellings.

"Why, Jem!" Don exclaimed suddenly, "why not now?"

"Eh?" said Jem, starting from watching a large bird dive down with a splash in the silvery water, and then rise again with a fish in its beak; "see that, Mas' Don?"

"Yes, yes," exclaimed Don impatiently; "why not now?"

"Why not now, Mas' Don?" said Jem, scratching his head; "is that what you call a connundydrum?"

"Don't be stupid, man. I say, why not now?"

"Yes, I heared you say so twice; but what does it mean?"

"We're quite alone; we have a boat and arms, with food and water. Why not escape now?"

"Escape, Mas' Don? What, run away now at once—desert?"

"It is not running away, Jem; it is not deserting. They have robbed us of our liberty, and we should only be taking it back."

"Ah, they'd preach quite a different sarmon to that," said Jem, shaking his head.

"Why, you are never going to turn tail?"

"Not I, Mas' Don, when the time comes; but it don't seem to have come yet."

"Why, the opportunity is splendid, man."

"No, Mas' Don, I don't think so. If we take the boat, 'fore we've gone far they'll ketch sight of us aboard, and send another one to fetch us back, or else make a cock-shy of us with the long gun."

"Then let's leave the boat."

"And go ashore, and meet our messmates and the captain."

"Go in another direction."

"Out of the frying-pan into the fire," said Jem, grinning. "Say, Mas' Don, how do they cook their food?"

"Don't talk nonsense, Jem; that's only a traveller's tale. I believe the people here will behave kindly to us."

"Till we got fat," said Jem, chuckling; "and then they'd have a tuck out. No, thank ye, Mas' Don; my Sally wouldn't like it. You see, I'm nice and plump and round now, and they'd soon use me. You're a great long growing boy, thin as a lath, and it 'd take years to make you fit to kill, so as it don't matter for you."

"There is a chance open to us now for escape," said Don bitterly; "to get right away, and journey to some port, where we could get a passage to England as sailors, and you treat it with ridicule."

"Not I, Mas' Don, lad."

"You do, Jem. Such a chance may never occur again;

and I shall never be happy till I have told my mother what is the real truth about our going away."

"But you did write it to her, Mas' Don."

"Write! What is writing to speaking? I thought you meant to stand by me."

"So I do, Mas' Don, when a good chance comes. It hasn't come yet."

"Ahoy!"

A hail came out of the dense growth some fifty yards away.

"There," said Jem, "you see we couldn't get off; some one coming back."

"Ahoy!" came again; "boat ahoy!"

"Ahoy! ahoy!" shouted back Jem, and the two boat-keepers watched the moving ferns in front of them, expecting to see the straw hat of a messmate directly; but instead there appeared the black white-tipped feathers, and then the hideously tattooed bluish face of a savage, followed directly after by another, and two stalwart men came out on to the sands, and began to walk slowly down toward the boat.

"Cock your pistol, Mas' Don," whispered Jem, "quiet like; don't let 'em see. They've got their spears and choppers. Precious ready too with their *ahoys*."

"Why, it's that tattooed Englishman, Jem, and that savage who called me his pakeha."

"And like his impudence!" said Jem. "You're right though, so it is."

"Morning, mate," said the Englishman, who, save that he was a little lighter in colour than his hideous-looking companion, could hardly be distinguished from him.

"Morning, my hearty," said Jem. "What is it? Want a passage home?"

"Do I want what?" growled the man. "Not I; too well off here."

"Wouldn't be safe to go back, p'r'aps," said Jem meaningly.

The man darted a fierce look at him, which told that the shaft had hit its mark.

"Never you mind about that," he said surlily.

"But you are a lifer, and have run away, haven't you?" continued Jem, in a bantering tone.

The man's aspect was for the moment so fierce that Don involuntarily stole his hand towards the pistol at his side. But his countenance softened directly after.

"That's neither here nor there, mate," said the man. "There's been chaps sent out abroad who were innocent, and others who have been punished more than they deserved; and you aren't the sort of fellow to go talking like that, and making trouble for a fellow who never did you any harm."

"Not I," said Jem; "it's no business of mine."

"And he isn't the fellow to make trouble," put in Don.

"That he isn't," said the man, smiling. "'Sides I'm a Maori chief now, and I've got a couple of hundred stout fellows who would fight for me. Eh, Ngati?" he said, addressing some words in the savage tongue.

"Pah, ha, ha!" roared the great fellow beside him, brandishing his spear; and seizing the greenstone paddle-like weapon, which hung from his neck, in his left hand, as he struck an attitude, turned up his eyes till the whites only were visible, distorted his face hideously, and thrust out his great tongue till it was far below his chin.

"Brayvo! brayvo! brayvo!" cried Jem, hammering the side of the boat; "brayvo, waxworks! I say, mate, will he always go off like that when you pull the string?"

"Yes," said the Englishman, laughing; "and two hundred more like him."

"Then it must be a werry pretty sight indeed; eh, Mas' Don?"

"Ah, it's all very well to laugh," said the Englishman good-humouredly; "but when they mean mischief, it's heads off and a feast."

"Eh?" cried Jem.

"They'll kill a man, and cook him and eat him after."

"Gammon!"

"Gammon, eh?" cried the Englishman; and he turned to his savage companion with a word or two.

The savage relapsed into his former quiescent state, uttered a loud grunt, and smacked his lips.

"And so you do do that sort of thing?" said Jem, grinning. "You look in pretty good condition, mate."

"No!" said the Englishman fiercely. "I've joined them, and married, and I'm a pakeha Maori and a great chief, and I've often fought for them; but I've never forgotten what I am."

"No offence meant, old chap," said Jem; and then from behind his hand he whispered to Don,—

"Look out, my lad; they mean the boat."

"No, we don't," said the Englishman, contemptuously; "if we did we could have it. Why, I've only to give the word, and a hundred fellows would be out in a canoe before you knew where you were. No, my lad, it's peace; and I'm glad of a chance, though I'm happy enough here, to have a talk to some one from the old home. Never was in the west country, I suppose? I'm an Exeter man."

"I've been in Exeter often," said Don eagerly; "we're from Bristol."

The Englishman waded rapidly into the sea, his Maori companion dashing in on the other side of the boat, and Jem and Don seized their pistols.

"Didn't I tell you it was peace?" said the Englishman, angrily. "I only wanted to shake hands."

"Ho!" said Jem, suspiciously, as their visitor coolly seated himself on the gunwale of the boat, his follower taking the opposite side, so as to preserve the balance.

"Enough to make you think we meant wrong," said the Englishman; "but we don't. Got any tobacco, mate?"

"Yes," said Jem, producing his bag. "'Tarn't very good. Say, Mas' Don, if he came to see us in Bristol, we could give him a bit o' real old Charlestown, spun or leaf."

"Could you, though?" said the man, filling his pipe.

"Yes; my uncle is a large sugar and tobacco merchant," said Don.

"Then how came you to be a sailor boy? I know, you young dog; you ran away. Well, I did once."

"No, no," said Don, hastily; "we did not run away; we were pressed."

"Pressed?" said the Englishman, pausing in the act of striking a light on one of the thwarts of the boat.

"You needn't believe unless you like," said Jem, sourly, "but we were; dragged off just as if we were—well, never mind what. Feel here."

He bent forward, took the man's hand, and placed it upon the back of his head.

"That's a pretty good scar, isn't it? Reg'lar ridge."

"Yes; that was an ugly crack, mate."

"Well, that's what I got, and a lot beside. Young Mas' Don here, too, was awfully knocked about."

"And you stood it?"

"Stood it?" said Don, laughing. "How could we help it?"

"Made you be sailors, eh, whether you would or no?"

"That's it," said Jem.

"Well, you can do as you like," said the man; "but I know what I should do if they'd served me so."

"Cut off?" said Jem.

"That's it, mate. I wouldn't ha' minded being a sailor, but not be made one whether I liked or no."

"You weren't a sailor, were you?" said Don

"I? No; never mind what I was."

"Then we had better cut off, Mas' Don," said Jem, grinning till his eyes were shut; "and you and me 'll be painted like he is in fast colours, and you shall be a chief, and I'll be your head man."

"To be sure," said the Englishman; "and you shall have a wife."

"Eh?" cried Jem fiercely; "that I just won't. And, Mas' Don, if we ever do get back, don't you never say a word to my Sally about this here."

"No, Jem, not I."

"But you'll leave the ship, mate?"

"Well, I dunno," said Jem, thoughtfully. "Will that there pattern all over your face and chest wash off?"

"Wash off? No."

"Not with pearl-ash or soda?"

"No, not unless you skinned me," said the man, laughing.

"Well, that part arn't tempting, is it, Mas' Don?"

Don shook his head.

"And then about that other part, old chap—cannibalism? I say, that's gammon, isn't it?"

"What do you mean?"

"Why, you know—the cooking a fellow and eating him. How dull you are!"

"Dull? You be here a few years among these people, talking their lingo, and not seeing an Englishman above once in two years, and see if you wouldn't be dull."

"But is that true?"

"About being cannibals? Yes it's true enough," said the man seriously; "and very horrid it is; but it's only when there's war."

He had succeeded in striking a light now, and was smoking placidly enough on the boat's edge, but dreamily thoughtful, as if he were recalling matters that were past.

"Has he ever—been at war?" said Don, altering the fashion of his inquiry when it was half uttered.

"Often."

"And——? you know," said Jem, who felt no delicacy about the matter.

The Englishman nodded his head slowly, and sent forth a tremendous puff of smoke, while his companion moved toward Don, and smiled at him, tapping him on the shoulder with his hand, and seeming to nod approval.

"Pakeha!" he said, excitedly; "my pakeha; Maori pakeha."

"What does he mean by that?" said Don, after he had suffered these attentions patiently for a few minutes.

"Means he wants you to be his pakeha."

"Yes: my pakeha; Maori pakeha!" cried the chief eagerly.

"But what is a pakeha?"

"Why, you're a pakeha, I'm a pakeha. They call foreigners pakehas; and he wants to claim you as his."

"What, his slave?" cried Don.

"No, no; he means his foreign brother. If you become his pakeha, he will be bound to fight for you. Eh, Ngati?"

The savage gave vent to a fierce shout, and went through his former performance, but with more flourish, as if he were slaying numbers of enemies, and his facial distortion was hideous.

"Well, when I was a little un, and went to school," said Jem, "I used to get spanks if I put out my tongue. Seems as if it's a fine thing to do out here."

"Yes; it's a way they have when they're going to fight," said the Englishman thoughtfully. "S'pose it would mean trouble if I were to set you on to do it; but it wouldn't be at all bad for me if you were both of you to leave the ship and come ashore."

"To be cooked?" said Jem.

"Bah! Stuff! They'd treat you well. Youngster here's all right; Ngati would make him his pakeha."

"My pakeha," cried the chief, patting Don again. "Much powder; much gun."

"Pupil of mine," said the Englishman, smiling; "I taught him our lingo."

"What does he mean?" said Don; "that he'd give me a big gun and plenty of powder?"

The Englishman laughed.

"No, no; he wants you to bring plenty of guns and powder ashore with you when you come."

"When I come!" said Don, thoughtfully.

"I sha'nt persuade you, my lad; but you might do worse. You'd be all right with us; and there are Englishmen here and there beginning to settle."

"And how often is there a post goes out for England?"

"Post? For England? Letters?"

"Yes."

"I don't know; I've been here a long time now, and I never had a letter and I never sent one away."

"Then how should I be able to send to my Sally."

"Dunno," said the man. "There, you think it over. Ngati here will be ready to take care of you, youngster; and matey here shall soon have a chief to take care of him."

"I don't know so much about that," said Jem. "I should be ready enough to come ashore, but you've got some precious unpleasant ways out here as wouldn't suit me."

"You'd soon get used to them," said the Englishman, drily; "and after leading a rough life, and being bullied by everybody, it isn't half bad to be a chief, and have a big canoe of your own, and make people do as you like."

"But then you're a great powerful man," said Don. "They'd obey you, but they wouldn't obey me."

"Oh, yes, they would, if you went the right way to work. It isn't only being big. They're big, much bigger all round than Englishmen, and stronger and more active. They're not afraid of your body, but of your mind; that's what they can't understand. If I was to write down something on a bit of wood or a leaf—we don't often see paper here—and give it to you to read, and you did the same to me, that gets over them: it's a wonder they can't understand. And lots of other things we know are puzzles to them, and so they think us big. You consider it over a bit, my lad; and if you decide to run for it, I'll see as you don't come to no harm."

"And him too?"

"Oh, yes; he shall be all right too; I'll see to that."

"Shouldn't be too tempting for 'em, eh? should I?" said Jem.

"Not for our tribes here," said the Englishman, laughing; 'but I may as well be plain with you. If we went to war with some of the others, and they got hold of you——"

"Say, Mas' Don," said Jem interrupting the speaker, "I don't like being a sort of white nigger aboard ship, and being kept a prisoner, and told it's to serve the king; but a man can go into the galley to speak to the cook without feeling that he's wondering which jynte of you he shall use first. No thankye; it's a werry lovely country, but I want to get home to my Sally some day; and if we cut and run here, I'm afraid I never should."

"You turn it over in your own minds, both of you, my lads. There, my pipe's out, and I think we'll go. Stop here long?"

"Do you mean the ship, or here with the boat?"

"Here with the boat," said the Englishman, holding out his hand.

"Till our party comes back," said Jem.

"I may see you again," said the Englishman; and shaking hands, he said a few words to his companion, and then began to wade ashore.

The savage smiled and shook hands in turn, after which he patted Don on the shoulder again.

"My pakeha," he said, sharply; "Maori pakeha—my."

He followed his leader; and Don and Jem watched them till they disappeared amongst the abundant growth.

CHAPTER XXII.

DON'S DECISION.

"IT'S tempting, Jem," said Don.

"Yes, Mas' Don; and it's untempting, too. I had a book once about manners and customs of foreign parts, but it didn't say things so plain as you've found 'em here."

"Yes, I'm afraid it won't do, Jem. Even if we got away from the ship, it might be to a life that would be worse."

"That's it, sir, as I said afore, 'out of the frying-pan into the fire.' Wonder how long they'll be 'fore they come back."

"Not till sundown. I say, shall we try it or sha'n't we?"

Jem scratched his head, and seemed to be hesitating.

"I don't know what to say, Jem. If they treated us well on board, I should be disposed to say let's put up with our life till we get back home."

"But then they don't treat us well, Mas' Don. I don't grumble to you, but it's a reg'lar dog's life I lead; bully and cuss and swear at you, and then not even well fed."

"But we are to be paid for it, Jem," said Don, bitterly.

"Paid, Mas' Don!" replied Jem, contemptuously. "What paying will make up for what we go through?"

"And I suppose we should have prize-money if we fought and took a French ship."

"But then we're sent right out here, Mas' Don, where there's no French ships to fight; and if there were, the prize-money is shared among them as aren't killed."

"Of course."

"Well, how do we know as we shouldn't be killed? No,

Mas' Don, they don't behave well to us, and I want to get home again, and so do you."

"Yes, Jem."

"P'r'aps it's cowardly, and they'll call it desertion."

"Yes, Jem."

"But we sha'n't be there to hear 'em call it so."

"No, Jem."

"Therefore it don't matter, Mas' Don; I've thought this all over hundreds o' times when you've been asleep."

"And I've thought it over, Jem, hundreds of times when you've been asleep."

"There you go again, sir, taking the ideas out of a man's brain. You shouldn't, Mas' Don. I always play fair with you."

"Yes, of course you do."

"Well, then, you ought to play fair with me. Now look here, Mas' Don," continued Jem, seating himself on the gunwale of the boat, so as to let his bare feet hang in the water.

"'Ware sharks, Jem," said Don quickly.

Jem was balanced on the edge, and at those words he threw himself backward with his heels in the air, and after he had struggled up with some difficulty, he stood rubbing his head.

"Where 'bouts—where 'bouts, sir?"

"I did not see a shark, Jem, but the place swarms with them, and I thought it was a risk."

"Well, I do call that a trick," grumbled Jem. "Hit my nut such a whack, I did, and just in the worst place."

"Better than having a leg torn off, Jem. Well, what were you going to say?"

"Bottom of the boat's nearly knocked it all out of my head," said Jem, rubbing the tender spot. "What I meant to say was that I was stolen."

"Well, I suppose we may call it so."

"Stolen from my wife, as I belongs to."

"Yes, Jem."

"And you belongs to your mother and your Uncle Josiah, so you was stolen, too."

"Yes, Jem, if you put it in that way, I suppose we were."

"Well, then," said Jem triumphantly, "they may call it cowardly, or desertion, or what they like; but what I say is this, a man can't be doing wrong in taking stolen goods back to them as they belong to."

"No, Jem, I s'pose not."

"Very well then, Mas' Don; the question is this—Will you or won't you?"

"I will, Jem."

"First chance?"

"Yes, I am decided."

"That's a bargain then, my lad. So shake hands on it. Why! how rough and hard and tarry your hands have grown!"

"Look out, Jem!"

Don caught hold of the grapnel rope ready to haul up and get away from the shore, but Jem seized his hand.

"It's all right, Mas' Don. Only them two running back with a basket, and I'm in that sort o' way of thinking that they've only got to coax me a bit, and swear as there shall be no tattooing and meat-pie nonsense, and I'd go ashore with them now."

"No, Jem, that would not do till we know a little more of them, and I can't help hesitating now it comes to the point."

"That's just what I felt, Mas' Don," said Jem, with a perplexed look on his face.

"Come, Jem, who's stealing some one else's ideas now?"

"Like fruit?" said the tattooed Englishman, coming down to the water's edge.

"That depends," said Jem, dubiously. "What is it?"

"Karaka," said their new friend, offering a basket of an olive-like fruit.

"Good to eat?"

"Yes; try it."

"S'pose you eat some first," said Jem suspiciously.

The Englishman laughed, and took some of the fruit, and began to chew it.

"Afraid these would drug you so that I could steal the boat?"

"I didn't know," said Jem sulkily. "Wouldn't be the first who has stolen a boat, I suppose."

Don took some of the berries, and began to eat, and this emboldened Jem, who tasted one in a very suspicious and doubting way.

"Hullo!" he said, with his countenance brightening; "know what these here taste like, Mas' Don?"

"Very mellow apple?"

"No; like the medlars that grew in my grandmother's garden."

"That's right!" said the Englishman; and his New Zealand companion began to select the best and ripest of the fruit from the basket and handed them to Don, watching him eat with what was meant for a pleasant smile; but as his face resembled one that had been carved in a piece of mahogany, and afterwards ornamented with streaks and scrolls, the effect was more repellent than attractive.

"My pakeha," said the great fellow with a childlike show of satisfaction; and he looked from one to the other and laughed.

"Here, he's took to you regular, youngster; only look out, for he'll want *utu* for it some time. Eh, Ngati? Utu?"

"*Utu, utu,*" said the chief, smiling.

"What's utu?" said Jem, in a surly tone.

"Payment."

"Oh, then we'll give him a bit of 'bacco."

He offered the New Zealander his tobacco-bag, which was quietly annexed with a smile.

"There, we'll leave you the fruit. They're good eating, my lads, and if at any time before you go, you feel disposed to settle down with us, there's plenty of room, and it won't be very long before you'll grow into chiefs."

He nodded, and then said a few words to his companion, who smiled at the two strangers in turn, after which they went off together into the forest, and were gone.

"Ugh!" ejaculated Jem. "Don't know whether it arn't safer aboard ship after all."

"Why do you say that?" cried Don.

"Because whenever that black chap looks at me, he gives me the shivers."

"Why?"

"Seems to me that he's too fond of you, Mas' Don, and as if he was thinking how good you'd be."

"Nonsense!" cried Don, who was enjoying the fruit. "Have some more of these. I wonder whether there are any more good kinds of fruit grow ashore."

"Sure to be."

"Do you think if we left the ship, Jem, and found our way right along the coast to some place where we could live till the ship had gone, and then wait till another ship came, we could get enough to eat?"

"Dessay we could."

"Because if we did, we should be quite independent, and could do as we liked."

"To be sure, that's the way it seems to me; but just now, Mas' Don, I can only think of one thing."

"What's that, Jem?"

"How to get a bit of sleep, for the sun has made me as drowsy as a beedle."

"Well, then, sit down and sleep."

Jem wanted no persuasion, and in five minutes he was breathing very heavily, while Don sat watching the beauties of nature, the clouds of steam floating above the volcanic island, the wondrous sheen of the sea in the sun, the great lace-like tree-ferns which drooped over the mossy growth at the forest edge, and the beautiful butterflies which floated about like gaily-painted flowers in the golden light.

Every now and then there was the sweet note of some bird ringing clearly in the air; then a loud and piercing screech heralded the coming of a parrot or cockatoo, which seemed tame enough to care little for the stranger who was watching its actions.

Then all would be still again—a dreamy, sleepy stillness that was wonderfully attractive to Don as he sat with his eyes half closed. In the distance he could see some of the Maories coming and going in a listless, careless way, as if their life was a very pleasant indolence without a care.

It was very beautiful and wonderfully attractive. On board the ship there were hard work, hard living, peremptory orders, and what seemed to the proud boy a state of slavery, while on shore offered itself a life of ease where there would be no battling with storm, and risk of war or shipwreck.

Why should he not take advantage of this or some other opportunity, and steal ashore?

It would be desertion, and setting aside the punishment held out to the one who forsook his ship after being forced into His Majesty's navy, there was a feeling troubling Don that it would be dishonourable to go.

On the other side there was home, the strong desire to be free, and a love of adventure prompting him to escape.

"No," he said decidedly at last; "it would be cowardly and base to desert. They treat me badly, but not hardly enough to make me run away. I'll stop and bear it like a man."

Somehow Don felt lighter in heart after coming to this determination; and after looking round and wondering how long the explorers would be before they returned, and also wishing he could have been of the party, he leaned his elbows on the side of the boat and gazed down into the clear water, and through it at the beautiful lace-like pattern made by the sun, casting the netted shadow of the ripples on the soft pebbly sand.

Now and then a shoal of fish glided in and dashed away. Then one brilliantly decked in gold and silver and blue came floating by, and Don watched it eagerly, wishing the while that he had a line.

He was leaning over the side in this way, gazing down at the water, now about four feet deep where the boat had swung, when he became aware of something pale and shadowy some little distance off. Looking at it in a sloping direction made the ocean water seem so dense that he could not make out what it was for some little time. At first it seemed to be a dimly-seen patch of seaweed; then it appeared to be too regular and rounded, and it struck him that it must be a large transparent jelly-fish floating in with the tide, till he made out that it was continued backward from him, and that it was larger than he had imagined; and as he looked the object gradually grew plainer and more distinct. It was still shadowy and grey, and had a peculiar, strange attraction, which made him lean more over the side till a curious nightmare-like sensation came over him, and as he realized that the object was alive, and that he was looking down at two strange dull eyes, he felt that he could not shrink back, although the creeping chilly feeling which came over him seemed like a warning of danger.

Then it all appeared more like a dream, in which he was striving hard to get away, and all the time obliged to crouch there gazing at that creature whose eyes were fixed upon him, and which imperceptibly grew plainer to his sight.

The intensity of the position grew more and more painful during what appeared to be a long time. He tried to call to Jem, who was asleep not six feet away, but his mouth felt dry. He endeavoured to reach out and kick him, but he could not stir, and still the creature advanced till, all at once, there was a tremendous disturbance in the water; something seemed to rise and strike him a violent blow in the chest, and the next moment he was seated in the bottom of the boat, which was rocking violently, and staring stupidly at Jem, who sat up staring back.

"What yer do that for?" cried Jem angrily. "I'd only just closed my eyes."

"I did not do anything," faltered Don, shivering.

"Yes, you did!" cried Jem. "Asked me to sit up and watch, and I'd ha' done it. Needn't ha' played tricks."

"I—I——"

"There, don't say you didn't, Mas' Don. Boat's rocking now, and you'd better swab up that water. Nice row there'd be if the skipper come back and found the boat all wet."

Jem picked up the swab and began to remove the water himself, and in doing so he noticed Don's face.

"Why, hullo, Mas' Don! What's the matter? You look as white as—— Why, what now?"

Jem was about to lean over the side and wring the swab, when Don sprang astern and dragged him back.

"Look! look!" he cried, pointing.

Jem followed the direction of the pointing finger, and shrank away with a shudder.

"What? A shark!" he exclaimed.

"Yes; it rose at me out of the water, and struck me in the chest, and I fell back, and so did he."

"Ugh!" ejaculated Jem, as he seized the boathook, and rested it on the gunwale.

"Don't touch it," whispered Don; "it may spring out of the water at you."

"It had better not," said Jem. "Hah!"

He drove the boathook down with all his might, striking the great fish just as it was slowly rising toward the surface, close to the boat; and so well aimed was the stroke, that there was a tremendous swirl in the water, the side near Jem resounded with a heavy blow from the fish's tail, and the boathook seemed to be snatched out of the striker's hand to go slowly sailing away oceanward.

"Look at that!" cried Jem. "Why, I must have driven it right into him. How are we to get it back?"

"Watch it," said Don, excitedly. "It will come out and float directly."

Don's prophecy did not come to pass, for as they watched, they saw about a foot of the boathook shaft stand sloping out of the water, and go here and there in a curious manner.

"Let's row after it," suggested Don.

"Wouldn't be no good, Mas' Don; and we've got nothing to fight him with but pistols. Let him be, and the thing will soon wriggle out."

Jem proved as far wrong as his companion, for, after a time, as they watched and saw the end of the shaft bob here and there; it suddenly disappeared about fifty yards away.

"Why, Mas' Don," said Jem, laughing, "it's like fishing; and after biting ever so long, the float's gone right under water. Now's your time. Strike!"

"And we've no line," said Don, who was beginning to get rid of his nervous sensation.

"No, we haven't a line," said Jem. "Keep your eye on the place where he went down; we musn't lose that hitcher. Say, it won't do to try and swim ashore. That's a shark, that is, and a big one, too. Did he hurt you?"

"Not much. It was like a tremendous blow with somebody's fist. Look!"

"Told you so!" cried Jem. "Here he comes with a rush to give us back the boathook."

"Or to attack the boat," said Don, as the end of the shaft suddenly appeared away to their right; and then came rapidly nearer in a direct line for where they were.

"Not he," said Jem sturdily. "Too stupid."

All the same, there was soon a peculiar rising in the water coming direct for them, as the boathook seemed to plough through the sea, which rapidly grew shallower. Onward it came, nearer and nearer, till Jem gave a warning shout, and placed one foot on the side ready to plunge overboard.

"Don't do that, Jem; it's certain death!" cried Don.

"Don't you stop, Mas' Don; that's certain death, too. Let's swim ashore. Now, my lad, now, now. Don't stop a fellow; don't!"

Jem shouted these words excitedly, as Don clung to him and held him back, gazing wildly all the time at the disturbed water, as the great fish swiftly approached, till, just as it was within a few yards, the shallowness of the water seemed to startle it, making it give quite a bound showing half its length, and then diving down with a kind of wallow, after which the occupants of the boat saw the wooden pole go trailing along the surface, till once more it was snatched, as it were, out of sight.

"Don't seem as if he's going to shake it out," said Jem.

"You must have driven the spike in right over the hook, and it acts like a barb. What a blow you must have given!"

"Well, I hit as hard as I could," said Jem. "He was coming at me. Can you see it now?"

"No."

"Keep a sharp look-out; it's sure to come up sometime."

The sharp look-out was kept; but they did not see the boathook again, though they watched patiently till nearly sundown, when a hail came from the woods; and as the boat-keepers got up the grapnel and ran the light vessel in shore, the captain and his men appeared slowly to their left, and came down as if utterly wearied out.

"Look at 'em, Mas' Don; they've been having a fight."

Jaded, their clothes torn in all directions, coated with mud, and with their faces smeared and scored, the blood stains on their cheeks and hands gave the returning party all the appearance of those who had been engaged in a fight for life.

But it had only been an encounter with the terrible thorns and spines of the wild land they had explored, and the wounds, much as they had bled, were but skin deep.

The boat-keepers leaped out, and ran the stern in as close as they could, and the captain was in the act of stepping in, placing a hand on Don's shoulder to steady himself, worn out as he was with his long tramp, when it seemed to Don that he felt the cold, slimy touch of a shark gliding up against his bare legs, and with a start of horror he sprang sidewise, with the result that the captain, who was bearing down upon the lad's shoulder, fell sidewise into the sea.

"You clumsy idiot!" cried the captain; and forgetting himself in his annoyance, worn out as he was, and irritable from his great exertions, he caught at Don's extended hand, and then as he rose struck the boy a heavy blow with his doubled fist right in the chest.

Don staggered heavily, fell into the water, and then struggled up drenched as the captain was before him. Then, forgetting in his hot rage everything about their relative positions and the difference in age, the boy made for the tall, frowning officer before him, and would have struck him in his blind wrath but for Bosun Jones, who had seen everything, and now hastily interposed.

"No, no, my boy," he said. "Keep back, you are too wet to do any good. Allow me, sir."

Don shrank back, realising the heinousness of the social sin he was about to commit, and a dead silence fell on the group, the men staring wonderingly as the captain accepted Bosun Jones' help, stepped into the boat, and stood wringing himself.

"Why, the young dog was going to strike me!" cried the captain.

"Surely not, sir," said the boatswain hastily. "Only going to help you, sir."

"Help me! I believe he was going to hit out. Here, sir, what made you start away like that?"

"He thought it was a shark, sir," cried Jem. "One's been about the boat all the aft'noon."

"Hold your tongue, sir!" cried the captain sternly. "Here, you boy, what made you flinch!"

"Thought I felt the shark touch me, sir," said Don, sullenly.

"Oh, then I am to be thrown into the water because you are a cowardly young idiot," cried the captain. "I'll talk to you to-morrow. In with you, my lads, and give way."

"There's no boathook!" cried the coxswain; and on the keepers being called to account, their story was received with such manifest doubt, that Don writhed and sat sullenly in his place in the boat, as it was rowed back to the sloop.

"Rather an absurd story that, Jones—about the boathook," said the captain as he stepped on board. "Mind it is reported to-morrow morning. I believe the young scoundrel was going to strike me."

"But you struck him first," said the boatswain to himself, as he saw the captain descend. "Hot-headed young rascal. Ah! here, Lavington, what about that boathook? Let's have the simple truth. One of the Maories stole it, and you were afraid to speak?"

"I was not afraid to speak the truth, sir," said Don; "and I told it."

"But that's such a wild story. Your messmate could not have driven it into a shark over the hook."

"I don't know whether it was driven in over the hook, sir,' replied Don; "but it stuck in the fish's back and would not come out."

The boatswain looked at him thoughtfully, while Don waited to hear his words.

"Look here, Lavington," he said, "I liked you, my lad, from the first, and I should be sorry for you to be in serious trouble. I have been your friend, have I not?"

"I can't see much friendship in dragging one away from home," said Don, coldly.

"I had my duty to do, young man, and a sailor is not allowed to ask questions as to what's right or wrong."

"But I was treated like a criminal," said Don.

"You were treated far better than pressed men are as a rule especially those who try to break away. But I can't argue that with you. You and your companion are king's men now, or king's boys, and have to do your duty. Let's come back to to-day's work. The captain's offended, and I want to save you from trouble if I can."

"It's very kind of you, sir," said Don.

"Now tell me this. Do you know what you were going to do when the captain knocked you backwards?"

Don was silent.

"Well, I'll tell you," said the boatswain. "You were going to strike him again. That's the truth, is it not?"

Don remained silent.

"It is the truth. Well, have you any idea of what a bit of madness that would have been here?"

Don shook his head.

"Why, my good lad, you could not commit a greater crime. It means death."

"Does it, sir?"

"Does it, sir! Why, goodness me, my lad, you must be half mad."

"People are sometimes, sir, when they are hit."

"Yes, that's true enough; but you must master your temper. Save all that sort of thing up till you fight the French, and then you will be allowed to grow quite mad if you like. Now once more, about that boathook. You did not lose it?"

"Yes, sir; we did lose it."

"Ah, I thought so."

"Because the great fish carried it off."

"Humph! Well, go and get yourself dry. If you are lucky, you will hear no more about this, only have the cost of the boathook deducted out of your pay, and perhaps the captain will have forgotten all about your conduct by to-morrow."

"What did he say to you?" said Jem, as Don went below.

Don told him.

"Pay for the boathook?" said Jem. "Well, I'll do that, my lad. But what did he say—the skipper would forget it by to-morrow?"

"Yes, Jem."

"I hope he will."

"But I can't forget that he hit me," said Don sternly.

"Now, now, Mas' Don, you mustn't speak like that."

"And you must not speak like that, Jem,—*Master Don*. You'll have some of the men hear you."

"Well, I'll mind; but you mustn't think any more about that, my lad. He's captain, and can do as he likes. You were going to hit him, weren't you?"

"Yes, Jem, I'm afraid I was. I always feel like that if I'm hurt."

"But you mustn't now you're a sailor. Say, my lad, things looks rather ugly, somehow. Think the captain will punish you?"

"We shall see, Jem."

"But hadn't we better—— I say, my lad," he whispered, "we could swim ashore."

"And the shark?"

"Ugh! I forgot him. Well, take a boat, and get right away, for I've been thinking, Mas' Don, it's a very horrid thing to have hit your officer."

"But I didn't hit him. He hit me."

"But you were going to, Mas' Don," whispered Jem. "Strikes me the time's come for running away."

Don shook his head.

"Why, you was red hot on it the other day, my lad."

"Yes, but I've been thinking a great deal about it since, Jem; and it seems to me that it would be too cowardly to run now we are king's sailors."

"But not if you were going to be punished for doing nothing."

"N—o, Jem," said Don hesitatingly.

"And for being hit as the captain hit you."

"N—no, Jem; but—but somehow—— There, don't say any more about it now."

CHAPTER XXIII.

BEFORE THE CAPTAIN.

BOSUN JONES was right in his hint. The captain forgot all about Don's offence as soon as he was comfortable and rested. He had struck out in his hasty irritation, but his anger soon passed, and had the matter been brought to his notice again, he would have laughed, and said that it was the boy's nature to resent being struck, and that he would make the better sailor.

The time passed pleasantly enough in the beautiful harbour, and every day a boat went ashore with a surveying or exploring party, all of whom were examined and cross-examined by their messmates on their return, as to the habits of the New Zealand savages, and many a yarn was invented about the Maoris' acts.

Both Don and Jem found their messmates rough, but good-tempered enough, and the days glided by rapidly; but the opportunity was never given Don for joining one of the exploring parties. In every case he was told he was too much of a boy.

"Never mind, Mas' Don. You'll grow into a man some day," Jem used to say.

The Maoris were quite friendly, and the very stringent rules made at first were relaxed. The officers and men who went ashore were always armed, and limits were placed to the number of savages allowed to visit the ship; but the boarding netting was dispensed with, and it was not deemed necessary to double the sentries.

More than once parties of men were allowed on shore, and upon these occasions Don and Jem encountered the tattooed Englishman.

"Haven't made up your minds to come and join us?" he said, laughing; and Don shook his head.

"Ah, well! I won't persuade you, my lad. P'r'aps you're best where you are. But if you do make up your mind, come to me."

"How should we find you?" said Jem, who was careful to acquire knowledge that might be useful.

"Ask the first man you see for Tomati Paroni, and he'll bring you to me."

"Tomati Paroni," said Don thoughtfully; "is that New Zealand for Tom—Tom—— ?"

"Tom Brown," said the chief, laughing. "They have all sorts of English words like that."

The country was so beautiful, and the shore presented so many attractions, that the officers kept a strict watch over the men for fear of desertion; but there was something which acted more as a deterrent than anything that the officers could say or do, and that was the report that the natives were cannibals.

"Lots of 'em would desert," Jem said one night, as he lay in his hammock so close to Don's that they touched, "only——"

"Well, only what?" said Don.

"They say they'd rather stick on board, and be roasted and basted by the captain and officers, than by the blacks."

"They're not blacks, Jem; and I don't believe about the cannibal work."

"Well, they arn't blacks certainly, Mas' Don; but I'm pretty suspicious about the other thing. I once thought as Tomati was laughing at us, but it's all true. Why, what d'yer think I see only yes'day?"

"Numbers of things. But what in particular?"

"Why, one of the big chiefs who come ashore in that long

canoe. You know; the one with a figure-head with its tongue sticking out?"

"Yes; I know."

"Well, he'd got a flute."

"What of that? Men have flutes at home. Uncle Josiah had one."

"What was it made on?" whispered Jem.

"Box-wood, with ivory mountings."

"Well, this chief's flute was of ivory altogether—I mean, of bone."

"Well?"

"Guess what bone it was."

"How can I tell?"

"Bone of a man's leg, Mas' Don; and he killed the man whose bone it was."

"How do you know?"

"Why, Tomati told me."

"Yes, but it might not be true; perhaps the man was boasting."

Don was wearied out with a long day's work, and soon dropped off asleep, to be roused up by the men to take the morning watch.

Jem and he rolled unwillingly out of their hammocks, and went on deck, to find all dark; and soon after, cold and uncomfortable, they were leaning over the bulwarks together, talking as they scanned the smooth black sea, and the faint outlines of forest and mountain along the silent shore.

"This is what I hate in being a sailor," grumbled Jem. "No sooner have you got comfortably off to sleep, and begun giving your mind to it, than you're roused up to keep some watch."

"Yes, it is wearisome, Jem."

"Wearisome's nothing to it. I was dreaming, Mas' Don, when they routed us up."

"So was I, Jem."

"What was you dreaming about, Mas' Don?"

"Home."

"Hah!" said Jem, with a sigh; "so was I. Wonder what my Sally's doing now."

"Sitting down to tea, Jem."

"What! in the middle of the night?"

"It's the middle of the afternoon now, perhaps, Jem, on the other side of the world."

"Dessay it is, sir, if you says so; but I never can understand that kind of talk. Say, my lad, how dark it is! Why if four or five of those great war canoes liked to come out now, with a lot of fighting men aboard, they could take this here ship before we could cry Jack Robinson. Look yonder. Isn't that one stealing out from behind that island?"

"No, Jem; I see nothing but shadow."

"Then p'r'aps it arn't; but I'm always thinking I see 'em coming out full of men."

"Fancy, Jem."

"So it is, I s'pose. Know how long we're going to stop here, Mas' Don?"

"No, Jem. Getting tired of it?"

"Tired? Ay, lad. I want to go home."

That morning, about a couple of hours after the watch had been relieved, Don was on deck, when he saw one of the long war canoes, with its hideously carved prow and feather-decorated occupants, come sweeping along close to the shore and dash right away at great speed.

"Wish we was in her," sighed a voice at his ear.

Don turned sharply, to find Jem gazing longingly after the flashing paddles of the canoe, one of which was waved at him as they passed.

"What for, Jem?"

"To get away from here, Mas' Don. Wish you'd alter your mind. I want to see my Sally once more."

"Here, you two! This way," said a severe voice; and the stern-looking master came up. "This way. The captain wants a word with both of you."

"The captain?" began Don, as his old trouble flashed into his mind.

"That will do. Now then, this way," said the master sternly; and he led them to the quarter-deck, where the captain was standing, with a couple of the officers by his side, and, a little distance in front, Ramsden, the sinister-looking seaman who, since the night they were pressed, had always seemed to bear the two Bristolians ill-will.

Don and Jem saluted, and stood before their officer, who looked them over searchingly, his eyes resting on theirs in a fierce, penetrating way that was far from pleasant.

Then, turning from them contemptuously, he signed to Ramsden to come forward.

"Now," he said sharply, "repeat what you told me just now."

"Yes, sir. I had to go below yes'day evening when, as I was going along 'tween the 'ammocks, I hears the word *desert* and I was that took aback, sir, I——"

"Ah! you are the sort of man who would be took aback on hearing such a word," said the first lieutenant, with a sneer.

"Yes, sir," said Ramsden.

"Let him speak," said the captain, scowling to hide a smile.

"Soon as I heard that word *desert*, I felt stopped short like; and then I heard voices making plans for going ashore."

"What did they say?"

"Can't rec'lect what they said exactly, sir; only as one talked about a boat, and the other about a canoe. It was Lavington as asked about the canoe; and just now, sir, they was watching a canoe that went by, and they exchanged signals."

"Yes, I saw them watching that canoe," said the captain, fixing his eyes on Jem.

"Yes, sir; and one of the chiefs waved a paddle to them."

The captain nodded, and Ramsden was going on with his charge, when he was stopped.

"That will do, my man," said the captain; "I know quite

enough. Now look here," he continued, turning to Don and Jem, "I am compelled to believe what this man says, for I saw enough to corroborate his testimony; but I will give you an opportunity for defending yourselves. Is what he says true?"

Don's lips parted to say it was only about half true; but a feeling of agonised shame checked his words. There was too much truth in it for him to make a bold denial, so he remained silent; and Jem, taking his cue from his companion, was silent too.

"Come," said the captain, "I like that. There is honesty in it, my lads; and as you are both young, and pressed men, I will not be so severe as I might for such an offence as yours."

"Didn't commit no offence," said Jem sturdily.

"Silence, sir! Now then, you know, I suppose, that though we are living a peaceful life out here, these are war times, and the punishment of deserters is—death."

Jem started, but Don did not stir.

"Now you are both very young, and you have worked so well, and with so much promise of making yourselves sailors, that I should be sorry for you—either of you—to be guilty of such a mad trick as desertion. If you tried it, you would almost certainly be retaken, and—the punishment must follow. If, on the other hand, you escaped, it would be into the savage country before you, where you would fall into the hands of some enemy tribe, who would kill you both like dogs. I daresay you have heard what takes place afterwards, when the Maori tribes have taken prisoners?"

Jem shuddered, but Don made no sign.

"Ah! I see you know," continued the captain, "so I need say little more. I am satisfied that you will neither of you be guilty of such an act of madness as you contemplated, especially now that I tell you that I stop at nothing which the law gives me power to do for the preservation of the discipline of my ship. These two lads," he said, turning to give an order, "will be placed in irons for the present."

He made a sign, and the two prisoners were taken below deck, and placed in irons.

"Better than being hung, my lads," said the armourer gruffly; and soon after they were alone, with a sentry on duty not far from where they were seated.

CHAPTER XXIV.

TOMATI'S PROMISE.

"WONDER whether Mike ever had a taste of this sort o' thing, Mas' Don," said Jem, after they had sat in silence some time, Don's face not inviting any attempt at conversation. "He never said anything about being in irons when he spun yarns about adventures."

"Jem!" said Don indignantly; and as if it only wanted his companion's words to start him in a furious outburst of passion; "it is shameful! It is a cruel indignity and disgrace."

"Hush, hush, my lad! Don't take it that way. They arn't so werry heavy, and they don't hurt much."

"Hurt? not hurt much? Why, they are treating us as if we were thieves."

"What, being ironed, sir? Well, it do seem a bit hard."

"It's cruel! it's horrible! and he had no right to do it for such an offence."

"Steady, my lad, steady. The sentry 'll hear you, and have his turn, p'r'aps, at telling tales."

"But he had no right to do this, I say."

"P'r'aps not, Mas' Don; but skippers does just what they please when they're out at sea in war time. I thought he was going to hang us once."

"He would not dare," said Don.

"Well, if he did, I should have liked to have a few words first with Mr. Ramsden; for of all the mean, dirty, sneaking chaps I ever set eyes on, he's about the worst."

"A mean, cowardly spy!" cried Don.

"Ah, that's it; so he is, Mas' Don; a mean, cowardly spy. I couldn't think o' them words, but they're just what he is.—Say, Mas' Don."

"Don't, don't, don't, Jem."

"Don't what, Mas' Don?"

"Don't do that. *Master Don.* It sounds so foolish, and it's ridiculous, seeing what we are."

"All right, my lad, I'll be careful; but what I wanted to say was, would there be any harm in taking Master Ramsden by his waistband, and dropping him some night over into the sea?"

"Do you want to commit murder, Jem?"

"Do I want to commit murder? Nay, Mas' Don, gently, gently; don't talk to a man like that. I only meant to give him a ducking."

"Amongst the sharks?"

"Ugh! I forgot all about the sharks, Mas' Don. I say, think there are many of 'em about?"

"They say there are plenty, and we saw a monster, Jem."

"So we did, my lad; so we did, and a nice lot o' worry he's got us in through stealing that boathook. But, look here, how do you feel now?"

"Heart-sick and tired of it all, Jem. I wish we had run off when we had the chance."

"You do?"

"I do. See how we have been served: dragged from our homes, roughly used; bullied and ill-treated; and with that man's word taken before ours. It's too bad — too bad."

"Well, it is, Mas' Don," whispered Jem. "But you see it was awkward. You couldn't swear as you hadn't thoughts of deserting."

"Deserting?" said Don hotly. "I will not have it called deserting. I say it is only claiming our liberty, when we have been seized upon and treated like slaves."

"What a weathercocky way you have got, Mas' Don. Only t'other day you was all on the other tack, and says, says you,

'It's deserting, and cowardly,' and a lot more to that tune, and the way you went on at me, sir, made my hair curl."

"I had not had this last blow, Jem. I had not been put in irons then like a common thief."

"Silence, below there!" cried an angry voice. "Sentry, stop that talking by the prisoners."

The marine marched slowly toward them, and growled out his orders. Then, settling his head in his stiff stock, he faced round and marched away.

"All right, Jolly," said Jem, good-humouredly; and then drawing closer to his companion in misfortune, he went on talking in a whisper.

"Say, Mas' Don, do you mean it now?"

"Mean what?"

"Going? It's now or never. If we waits till we goes off to sea again our chance is gone."

"I mean it, Jem."

"That's a good bargain, my lad," said Jem, slapping him on the knee. "Then the sooner we're off the better."

"How can we go?"

"How? Easy enough. Get on deck, slide down a rope over the side when it's dark."

"In irons?"

"They don't weigh much. We could get hold of an oar or two, or lower down a grating, and hold on by that till we'd swam ashore."

"And the sharks, Jem?"

"Oh, those sharks!" cried Jem, pettishly. "I always forget them. I wish there wasn't such a thing as a shark on the face of the earth. Well, we must try some other way."

"That's easy enough to say, Jem; but what way is there?"

"Oh, I don't know yet, Mas' Don; but they say, 'where there's a will there's a way.' P'r'aps I can think it out. 'Member that big case as was too wide to come into the lower warehouse?"

"Yes."

"Well, your uncle said he'd be obliged to have the door-posts cut, but I thought that out after I'd measured it, and I found that it would just go in at the top warehouse doors if we hauled it up with the crane."

"You used to call it winding anything up, Jem."

"Ay, but I hadn't been to sea then, Mas' Don. Well, didn't I have that there case up to the top floor, and then lower it down through all the traps, and get it into the ground floor without the door being cut; and when your uncle come in, he stared, and asked me how I'd managed it?"

"Yes, I remember it all," said Don sadly.

"Look here, you two. I don't want to be hard," said the marine; "but you'll get me into a row. Now, are you going to clap on the hatchways, or am I to report you?"

"All right, Jolly; we won't talk any more," said Jem; and he kept his word that night.

There was no release next day, and very drearily it passed till towards evening, when Jem waited till the sentry's back was turned, and put his lips to Don's ear.

"I've got it, Mas' Don," he said.

"What, can you see your way to escape?"

"I've hit it out, my lad. Look here. Do you know them's men's irons you've got on?"

"Yes. They don't make irons for boys."

"Then look here, my lad; it may mean a bit of skin off; but all you've got to do is to squeeze your feet through those rings, and then I'll be bound to say a thin slip of a fellow like you can creep out of the iron round your waist."

"I don't think so, Jem. I'm stouter than you fancy."

"Oh no, you're not, and I dessay it'll be a tight fit; but you do it."

"And suppose I do get out of them, what about you?"

"About me, Mas' Don? ah, I don't know about me; but you could get right away, slide down the rope, get the gig up alongside——"

"When it's swinging from the davits, Jem?"

"There you go again," grumbled Jem. "I never did see

such a fellow for chucking stumbling-blocks all over the place for a man to hit his shins against."

"Then propose something possible. And besides, you don't suppose I'm going away without you."

"But I can't get my irons off, and you can get yours."

"I don't know that," said Don, trying; and, to his great surprise, finding that he could drag the ring over his ankle without much difficulty.

"There, I told you so. Slip it on again 'fore the sentry sees."

The marine was not likely to see, for the place was very dark where they sat, and for a long time they discussed the matter in a whisper, but only to be obliged to come to the conclusion that it was impossible to escape, unless Don would go alone.

"Well, if you won't go alone, you won't, Mas' Don," said Jem, in an ill-used tone; "but I do say as it's shabby of you, after I've thought about it so much."

The second night of their imprisonment passed slowly, and they were cudgelling their brains next day, when they were summoned on deck, received a severe reprimand, and, after their irons had been taken off, were told to go to their duty.

Then a week passed of land surveying and chart making, during which time the intercourse with the natives had been kept on a very friendly footing; and then a rumour ran round the ship that they were to sail after a certain channel had been sounded and the chart made.

"It's all over, Mas' Don," said Jem gloomily. "We shall go sailing away all over the world, and be took by the French, and never see home again!"

Don made no reply, but went about his duty gloomily enough till toward afternoon, when a canoe came off from the shore, manned by about fifty of the New Zealanders, and with Tomati and Ngati in the stern.

These two were soon on board, and were entertained by the captain, who made them several useful presents.

How he managed it Don hardly knew himself, but he contrived to get close behind the tattooed Englishman, and said softly, just as the officers were laughing and watching Ngati, who was going through his war-dance for their delectation, and distorting his features to the greatest extent,—

"Could you come after dark to-night in your canoe, and take us ashore?"

"Hist! mind what you're saying," replied the man, clapping his legs loudly, as if to encourage his companion to fresh exertions and distortions of his countenance.

"I want to come," said Don softly, in the midst of the applause.

"I daren't do it, my lad. They'd come down after me if I did; but I'll send Ngati. He'll come in his little canoe."

Don's heart beat wildly at these words, and he had no chance to say more, for Tomati went toward the officers, talked with them for a while; and then, as Don watched, he saw him go to the big chief, clap him on the shoulder, and say something which made the great fellow smile.

The New Zealanders seemed to show more interest in the appointments of the ship than they had displayed before, and the officers were civil enough to them, exchanging presents, and getting from the dusky warriors greenstone ornaments and weapons in exchange for powder and tobacco.

Don's heart had ceased to beat, and he was thinking despondently that he might as well give up all idea of evasion, when a hand was laid upon his shoulder, and looking up, it was to encounter the hideous face of the big chief, who said, with a peculiar laugh,—

"My pakeha. Bring gunpowder plenty. Wait by big ship. Dark."

It was not a very clear promise, but Don realised that it meant a chance of escape, and his eyes flashed with excitement, as the chief went on.

"Plenty gunpowder. Bring, bring. My pakeha."

He went off directly to where some of his fellows were standing about the deck, and hardly realising whether the chief was to be depended on, Don was about to go in search of Jem, when he felt a chill of despair, for, as he turned, he encountered the sinister countenance of Ramsden, his eye fixed upon him in a watchful way, and a satisfied smile playing about his lips.

Did he hear? Did he know? If he did, Don felt certain that the scoundrel would go and report all to one of the officers, and so get it to the captain's ears.

Still there was hope. He might not have heard, and as to the New Zealand men speaking to him, they were doing that to nearly every sailor they encountered on the deck.

Still he felt that it would be better not to be seen speaking to Jem, and he crossed to another part of the ship, and stood watching the leave-taking of the visitors, who descended into their canoe laden with presents and the objects they had obtained by barter.

Tomati was the last to descend, and he was standing in the gangway with a bottle of rum and a canister of powder in his hands, when Don heard the first lieutenant say to him jocularly,—

"I say, my fine fellow: I believe if the truth was known, you slipped off from Norfolk Island, and took up your residence here."

The man made no answer for a few moments, but stood looking the officer full in the face.

"What island did you say, sir?" he said at last.

"Norfolk Island. Am I right?"

"I'm a chief of this tribe, sir," said the man sturdily, "and these are my people. I'm not an Englishman now."

He went down into his canoe, and it darted away, propelled by fifty paddles, while the lieutenant turned away laughing, and went to the captain.

"That man's an escaped convict, or I'm a Dutchman, sir," he said; and they went forward talking.

Don cast an eye round for Jem, but he was not in sight. Ramsden was though; and, go where he would for the rest of that day, Don always woke to the fact that this man was at hand, apparently taking no notice, but watching him.

It seemed as if he would never have a chance to speak to Jem about what had passed; but at last Ramsden went below, and after a little inquiry Don learned that Jem was aloft in the foretop, helping a couple more men at repairing some of the toggles and reef points of a sail.

Don ran up as fast as his skill would allow, and had hardly reached the top when Ramsden came back on deck, and began seeking him out.

Don paused, out of sight now, to watch the man in turn, and saw him go from place to place, looking about searchingly, and undoubtedly for him.

"Hullo, my lad!" said Jem cheerily; "come to help?"

Don shook his head, and remained watching the progress of the men, but giving Jem a meaning look from time to time, sufficient to stimulate his curiosity, and make him on the *qui vive*. Then to avoid suspicion, he hurried down, and had hardly reached the deck again before Ramsden, who had again been below, came once more on deck, and remained watching him till dark.

"Let's get under the lee of this bulwark," said Don, when at last he found an opportunity for speaking to Jem alone.

"We shall get in a row if we are seen," said Jem.

"But it's too dark for us to be seen," whispered Don; and this seeming to be the case, they went into the shadow cast by one of the quarter boats, and lay down.

"What is it, Mas' Don?" said Jem in a whisper, as soon as they had satisfied themselves that they were alone.

Don related what had passed; but Jem did not seem to take to it.

"No," he said; "he is not likely to come, and if he did, they'd hear his canoe, and nail him. What time did he say?"

"Time? There was no time named."

"Then how shall we know, my lad? We can't watch for him all night.'

"Why not?" said Don excitedly. "It seems to be our last chance.'

"Well, I dunno," said Jem, gloomily; "it don't seem to me like a chance at all. But I'll do what you do, my lad. I'll stand by you."

"Then let's begin our watch at once, after we've put a rope overboard from the forechains, so as to slip down when the canoe comes."

"And what then?"

"Then, Jem, we must swim to it, and they'll take us aboard."

"And the sharks, my lad?"

"Sharks!" said Don despairingly. "I'd forgotten them.'

"That's what I used to do, but you always remembered."

"Jem," said Don, after a pause, "we must chance the sharks. They will not see us in the dark."

"But if—— No; I won't show the white feather, Mas' Don," said Jem. "Come on, and we'll get a rope over to starboard and larboard too."

"No need, Jem," said Don. "The canoe is sure to come from the land side."

"All right, sir. Come on, and don't say another word."

Jem crept away, keeping in the shadow, and moving very slowly, so as not to attract the attention of the watch, and Don followed, while, as soon as he had gone a few yards, what looked like a dog slowly crept by on all fours close beneath the bulwark, after getting up from a crouching position just by where the pair had been discussing their chances of escape.

CHAPTER XXV.

THE ALARM.

THERE were so many opportunities for lying *perdu* on the deck of a man-of-war on a dark night that the shadowy figure had no difficulty in keeping pretty close to Don Lavington and his companion as, decided now upon their course of action, they laid hold upon a stout line where it was coiled up, and after running a sufficiency over the side to touch water, made it fast close to the main chains.

This done, they went cautiously forward so as to avoid the watch, and after being nearly seen, more than once, succeeded in getting a second line over the side close to the fore chains, in happy unconsciousness of the fact that the shadowy-looking figure was watching every movement.

As is the fashion aboard a man-of-war, the actors in this scene were barefooted, and thus able to pass quietly along the well-scrubbed deck; but unfortunately for them, the sailor playing the spy had the same advantage, and kept them in view unnoticed and unheard.

Now he was lying under the bulwarks, and so close that Jem's foot almost touched his shoulder. Another time he was lying in one of the boats slung from the davits—then behind a coil of rope—behind the cook's galley—in the lee of a cask—once in a water barrel which was to be filled with the icy fluid of the river which came down from one of the mountains; always, with the activity of a monkey, contriving to be somewhere close at hand, till they stood at last, silent and watchful, about mid-way between the fore and main chains, peering out into the darkness shoreward and listening for the faintest sound from off the sea.

It was a wonderfully still night, and though out to the east the restless waves beat heavily on reef and shore, their action here was a slow heaving and curling over on the black metallic sand with a sound that to those on shipboard was like a whisper, but whose movement could be seen by a faint line of lambent light just in the blackest part to leeward of the ship, where sea touched shore. Sometimes this was so faint as to be hardly visible to the best-trained sight; at others it was as if some phosphorescent serpent was gliding swiftly along the sands, and it was in this direction that Don strained his eyes in the hope of catching sight of Ngati's canoe, whose paddles would churn up the water and shed on either side a faint golden light.

On board there were the customary anchor lanterns, and the faint glow thrown up from the skylights; but these seemed to have scarcely any effect upon the darkness, which hung down like a pall over the vessel, and Don's spirits rose as he felt how well they were concealed. Then they sank once more, for Jem placed his lips close to his ear and whispered,—

"It's too dark, my lad; we shall never be able to see the canoe if she comes."

Just then Don pressed his arm, and they listened together to what sounded like a faint sawing noise, which stopped and was renewed several times, and was followed by a slight splash.

The sounds came from forward, apparently somewhere in the direction of the foreshrouds; but though they listened intently it was heard no more.

"Fish," said Jem in a whisper, "trying to climb up into the ship, and then tumbled back into the sea."

"Nonsense!" said Don, shortly. "Now you look to the left, and I'll look to the right."

"Right, my lad. I'll look, but she won't come."

The searching scrutiny went on, and to Don, as he strained his eyes, it seemed as if all kinds of uncouth-looking monsters kept looming up out of the sea and disappearing; and though from time to time he told himself that it was all fancy, the various objects that his excited vision formed were so real that it was hard to believe that they were only the coinage of his fancy.

He turned and looked on board at the various lights, faintly seen, with the result that his eyes were rested, while he listened to the monotonous talking of the watch and an occasional burst of laughter from the gunroom, or the regular murmur from the forecastle.

Then he watched shoreward again for the faint golden flash made by the paddles of Ngati's canoe.

No lambent glow, no sound of paddling, not even a murmur from the shore, where the native huts were gathered together, and the great *whare* stood with its singularly carved posts representing human form over human form in strange combinations, with grotesque heads, pearly shell eyes, and tongues protruding from distorted mouths.

Then Jem caught Don's arm in turn, for there was a splash far away to the left, below where, faintly seen, a great sugar-loaf mountain rose high into the heavens.

The splash was not repeated, but, just as they had given up listening for it, once more the dull sawing sound came out of the darkness, but this time, instead of being forward it was away aft—how far they could not tell, for in the darkness sounds, like lights, may be close at hand or a couple of hundred yards away—it is hard to tell which.

The faint sawing went on for some time, ceased, and was renewed, to finish as before with a curious rustling and a splash.

"What can that be, Jem?" whispered Don.

"Not going to wenture an observation again," replied Jem, sourly.

Then all was still save the murmurs of voices inboard, and Don stood pressed against the bulwark listening intently, and thinking that before they went below to their hammocks they must haul up the lines again and coil them down, or their appearance would betray that something had been going on.

How long they had been waiting since the last sound was heard, Don could not tell; but all was so wonderfully still that the silence was oppressive; and after arriving at the conclusion that the canoe would not come, as from the utter absence of light or movement ashore it was evident that none of the natives were stirring, he turned to Jem.

"Asleep?" he whispered.

"I arn't a horse, am I?" was the surly reply. "Nice place to go to sleep standing up, Mas' Don.—Think he'll come?"

"I m afraid not, now."

"What shall us do?"

Don was silent.

"Say, Mas' Don," whispered Jem, after a thoughtful pause, "seems a pity to waste them ropes after——"

"Hist!"

Don's hand was on his lips, for voices were heard from aft, and directly after they heard the captain say,—

"Yes; extremely dark. Think we shall have a storm?"

"No," said the first lieutenant, "the glass is too high. Very dark indeed."

Then two faint sparks of light could be seen, indicating that the speakers were smoking, and the low murmuring of their voices suggested that they were chatting carelessly together.

"Keep your hand down, Mas' Don," said Jem in a whisper, after removing it. "They can't hear us, and if they did they'd think it was the watch. Say, look here, seems a pity to waste them ropes after we've got 'em down ready."

"Yes, Jem, it does."

"Such a short way to slide down, and no fear o' their breaking, same as there was in that cock-loft. What d'yer say?"

"What to?"

"Let's slide down and swim for it. 'Tarn't quarter of a mile. You could do that easy.'

"Yes, Jem; I think so."

"And I'd help you if you got tired. Let's go."

"But the sharks.'

"There I goes again. I always forgets them sharks; but look here, my lad, it's dark as pitch."

"Quite, Jem."

"We can't see twenty yards afore us, not clear."

"Not ten, Jem."

"Well, that's through the air. We couldn't see an inch through water."

"What of that?"

"More couldn't the sharks."

"Think not, Jem?'

"I feel 'bout sure on it. Look here, Mas' Don, I arn't got any money, but if I had, I'd wager half-a-guinea that all the sharks are at home and fast asleep; and if there's any of 'em shut out and roaming about in the streets—I mean in the sea—it's so dark that they couldn't see more than an inch before their noses; so let's open our knives ready, in case one should come, so that we could dive down and stab him, same as the natives do, and then swim on ashore. I'll risk it : will you?"

Don was silent for a few moments.

"Don't say *yes*, my lad, if you'd rayther not," said Jem, kindly. "I don't want to persuade you."

"I'm ready, Jem. I was thinking whether it was right to let you go."

"Oh, never you mind about me, my lad. Now, look here, shall us one go down each rope, or both down one?"

"Both down this one close here, and whoever goes down first can wait for the other. Yes, Jem; I'll go first."

"When?"

"Now, at once."

"Hoo—ray!" whispered Jem in Don's ear, so sharply that it produced a strange tickling sensation.

"Open your knife, Jem."

"Right, my lad; I'm ready."

"This way, then. Hist!"

Don caught Jem's arm in a firm grip as he was moving along the deck, each feeling somewhat agitated at the daring venture of exchanging firm planks for the treacherous sea, infested as they knew it was by horrible creatures which could tear them limb from limb.

Jem had heard a sound at the same moment, and he needed no telling that he should listen.

For from some distance off along the shore there was a faint splash, and, as they strained their eyes in the direction from whence it had come, they could see flashes of pale light, which they knew were caused by paddles.

"It's them, Jem," whispered Don, excitedly. "We must not start yet till the canoe is close up. I wish I had told him that I would make some signal."

"It'll be all right, my lad," said Jem huskily. "Give 'em time. Think the watch 'll see 'em?"

"I hope not," panted Don, as he strained his eyes in the direction of the faintly flashing paddles, which seemed to be moved very cautiously.

"Think it is them, Jem?"

"Who could it be?"

"Might it be a war canoe coming to try and capture the ship?"

"Not it," said Jem sturdily; "it's Ugly, as put out his tongue, coming to help us away. My, Mas' Don, how I should like to chop him under the chin next time he does that pretty trick of his."

"Silence, man! Listen, and look out. Let's get close to the rope first."

They crept softly toward the rope hanging down from the main chains, ready to their hand, and, as they crept, the dark figure that had seemed to be spying over their movements crept too, but on toward the quarter-deck, where the captain and the first lieutenant were lolling over the rail, and talking gently as they smoked—rather a rare custom in those days.

"It's the canoe, Jem," whispered Don; "and it's coming closer."

They strained their eyes to try and make out the men in the long, low vessel, but it was too dark. They could not even hear the plash of a paddle, but they knew that some boat—

that of friend or foe—was slowly coming toward the ship, for the flashing of the paddles in the phosphorescent water grew more plain.

"Ready, Jem?"

"Yes, I'm ready, lad. Rope's just where you stand."

"What!" cried the captain's voice loudly, and then there was a quick murmur of talking.

"What's that mean, Mas' Don?"

"Don't know. Some order."

"Boat ahoy!" cried one of the watch forward, and there was a buzz of excitement which told that the paddling of the canoe had been seen.

"Watch there forward!" roared the captain.

"Ay, ay, sir," came back.

"Follow me, Jem; we must swim to her now."

"I'm after you, my lad."

"Jem!" in a tone of despair.

"What is it!"

"The rope's cut!"

"What? So it is. Never mind. After me! There's the one in the forechains."

In the midst of a loud buzz of voices, and the pad, pad—pad, pad of bare feet on the deck, Jem and Don reached the forechains; and Jem ran his hand along in the darkness till he felt the knot by which he had secured the rope.

"Here she is, Mas' Don. Now, then, over with you quick, or I shall be atop of your head."

"I've got it," whispered Don.

Then in a voice full of despair,—

"This is cut, too!"

At the same moment the captain's voice rang out,—

"Look out there, you in the watch forward; two men are trying to leave the ship!"

CHAPTER XXVI.

WHAT MR. JONES THOUGHT.

"WHAT'S to be done, Mas' Don?" whispered Jem, whom this second proof of treachery against them seemed to have robbed of the power to act.

"This way," cried a voice, which they recognised as Ramsden's. "By the forechains."

"Oh, if I had hold of you," snarled Jem, as he ground his teeth.

"Do you hear me?" whispered Don. "Come on."

He spoke from where he stood on the bulwark, holding by one of the shrouds, and offering his hand to Jem, who could not see it, but climbed to his side.

"Header?" he whispered.

"Yes.—Off!"

Don gave the word as he glanced in the direction where he believed the canoe to lie; and then, raising his hands above his head, he sprang right off the bulwark into the sea.

Splash!

A moment's pause and then—

Splash!

Jem had followed suit, and there was a faint display—if the expression is allowable—of water fireworks, as innumerable pinhead-like beads of light flashed away in every direction.

"Lanthorns here!" cried the captain. "Sentries, quick! this way."

He reached the spot from which Don and Jem had taken their daring leap, and in less than a minute the light of a couple of lanthorns was thrown upon the sea.

"Come back!" roared the captain, "or I fire. Marines, make ready."

The lanthorns' light gleamed further on the sea as those who held them clambered up the shrouds and held them at arms' length, and then dimly seen were the backs of the heads of the two swimmers, who made the water swirl as they struck out with all their might.

"Do you hear, you scoundrels?" roared the captain again. "Come back, or I fire."

There was no reply and the heads began to grow more faint in the gloom, while now the news had spread through the ship, and officers and men came tumbling up the companion ladder and out of their cabins.

"Marines, present—fire!" cried the captain.

There were two sharp clicks and as many tiny showers of sparks. That was all.

"Why, you were not loaded!" cried the captain, fiercely, "Where is the lieutenant? Where is the sergeant? Load, you scoundrels, load!"

The men grounded arms, and began to load quickly, the thudding of their iron ramrods sounding strangely in the still night air.

"Pipe away the first cutter!" cried the captain. "Mr. Rogerson, bring those scoundrels back."

The shrill pipe of the boatswain was heard, and there was a rush of feet as the captain shouted again,—

"Present—fire!"

There was a sharp flash, a loud report, and the captain stamped with rage.

"Fire, you scoundrel, fire!" he roared at the second man, who was about to lower his clumsy musket, after tugging in vain at the trigger, when the piece went off, and the bullet fled skyward, sending the nearest lanthorn held up in the shrouds out of its holder's hand, to fall with a splash in the sea, and float for a few moments before it filled and sank, the candle burning till the water touched the wick.

"'Pon my word!" cried the captain. "Nice state o

discipline. Now you—fire again. And you, sir, load. Can you see the men, marines?"

"No, sir. Right out of sight."

"Then fire where they were when you saw them last."

"'COME BACK!' ROARED THE CAPTAIN, 'OR I FIRE.'"

"But they won't be there now, sir."

"Silence, you scoundrel! How dare you? Fire!"

Bang.

"Now you: are you ready?"

"Yes, sir."

"Fire!"

Bang.

"Load again!" cried the captain. "Now, you scoundrels, come back or you shall have a volley."

A strange noise came off the sea.

"Hark! what's that?" cried the captain. "A cry for help!"

"No, sir."

"What was it, then?"

"Beg pardon, sir; but I think it was one on 'm a-larfin."

The captain gave the speaker—one of the warrant officers—a furious look.

"Now, then, is that boat going to be all night?" he shouted.

"All ready, sir. Lower away."

The boat kissed the sea with a faint splash; she was thrust off; and as the oars dropped and the men gave way the cutter went rapidly through the water, at a rate which would have soon made the fugitives prisoners but for the fact that boat and swimmers were taking different directions, and the distance between them increased at every stroke.

"They've taken no lanthorn!" cried the captain. "Surely no one's orders were ever worse obeyed."

"Shall I call them back, sir?" said the second lieutenant.

"No, no; let them find it out for themselves. Here, marines, ten of you load. Quick, my lads, clear the way from up here."

"Make ready, take good aim at the scoundrels—present—fire!"

This time the whole of the pieces went off with a loud rattle, which brought lights out in the New Zealand village, and a buzz of excitement came from the men.

"More lanthorns there!" cried the captain. "See them?" he cried, to the officer in the boat.

"Not yet, sir."

"Take a sweep round to the southward. They're more there."

"Ay, ay, sir!" came faintly out of the darkness; and the dull rattle of the oars reached those on deck.

"I'll have those two back, dead or alive!" cried the captain, stamping about in his rage. "Pipe down the second cutter."

His orders were obeyed, and in a short time, with a lanthorn in bow and stern, the second boat touched the water, and rowed off, the officer in command receiving instructions to bear off more still to the southward, and finally sweep round so as to meet the first boat.

Directly this was started a happy thought seemed to strike the captain, who had a third boat lowered, with instructions to row right ashore, land the men, and divide them in two parties, which would strike off to right and left, stationing a man at every fifty yards; and these were to patrol the beach to and fro, keeping watch and a sharp look out for the fugitives.

"That will checkmate them, Mr. Jones," he said. "I wish I had thought of this before. Now go."

Mr. Bosun Jones was in command of this boat, and he gave orders to his men, the oars splashed, and away they went into the darkness, their lights growing fainter and fainter, till they seemed to be mere specks in the distance; but they did not die out, and as those left on deck watched the progress, they saw the lanthorns of the last boat become stationary, and knew that the men had reached the shore, while the lanthorns of the second cutter were faintly visible, moving slowly far away to the south.

The captain rubbed his hands with satisfaction, and kept walking to the gangway and using his night-glass without any greater result than that of seeing a couple of faint specks of light, when he got the boats' lanthorns into the field. Then he listened in the hope of hearing shouts, which would suggest the capture of the fugitives; but half an hour—an hour—glided by, and all was still. The buzz and cries which had arisen from the collection of huts had ceased, and the lights shown there had been extinguished, while the darkness which hung over the sea appeared to grow more dense.

At last there was a hail about a hundred yards away, and the officer in the first boat answered the captain's eager inquiry.

"No, sir; no luck. Not a sign of any one. I'm afraid——"

" They have got ashore and escaped ? "

" No, sir," said the lieutenant, gravely; " I don't think a man could swim ashore in this darkness and escape."

" Why, the distance is very short ! "

"Yes, sir ; but there are obstacles in the way."

" Obstacles ? "

" Well, sir, I've seen some tremendous sharks about in the clear water ; and I don't think any one could get any distance without having some of the brutes after him."

A terrible silence followed this declaration, and the captain drew his breath hard.

" Come aboard," he said. " It is too dark for further search to be made."

The boat was rowed alongside, the falls lowered, the hooks adjusted, and she was hoisted up and swung inboard.

" I'd give anything to capture the scoundrels," said the captain, after walking up and down for a few minutes with the lieutenant ; " but I don't want the poor fellows to meet with such a fate as that. Do you think it likely ? "

" More than likely, sir," said the lieutenant, coldly.

The captain turned aft, made his way to the quarter deck, and remained there attentively watching shoreward to where he could faintly see the lights of the last boat.

" We must leave further search till morning," muttered the captain ; and giving his order, signal lamps were run up to recall the boats ; and before very long they were answered, and the lanthorns of Bosun Jones' boat could soon after be seen heading slowly for the ship, the second boat following her example a few minutes later.

" No signs of them, Mr. Jones ? " said the captain, as his warrant officer reached the deck to report himself.

" No, sir," said the boatswain, sadly ; " but I heard a sound, and one of my men heard it too."

" A sound ? What sound ? "

" Like a faint cry of distress, sir."

"Yes; and what did you make of that?"

The boatswain was silent a moment.

"The harbour here swarms with sharks, sir, and the cry sounded to me like that of a man being drawn under water."

"No, no; no, no; not so bad as that," said the captain, rather excitedly. "They've got to shore, and we will have them back to-morrow. The people will give them up either by threats or bribes."

"I hope so, sir," said the boatswain, coldly. And, then, as he went below, "Poor lad! I'd have given a year of my life rather than it should have happened. This pressing is like a curse to the service."

By this time the officer in the last boat had reported himself, the crews were dismissed, the watch set, and all was silence and darkness again.

About dawn the captain, after an uneasy night, came on deck, glass in hand, to search the shore, and try to make out some sign of the fugitives; but just as he had focussed his glass, he caught sight of some one doing the very same thing, and going softly to the bows he found that the officer busy with the glass was Bosun Jones, who rose and saluted his superior.

"See anything, Mr. Jones?" the captain said.

"No, sir; only the regular number of canoes drawn up on the beach."

"Have you thought any more about what you said you heard last night?"

"Yes, sir, a great deal."

"But you don't think the poor lad met such a fate as you hinted at?"

"Yes, sir, I do," said the boatswain sternly; "and I feel as if I had helped to bring him to such a death."

"Mr. Jones," said the captain, haughtily, "you merely did your duty as a warrant officer in the king's service. If that unfortunate boy met such a disastrous fate, it was in an attempt to desert."

The captain closed his glass with a loud snap, and walked away, while Bosun Jones stood with his brow knit and his lips compressed, gazing straight before him as the sun rose and shed a flood of light over the glorious prospect.

But to the bluff petty officer everything seemed sad and gloomy, and he went below seeing nothing but the frank, manly features of young Don Lavington, as he muttered to himself,—

"Not a chance of escape. Poor boy! poor boy!"

CHAPTER XXVII.

THE FUGITIVES.

DON and Jem plunged almost simultaneously into the black, cold water, and felt the sea thundering in their ears.

Then Jem, being broader and stouter than his companion, rose to the surface and looked round for Don; but a few seconds of agony ensued before the water parted and the lad's head shot up into the faint light shed by the lanthorns.

"Now for it, Mas' Don," whispered Jem; "think as it's a race, and we're going to win a cup at a 'gatta. Slow and sure, sir; slow and sure, long, steady strokes, and keep together."

"They're calling to us to stop, Jem," whispered Don.

"Let 'em call, Mas' Don. Somebody else seems a-calling of me, and that's my Sally. Oh, don't I wish I hadn't got any clothes."

"Can they see us?" whispered Don, as they swam steadily on."

"I don't believe they can, sir; and if they can, they won't see us long. Shouldn't be surprised if they lowered a boat."

"Ah! look out!" whispered Don. "Shall we dive?"

For he heard the clicking of the muskets as they missed fire.

"Well, I do call that cowardly," said Jem, as he heard the order to load; "shooting at a couple of poor fellows just as if they was wild duck."

"Swim faster, Jem," said Don, as he gazed back over his shoulders at the lights as the shots rang out.

"No, no; swim slower, my lad. They can't see us; and if they could, I don't believe as the men would try and hit us. Ah! Not hit, are you?"

"No, Jem; are you?"

"Not a bit of it, my lad. There they go again. Steady. We're all right now, unless a boat comes after us. We shall soon get ashore at this rate, and the tide's helping up, and carrying us along."

"Toward shore, Jem, or out to sea?"

"Shore, of course," said Jem, as he swam on his side, and kept an eye on the faint lights of the ship. "Say, Mas' Don, they won't hang us, will they, if they ketches us?"

"What made you say that?"

"Because here comes a boat after us.—Hear the skipper?"

"Yes; but the canoe—where is the canoe?"

Don raised himself, and began to tread water, as he looked in the direction where they had seen the water flash beneath the paddles.

"I dunno, my lad. Can't see nothing but the lights of the ship. Better swim straight ashore. We sha'n't be able to see no canoe to-night."

They swam steadily on, hearing only too plainly the plans made for their recapture. The orders, the creaking of the falls, even the plash made by the boats, as they kissed the water, and the dull rattle of the oars in the row-locks was carried in the silence of the night distinctly to their ears, while the regular plash, plash, plash, as the oars dipped, sent a thrill through Don, and at times seemed to chill his energy.

But these checks were almost momentary. There was a sense of freedom in being away from the ship, and, in spite of the darkness, a feeling of joyous power in being able to breast the long heaving swell, and pass on through the water.

"Better not talk, Mas' Don," whispered Jem, as they swam; "sound goes so easily over the water."

"No, I'm not going to talk," said Don; "I want all my breath for swimming."

"Don't feel tired, do you?"

"Not a bit."

"That's right, lad. Stick to it steady like. Their lanthorns aren't much good. Don't you be skeart; we can see them plain enough, but they can't see us."

"But it seems as if they could," whispered Don, as they saw a man standing up in the bows of one of the boats, holding a lanthorn on high.

"Yes, seems," whispered Jem; "but there's only our heads out of water, and only the tops o' them sometimes. Say, that must ha' been fancy about the canoe."

"No, Jem; she's somewhere about."

"Glad on it: but I wish she'd come and pick us up."

They swam on silently toward the shore, listening to the shouts of the men, and watching alternately the lights of the boats and those of the ship.

All at once a curious noise assailed Don's ear.

"What's the matter, Jem?" he whispered, in alarm.

"Matter?" said Jem, greatly to his relief. "Nothing, as I knows on."

"But that noise you made?"

"I didn't make no noise."

"You did, just now."

"Why, I was a-larfin' quiet-like, so as to make no row."

"Oh!"

"Thinking about them firing a volley at us in the dark. Wonder where the bullets went?"

"Don't talk, Jem; they may hear us."

"What! a whisper like that, my lad? Not they. Boats is a long way off, too, now."

The excitement had kept off all sense of fear, and so far Don had not seemed to realise the peril of their position in swimming through the darkness to land; for even if there had been a canoe coming to their help, the lowering of the boats seemed to have scared its occupants away, and though the sea was perfectly calm, save its soft, swelling pulsation, there were swift currents among the islands and points, which, though easily mastered by canoe or boat with stout rowers, would carry in an imperceptible manner a swimmer far from where he wished to go.

But they swam steadily on for some time longer, Jem being the first to break the silence.

"Say, Mas' Don," he whispered, "did you hear oars?"

"No, Jem."

"I thought I did. I fancy one of the boats put off without a lanthorn. Weren't there three?"

"Yes, I think so."

"Well, you can see two of 'em easy like."

"Yes, Jem; I can see."

"Then there's another cruising about in the dark, so we must be careful."

There was another interval of steady swimming, during which they seemed to get no nearer to the shore, and at last Jem spoke again.

"Say, Mas' Don, don't you feel as if you'd like a cup o' tea?"

"No."

"I do. I'm as dry as sawdus'. S'pose we're nearly there, but I can't touch bottom. I tried just now."

They swam on, with the lights of the boat farther off than ever, and the ship more distant still.

"Getting tired, Jem?"

"N—no. Could go on for about another week. Are you?"

"My clothes seem so heavy. Can you see the shore?"

"I can see the beach right afore us, but can't tell how nigh it is. Never mind about your clothes, my lad; but they're a great noosance at a time like this. Take your strokes long, and slow as you can."

"That's what I'm doing, Jem, but—do you think it's much further?"

"Now, lookye here, Mas' Don; if ever there was a good-tempered chap it was—I mean is—Jem Wimble; but if you gets talking like that, you aggravates me to such a degree that I must speak."

Jem spoke angrily, and with unwonted excitement in his manner.

"Is it much furder, indeed? Why, of course it arn't. Swim steady, and wait."

Jem closed in as much as was possible after raising himself in the water, and scanning the distant shore; and as he did so a cold chill of dread—not on his own account—ran through him, for he felt that they were certainly no nearer shore than they were before.

"Throw your left shoulder a little more forward, Mas' Don," he said calmly; "there's a p'int runs out here, I think, as'll make the journey shorter."

Don obeyed in silence, and they swam on, with Jem watchfully keeping his eyes upon his companion, who was now deeper in the water.

"Jem," said Don, suddenly.

"Yes, Mas' Don. Take it coolly, my lad. We're getting close there. Oh, what a lie!" he added to himself, with a chill of misery unnerving him.

"Jem."

"Ay, ay, Mas' Don."

"If you escape——"

"If I escape!" whispered Jem, angrily. "Now, what's the use o' your talking like that? Escape, indeed! Why, I feel as if I could live in the water, if I had plenty to eat and drink."

"Listen to me," said Don, hoarsely. "If you escape, tell my mother I always loved her, even when I was obstinate. Tell her we didn't run away, and that—that I didn't take that money, Jem. You'll tell her that?"

"I won't tell her nor nobody else nothing of the sort," said Jem. "I'm too busy swimming to think o' no messages, and so are you. Steady—steady. Bit tired, lad?"

"Tired, Jem? My arms feel like lead."

"Turn over and float a bit, dear lad, and rest yourself."

"No," said Don. "If I turn over I shall be too helpless to keep up, and I can't turn back.—Jem, I'm beat out."

"You're not!" cried Jem, in so loud and angry a voice, that the occupants of the pursuing boats must have heard them if they had been near. "You've got to keep on swimming steady, as I tells you, and if you says another word to me 'bout being beat, I'll give you such a shove aside o' the head as'll duck you under."

Don made no answer, but swam on feebly, with the water rising over his lips at every stroke; and as Jem swam by him he could hear the lad's breath come quickly, and with a hoarse, panting sound.

"And I can't leave him, even to save myself," groaned Jem. "Oh, Sally, Sally, my gal, I did love you very true; and if I never see you again, good-bye—good-bye!"

It seemed to poor Jem Wimble that his thoughts were so heavy that they sank him lower in the water; but he had a buoyant heart, which is the surest and best of life preservers; and taking a long breath, and setting his teeth, he swam on.

"Not so very far now, Mas' Don," he said. "You feel better now, don't you?"

"Jem."

"Yes, lad."

"It's getting darker. I want to keep on, but I can't. Can you shake hands?"

"No!" cried Jem, fiercely. "You turn over and float."

Don uttered a sigh, and obeyed in a feeble way, while Jem ceased his striking out for shore, and placed one arm under Don's neck.

"It's all right, my lad. Don't lose heart," he said. "It's wonderful easy to float; but you're tired. It's your clothes does it. You're a wonderful good swimmer, Mas' Don; but the wonderflest swimmers can't swim for ever in clothes. That's resting you, arn't it? I'm fresh as a lark, I am. So 'll you be dreckly, lad. Keep cool. Just paddle your hands a bit. We're close in shore, only it's so dark. We've done 'em. Boats is right away."

"Are they—are they right away, Jem?"

"Yes, my lad, thank goodness!"

Don groaned.

"Don't do that, my lad. You do make me savage when you won't be plucky. Why, you can swim miles yet, and you shall, as soon as you're rested. I say, how savage the capen will be when he finds he can't ketch us!"

"Jem, my lad," said Don, quietly; "don't talk to me as if I were a child. It's very good of you, and—kind—but—but I'm done, Jem—I'm done."

"You're not!" cried Jem, savagely. "Say that again, and I'll hit you in the mouth. You arn't done, and it's the way with you. You're the obsnittest chap as ever was. You've got to swim ashore as soon as you're rested, and I say you shall."

Don made no reply, but he floated with his nostrils clear of the water, and smiled as he gazed straight up in the dark sky.

"There. It was time I spoke," continued Jem. "Some chaps loses heart about nothing."

"Nothing, Jem?"

"Well, next to nothing, my lad. Why, mussy me! what a fuss we are making about a few hundred yards o' smooth water. I've swum twice as far as this. Rested?"

Don made no reply.

"Ah, you will be soon. It's the clothes, my lad. Now look here, Mas' Don. You take my advice. Never you try a long swim again like this with your clothes on. They makes a wonderful deal of difference."

"Jem," said Don, interrupting him.

"Ay, ay, my lad."

"Are the boats very far away?"

"Well, a tidy bit; say half-mile."

"Then swim ashore and leave me; save yourself."

"Oh, that's it, is it?"

"And tell my mother——"

"Now, look here," cried Jem. "I should look well going and telling your mother as I left you in the lurch; and my Sally would spit at me, and serve me right. No, Mas' Don, I've tried it easy with you, and I've tried it hard; and now I says this: if you've made up your mind to go down, why, let's shake hands, and go down together, like mates."

"No, no; you must swim ashore."

"Without you?"

"Jem, I can do no more."

"If I leaves you, Mas' Don—— Ahoy! Boat!—boat!"

Jem meant that for a sturdy hail; but it was half choked, for just at that moment Don made a desperate effort to turn and swim, lost his remaining nerve, and began to beat the water like a dog.

"Mas' Don, Mas' Don, one more try, dear lad, one more try!" cried Jem, passionately; but the appeal was vain. He, with all his sturdy manhood, strength hardened by his life of moving heavy weights, was beaten in the almost herculean task, and he knew at heart that Don had struggled bravely to the very last, before he had given in.

But even then Don responded to Jem's appeal, and ceased paddling, to make three or four steady strokes.

"That's it! Brave heart! Well done, Mas' Don. We shall manage it yet. A long, steady stroke—that's it. Don't give up. You can do it; and when you're tired, I'll help you Well done—well done. Hah!"

Jem uttered a hoarse cry, and then his voice rose in a wild appeal for help, not for self, but for his brave young companion.

"Boat! boat!" he cried, as he heard Don, deaf to his entreaties, begin the wild paddling action again; and he passed his arm beneath his neck, to try and support him.

But there was no reply to his wild hail. The boats were out of hearing, and the next minute the strangling water was bubbling about his lips, choking him as he breathed it in; and with the name of his wife on his lips, poor Jem caught

Don in a firm grip with one hand, as he struck wildly out with the other.

Four or five steady strokes, and then his arm seemed to lose its power, and his strokes were feeble.

"Mas' Don," he groaned; "I did try hard; but it's all over. I'm dead beat, too."

CHAPTER XXVIII.

FRIENDLY ATTENTIONS.

A PECULIAR pale light played and flashed from the surface of the black water which was being churned up by the desperate struggles of the drowning pair. It was as if myriads of tiny stars started into being where all was dark before, and went hurrying here and there, some to the surface, others deep down into the transparent purity of the sea.

A minute before Jem Wimble had kept command of himself, and swam as a carefully tutored man keeps himself afloat; that minute passed, all teaching was forgotten in a weak, frantic struggle with the strangling water which closed over their heads.

A few moments, during which the phosphorescent tiny creatures played here and there, and then once more the two helpless and nearly exhausted fugitives were beating the surface, which flashed and sent forth lambent rays of light.

But it was not there alone that the phosphorescence of the sea was visible.

About a hundred yards away there was what seemed to be a double line of pale gold liquid fire changing into bluish green, and between the lines of light something whose blackness was greater than the darkness of the sea or night. There was a dull low splashing, and at every splash the liquid fire seemed to fly.

The double line of fire lengthened and sparkled, till it was as so much greenish golden foam reaching more and more toward where the drowning pair were struggling.

Then came a low, growling, grinding sound, as if the long lines of light were made by the beating fins of the dark object, which was some habitant of the deep roused from slumbers by the light of the golden foam formed by those who drowned.

And it rushed on and on to seize its prey, invisible before, but now plainly seen by the struggles and the resulting phosphorescent light.

Long, low, and with its head raised high out of the water, horrent, grotesque and strange, the great sea monster glided along over the smooth sea. Full five-and-twenty fins aside made the water flash as it came on, and there was, as it were, a thin new-moonlike curve of light at its breast, while from its tail the sparkling phosphorescence spread widely as it was left behind.

The low grumbling sound came again, but it was not heard by those drowning, nor was the light seen as it glided on nearer and nearer, till it reached the spot.

One dart from the long raised neck, one snap of the fierce jaws—another dart and another snap, and the sea monster had its prey, and glided rapidly on, probably in search of more in its nightly hunt.

Nothing of the kind! The long creature endued with life darted on, but the long neck and horned head were not darted down, but guided past those who where drowning. Everything was stiff and rigid but the playing fins. But there was another dull, low grunt, the fins seemed to cease by magic; and, instead of being snapped up by the monster's mouth, the two sufferers were drawn in over its side.

Then the water flashed golden again, the monster made a curve and rushed through the water, and sped away for miles till, in obedience to another grunting sound, it turned and dashed straight for a sandy beach, resolving itself into a long New Zealand war canoe, into which Don and Jem had been drawn, to lie half insensible till the beach was neared, when Jem slowly and wonderingly sat up.

"Where's Mas' Don?" he said in a sharp ill-used tone.

"Here he is," said a gruff voice, and Jem looked wonderingly in a savage's indistinctly seen face, and then down in the bottom of the long canoe, into which they had been dragged.

"Mas' Don—don't say you're drowned, Mas' Don," he said pitifully, with a Somersetshire man's bold attempt at the making of an Irish bull.

"My pakeha! My pakeha!" said a deep voice; and Jem became aware of the fact that the big chief he had so often seen on board the ship, and who had come to them with the present of fruit when they were guarding the boat, was kneeling down and gently rubbing Don.

"Is he dead?" said Jem in a whisper.

"No, not this time," said the gruff voice out of the darkness. "Pretty nigh touch, though, for both of you. Why didn't you hail sooner?"

"Hail sooner?" said Jem.

"Yes. We came in the canoe to fetch you, but you didn't hail, and it was too dark to see."

"We couldn't hail," said Jem, sulkily. "It would have brought the boats down upon us."

"Ah, so it would," said the owner of the gruff voice. "There's three boats out after you."

"And shall you give us up?"

"Give you up? Not I. I've nothing to do with it; you must talk to him."

"My pakeha!" cried the big chief excitedly.

"That isn't his name, is it?" said Jem.

"No. Nonsense! Pakeha means white man. I was a pakeha once."

"Let me help him up," said Jem eagerly.

"My pakeha! my pakeha!" said the chief, as if putting in a personal claim, and ready to resist Jem's interference.

The difficulty was ended by Don giving himself a shake, and slowly rising.

"Jem! Where's Jem?"

"Here! All right, Mas' Don. We're in the canoe."

"Hah!" ejaculated Don; and he shuddered as if chilled. "Where are the boats?"

"Miles away," said the tattooed Englishman. "But look here, I'm only on board. This is Ngati's doing. I know nothing about you two."

"My pakeha! my pakeha!" cried the chief.

"Lookye here," cried Jem, speaking in the irritable fashion of those just rescued from drowning; "if that there chief keeps on saying, '*My pakeha*' at me in that there aggravating way, I shall hit him in the mouth."

"Ah! you're rusty," said the tattooed Englishman. "Man always is when he's been under water."

"I dunno what you mean by being rusty," said Jem snappishly. "What I say is, leave a man alone."

"All right!" said the Englishman. "I'll let you alone. How's your young mate?"

"My head aches dreadfully," said Don; "and there's a horrible pain at the back of my neck."

"Oh, that'll soon go off, my lad. And now what are you going to do?"

"Do?" interrupted Jem. "Why, you don't mean to give us up, do you?"

"I don't mean to do anything or know anything," said the man. "Your skipper'll come to me to-morrow if he don't think you're drowned, or—I say, did you feel anything of 'em?"

"Feel anything—of what?" said Don.

"Sharks, my lad. The shallow waters here swarm with them."

"Sharks!" cried Don and Jem in a breath.

"Yes. Didn't you know?"

"I'd forgotten all about the sharks, Jem," said Don.

"So had I, my lad, or I dursen't have swum for it as we did. Of course I thought about 'em at first starting, but I forgot all about 'em afterwards."

"Jem," said Don, shuddering; "what an escape!"

"Well, don't get making a fuss about it now it's all over,

Mas' Don. Here we are safe, but I must say you're the wussest swimmer I ever met.—Here, what are they going to do?"

"Run ashore," said the Englishman, as there was a buzz of excitement among the New Zealanders, many of whom stepped over into the shallow water, and seized the sides of the boat, which was rapidly run up the dark shore, where, amidst a low gobbling noise, the two wet passengers were landed to stand shivering with cold.

"There you are," said the Englishman, "safe and sound."

"Well, who said we weren't?" grumbled Jem.

"Not you, squire," continued the Englishman. "There; I don't know anything about you, and you'd better lie close till the ship's gone, for they may come after you."

"Where shall we hide?" said Don eagerly.

"Oh, you leave it to Ngati; he'll find you a place where you can lie snug."

"Ngati," said the owner of the name quickly, for he had been listening intently, and trying to grasp what was said. "Ngati! my pakeha."

"Oh, I say: do leave off," cried Jem testily. "Pakeha again. Say, Mas' Don, him and I's going to have a row before we've done."

The chief said something quickly to the Englishman, who nodded and then turned to the fugitives.

"Ngati says he will take you where you can dry yourselves, and put on warm things."

"He won't be up to any games, will he?" said Jem.

"No, no; you may trust him. You can't do better than go with him till the search is over."

The Englishman turned to a tall young savage, and said some words to him, with the result that the young man placed himself behind Don, and began to carefully obliterate the footprints left by the fugitives upon the sand.

Don noticed this and wondered, for in the darkness the footprints were hardly perceptible; but he appreciated the act, though he felt no one but a native would distinguish between the footprints of the two people.

"My pakeha," said Ngati just then, making Jem wince and utter an angry gesticulation. "Gunpowder, gun, pow-gun, gun-pow."

"Eh?" said Jem harshly.

"My pakeha, powder-gun. Pow-gun, gun-pow. No?"

"He says his pakeha was to have brought plenty of guns and powder, and he has not brought any."

"No," said Don, shivering as he spoke. "The guns are the king's. I could not bring any."

The New Zealand chief seemed to comprehend a good deal of his meaning, and nodded his head several times. Then making a sign to a couple of followers, each took one of Don's arms, and they hurried him off at a sharp run, Jem being seized in the same way and borne forward, followed by the rest of the men who were in the boat.

"Here, I say. Look here," Jem kept protesting, "I arn't a cask o' sugar or a bar'l o' 'bacco. Let a man walk, can't yer? Hi! Mas' Don, they're carrying on strange games here. How are you getting on?"

Don heard the question, but he was too breathless to speak, and had hard work to keep his feet, leaving everything to the guidance of his companions, who kept on for above a quarter of a mile before stopping in a shadowy gully, where the spreading ferns made the place seem black as night, and a peculiar steaming sulphurous odour arose.

But a short time before Don's teeth were chattering with the cold, but the exercise circulated his blood; and now, as his eyes grew more used to the obscurity, he managed to see that they were in a rough hut-like place open at the front. The sulphurous odour was quite strong, the steam felt hot and oppressive, and yet pleasant after the long chilling effect of the water, and he listened to a peculiar gurgling, bubbling noise, which was accompanied now and then by a faint pop.

He had hardly realised this when he felt that his clothes were being stripped from him, and for a moment he felt disposed to resist; but he was breathless and wearied out, and rough as was the attention, it struck him that it was only preparatory to giving him a dry blanket to wear till his drenched garments were dry, and hence he suffered patiently.

But that was not all, for, as the last garment was stripped off, Ngati said some words to his people, and before he could realise what was going to be done, Don felt himself seized by four men, each taking a wrist or ankle, and holding him suspended before Ngati, who went behind him and supported his head.

"Hah!" ejaculated Ngati, with a peculiar grunt. His men all acted with military precision, and, to Don's astonishment, he found himself plunged into a rocky basin of hot water.

His first idea was to struggle, but there was no need. He had been lowered in rapidly but gently, and he felt Ngati place the back of his head softly against a smooth pleasantly-warm hollowed-out stone, while the sensation, after all he had gone through, was so delicious that he uttered a sigh of satisfaction.

For now he realised the hospitality of the people who had brought him there, and the fact that to recover him from the chill of being half drowned, they had brought him to one of their hot springs, used by them as baths.

Don uttered another sigh of satisfaction, and as he lay back covered to his chin in the hot volcanic water, he began to laugh so heartily that the tears came into his eyes.

For the same process was going on in the darkness with Jem, who was a less tractable patient, especially as he had taken it into his thick head that it was not for his benefit that he was to be plunged into a hot water pool, but to make soup for the New Zealanders around.

"Mas' Don!" he cried out of the darkness, "where are you? I want to get out of this. Here, be quiet, will yer? What yer doing of? I say. Don't. Here, what are you going to do?"

Don wanted to say a word to calm Jem's alarms, but after the agony he had gone through, it seemed to him as if his nerves were relaxed beyond control, and his companion's perplexity presented itself to him in so comical a light, that he could do nothing but lie back there in his delicious bath, and laugh hysterically; and all the while he could hear the New Zealanders gobbling angrily in reply to Jem's objections, as a fierce struggle went on.

"That's your game, is it? I wouldn't ha' thought it of a set who calls theirselves men. Shove me into that hot pot, and boil me, would you? Not if I knows it, you don't. Hi! Mas' Don! Look out! Run, my lad. They're trying to cook me alive, the brutes. Oh, if I only had a cutlash, or an iron bar."

Don tried to speak again, but the words were suffocated by the gurgle of laughter.

"Poor old Jem!" he thought.

"I tell you, you sha'n't. Six to one, eh? Leave off. Mas' Don, they're going to scald me like a pig in a tub. Hi! Help!"

There was the sound of a struggle, a loud splash, and then silence, followed by Jem's voice.

"Oh!" he ejaculated. "Then why didn't you say so? How was I to know you meant a hot bath? Well, it arn't bad. —Mas' Don!"

"Yes."

"What! ha' you been there all the time?"

"Yes."

"What yer been doing of?"

"Laughing."

"Larfin'? Are they giving you a hot bath?"

"Yes."

"Arn't it good?"

"Glorious!"

"I thought they was going to scald me like a pig, so as to eat me afterwards. Did you hear me holler?"

"Hear you? Yes.—How delicious and restful it feels."

"Ah, it do, my lad; but don!t you let any on it get into your mouth. I did, and arn't good. But I say; what's it mean? Seems so rum to me coming to meet us in a canoe and bringing us ashore, and giving us hot baths. I don't seem to understand it. Nobody does such things over at home."

As they lay in the roughly made stone slab baths, into which the volcanic water effervesced and gurgled, the followers of Ngati came and went busily, and a curious transformation came over the scene—the darkness seemed to undergo a change and become grey. Then as Don watched, he saw that above his head quite a cloud of steam was floating, through which a pale, sad light began to penetrate; and as he watched this, so pleasant and restful was the sensation that he felt as if he could sleep, till he took into consideration the fact that if he did, his body would become relaxed, and he would slip down with his head beneath the surface.

As it grew lighter rapidly now, he could make out that the roughly thatched roof was merely stretched over a rough rocky nook in which the hot spring bubbled out of the mountain slope, and here a few rough slabs had been laid together, box-fashion, to retain the water and form the bath.

Before he had more than realised the fact that Jem was in a shelter very similar to his own, the huge New Zealander was back with about a dozen of his men, and himself bearing a great native flax cloth marked with a broad pattern.

Just as the sun had transformed everything without, and Don was gazing on a glorious prospect of lace-like tree-fern rising out of the steaming gully in which he stood, Jem Wimble came stalking out of the shelter where he had been dressing—a very simple operation, for it had consisted in draping himself in a great unbleached cloth—and looking squat and comical as a man in his circumstances could look.

Ngati was close at hand with his men all standing in a group, and at first sight it seemed as if they were laughing at the little, stoutly-built, pink-faced man, but, on the contrary, they were smiles of admiration.

"I couldn't ha' believed it, Mas' Don," said Jem; "I feel as fresh as a daisy, and—well, I never did! Mas' Don, what a guy you do look!"

Don, after a momentary thought that he looked something like one of the old Romans in a toga, just as he had seen them in an engraving, had been so taken up with the beauty of the ferny gully, with the sun gilding here and there the steamy vapour which rose from the hot springs, that he had thought no more of his personal appearance till Jem spoke.

"Guy?" he said, laughing, as he ran his eye over Jem. "I say, did you ever hear the story of the pot and the kettle?"

"Yes, of course; but I say, my lad, I don't look so rum as you, do I?"

"I suppose you look just about the same, Jem."

"Then the sooner they gets our clothes dry and we're into 'em again, the sooner we shall look like human beings. Say, Mas' Don, it's werry awkward; you can't say anything to that big savage without him shouting 'pakeha.' How shall we ask for our clothes?"

"Wait," said Don. "We've got to think about getting further away."

"Think they'll send to look for us, Mas' Don?"

"I should say they would."

"Well, somehow," said Jem, "I seem to fancy they'll think we're drowned, and never send at all. But, look here; what's all this yaller stuff?"

"Sulphur."

"What, brimstone? Why, so it is. Think o' their buying brimstone to lay down about their hot baths. I know!" cried Jem, slapping his thigh, "they uses it instead of coal, Mas' Don; burns it to make the water hot."

"No, no, Jem; that's natural sulphur."

"So's all sulphur nat'ral."

"But I mean this is where it is found, or comes."

"G'long with you."

"It is, Jem; and that water is naturally hot."

"What, like it is at Bath?"

"To be sure."

"Well, that caps all. Some one said so the other day aboard ship, but I didn't believe it. Fancy a set o' savages having hot water all ready for them. I say, though, Mas' Don, it's very nice."

Just then Ngati came up smiling, but as Jem afterwards said, looking like a figure-head that was going to bite, and they were led off to a *whare* and furnished with a good substantial meal.

CHAPTER XXIX.

AN UNWELCOME RECOGNITION.

"IT arn't bad," said Jem; "but it's puzzling."

"What is?" said Don, who was partaking of broiled fish with no little appetite.

"Why, how savages like these here should know all about cooking."

The breakfast was eaten with an admiring circle of spectators at hand, while Ngati kept on going from Don to his tribesmen and back again, patting the lad's shoulder, and seeming to play the part of showman with no little satisfaction to himself, but with the effect of making Jem wroth.

"It's all very well, Mas' Don," he said, with his mouth full; "but if he comes and says 'my pakeha' to me, I shall throw something at him."

"Oh, it's all kindly meant, Jem."

"Oh, is it? I don't know so much about that. If it is, why don't they give us back our clothes? Suppose any of our fellows was to see us like this?"

"I hope none of our fellows will see us, Jem."

"Tomati Paroni! Tomati Paroni!" shouted several of the men in chorus.

"Hark at 'em!" cried Jem scornfully. "What does that mean?"

The explanation was given directly, for the tattooed Englishmen came running up to the *whare*.

"Boats coming from the ship to search for you," he said quickly, and then turned to Ngati and spoke a few words with the result that the chief rushed at the escaped pair, and signed to them to rise.

"Yes," said the Englishman, "you had better go with him and hide for a bit. We'll let you know when they are gone."

"Tell them to give us our clothes," said Jem sourly.

"Yes, of course. They would tell tales," said the Englishman; and he turned again to Ngati, who sent two men out of the *whare* to return directly with the dried garments.

Ngati signed to them to follow, and he led them, by a faintly marked track, in and out among the trees and the cleared patches which formed the natives' gardens, and all the while carefully avoiding any openings through which the harbour could be seen.

Every now and then he turned to speak volubly, but though he interpolated a few English words, his meaning would have been incomprehensible but for his gestures and the warnings nature kept giving of danger.

For every here and there, as they wound in and out among the trees, they came upon soft, boggy places, where the ground was hot; and as the pressure of the foot sent hissing forth a jet of steam, it was evident that a step to right or left of the narrow track meant being plunged into a pool of heated mud of unknown depth.

In other places the hot mud bubbled up in rounded pools, spitting, hissing, and bursting with faint cracks that were terribly suggestive of danger.

Over these heated spots the fertility and growth of the plants was astounding. They seemed to be shooting up out of a natural hothouse, but where to attempt to pass them meant a terrible and instant death.

"Look out, Mas' Don! This here's what I once heard a clown say, 'It's dangerous to be safe.' I say, figgerhead, arn't there no other way?"

"Ship! Men! Catchee, catchee," said Ngati, in a whisper.

"Hear that, Mas' Don? Any one'd think we was babbies. Ketchy, ketchy, indeed! You ask him if there arn't no other way. I don't like walking in a place that's like so much hot soup."

"Be quiet, and follow. Hist! hark!"

Don stopped short, for, from a distance, came a faint hail, followed by another nearer, which seemed to be in answer.

"They're arter us, sir, and if we're to be ketched I don't mean to be ketched like this."

"What are you going to do, Jem?"

"Do?" said Jem, unrolling his bundled-up clothes, and preparing to sit down, "make myself look like an ornery Chrishtun."

"Don't sit down there, Jem!" cried Don, as Ngati gave a warning cry at the same moment, and started back.

But they were too late, for Jem had chosen a delicately green mossy and ferny patch, and plumped himself down, to utter a cry of horror, and snatch at the extended hands. For the green ferny patch was a thin covering over a noisome hole full of black boiling mud, into which the poor fellow was settling as he was dragged out.

"Fah!" ejaculated Jem, pinching his nose. "Here, I've had 'most enough o' this place. Nice sort o' spot this would be to turn a donkey out to graze. Why, you wouldn't find nothing but the tips of his ears to-morrow morning."

Another hail rang out, and was answered in two places.

"I say, Mas' Don, they're hunting for us, and we shall have to run."

He made signs to the chief indicative of a desire to run, but Ngati shook his head, and pointed onward.

They followed on, listening to the shouts, which came nearer, till Ngati suddenly took a sharp turn round a great buttress of lava, and entered a wild, narrow, forbidding-looking chasm, where on either side the black, jagged masses of rock were piled up several hundred feet, and made glorious by streams which coursed among the delicately green ferns.

"Look's damp," said Jem, as Ngati led them on for about fifty yards, and then began to climb, his companions following him, till he reached a shelf about a hundred feet up, and beckoned to them to come.

"Does he think this here's the rigging of a ship, and want us to set sail?" grumbled Jem. "Here, I say, what's the good of our coming there?"

The chief stamped his foot, and made an imperious gesture, which brought them to his side.

He pointed to a hole in the face of the precipice, and signed to them to go in.

"Men—boat," he said, pointing, and then clapping his hand to his ear as a distant hail came like a whisper up the gully, which was almost at right angles to the beach.

"He wants us to hide here, Jem," said Don; and he went up to the entrance and looked in. A hot, steamy breath of air came like a puff into his face, and a strange low moaning noise fell upon his ear, followed by a faint whistle, that was strongly suggestive of some one being already in hiding.

"I suppose that's where they keeps their coals, Mas' Don," said Jem. "So we've got to hide in the coal-cellar. Why not start off and run?"

"We should be seen," said Don anxiously. "Don't let us do anything rash."

"But p'r'aps it's rash to go in there, my lad. How do we know it isn't a trap, or that it's safe to go in?"

"We must trust our hosts, Jem," replied Don. "They have behaved very well to us so far."

There was another hail from the party ashore, and still Jem hesitated.

"I don't know but what we might walk straight away, Mas' Don," he said, glancing down at the garb he wore. "If any of our fellows saw us at a distance they'd say we was savages, and take no notice."

"Not of our white faces, Jem? Come, don't be obstinate; I'm going on."

"Oh, well, sir, if you go on, o' course I must follow, and look arter you; but I don't like it. The place looks treacherous. Ugh! Wurra! wurra! wurra!"

That repeated word represents most nearly the shudder given by Jem Wimble as he followed Don into the cave, the chief pointing for them to go farther in, and then dropping rapidly down from point to point till he was at the bottom, Jem peering over the edge of the shelf, and watching him till he had disappeared.

"Arn't gone to tell them where we are, have he, Mas' Don?"

"No, Jem. How suspicious you are!"

"Ah, so'll you be when you get as old as I am," said Jem, creeping back to where Don was standing, looking inward. "Well, what sort of a place is it, Mas' Don?"

"I can't see in far, but the cavern seems to go right in, like a long crooked passage."

"Crooked enough, and long enough," grumbled Jem. "Hark!"

Don listened, and heard a faint hail.

"They're coming along searching for us, I suppose."

"I didn't mean that sound; I meant this. There, listen again."

Don took a step into the cave, but went no farther, for Jem gripped his arm.

"Take care, my lad. 'Tarn't safe. Hear that noise?"

"Yes; it is like some animal breathing hard."

"And we've got no pistols nor cutlashes. It's a lion, I know."

"There are no lions here, Jem."

"Arn't there? Then it's a tiger. I know un. I've seen 'em. Hark!'

"But there are no tigers, nor any other fierce beasts here, Jem."

"Now, how can you be so obstinate, Mas' Don, when you can hear 'em whistling, and sighing and breathing hard right in yonder. No, no, not a step farther do you go."

"Don't be so foolish, Jem."

"'Tarn't foolish, Mas' Don; and look here: I'm going to take advantage of them being asleep to put on my proper costoom, and if you'll take my advice, you'll do just the same."

Don hesitated, but Jem took advantage of a handy seat-like piece of rock, and altered his dress rapidly, an example that, after a moment or two of hesitation, Don followed.

"Dry as a bone," said Jem. "Come, that's better. I feels like a human being now. Just before I felt like a chap outside one of the shows at our fair."

He doubled up the blanket he had been wearing, and threw it over his arm; while Don folded his, and laid it down, so that he could peer over the edge of the shelf, and command the entrance to the ravine.

But all was perfectly silent and deserted, and, after waiting some time, he rose, and went a little way inside the cavern.

"Don't! Don't be so precious rash, Mas' Don," cried Jem pettishly, as, urged on by his curiosity, Don went slowly, step by step, toward what seemed to be a dark blue veil of mist, which shut off farther view into the cave.

"I don't think there's anything to mind, or they wouldn't have told us to hide here."

"But you don't know, my lad. There may be dangerous wild critters in there as you never heard tell on. Graffems, and dragons, and beasts with stings in their tails—cockatoos."

"Nonsense! Cockatrices," said Don laughing.

"Well, it's all the same. Now, do be advised, Mas' Don, and stop here."

"But I want to know what it's like farther in."

Don went slowly forward into the dim mist, and Jem followed, murmuring bitterly at his being so rash.

"Mind!" he cried suddenly, as a louder whistle than ordinary came from the depths of the cave, and the sound was so weird and strange that Don stopped short.

The noise was not repeated, but the peculiar hissing went on, and, as if from a great distance, there came gurglings and rushing sounds, as if from water.

"I know we shall get in somewhere, and not get out again, Mas' Don. There now, hark at that!"

"It's only hot water, the same as we heard gurgling in our bath," said Don, still progressing.

"Well, suppose it is. The more reason for your not going. P'r'aps this is where it comes from first, and nice place it must

"THERE WAS A RUSTLING SOUND, AND THE FIGURE OF A MAN APPEARED."
(*p.* 238).

be where all that water's made hot. Let's go back, and wait close at the front."

"No; let's go a little farther, Jem."

"Why, I'm so hot now, my lad, I feel as if I was being steamed like a tater. Here, let's get back, and——"

"Hist!"

Don caught his arm, for there was another whistle, and not from the depths of the dark steamy cave, but from outside, evidently below the mouth of the cave, as if some one was climbing up.

The whistle was answered, and the two fugitives crept back a little more into the darkness.

"Ahoy! Come up here, sir!" shouted a familiar voice, and a hail came back.

"Here's a hole in the rocks up here," came plainly now.

"Ramsden," whispered Don in Jem's ear.

They stole back a little more into the gloom, Jem offering no opposition now, for it seemed to them, so plainly could they see the bright greenish-hued day-light, and the configuration of the cavern's mouth, that so sure as any one climbed up to the shelf and looked in they would be seen.

Impressed by this, Don whispered to Jem to come farther in, and they were about to back farther, when there was a rustling sound, and the figure of a man appeared standing up perfectly black against the light; but though his features were not visible, they knew him by his configuration, and that their guess at the voice was right.

"He sees us," thought Don, and he stood as if turned to stone, one hand touching the warm rocky side of the cave, and the other resting upon Jem's shoulder.

The man was motionless as they, and his appearance exercised an effect upon them like fascination, as he stood peering forward, and seeming to fix them with his eyes, which had the stronger fancied effect upon them for not being seen.

"Wonder whether it would kill a man to hit him straight in the chest, and drive him off that rock down into the gully below," said Jem to himself. "I should like to do it."

Then he shrank back as if he had been struck, for the sinister scoundrel shouted loudly,—

"Ahoy there! Now, then out you come. I can see you hiding."

CHAPTER XXX.

A DETERMINED ENEMY

DON drew a long breath and took a step forward to march out and give himself up, but Jem's hands clasped him round, a pair of lips were placed to his ear, and the yardman's voice whispered,—

"Stand fast. All sham. He can't see."

Don paused, wondering, and watched the dark figure in the entrance to the cave, without dismay now, till, to his surprise, the man began to whistle softly.

"Likely place too," he muttered. "Are you coming up here, sir?"

"What is it?"

"Likely looking cave, sir; runs right in; looks as if they might be hiding in here."

There was a rattling and rustling of stones and growth, and then the man at the entrance stooped down and held out his hands to assist some one to ascend, the result being that the broad heavy figure of Bosun Jones came into view.

"Not likely to be here, my lad, even if they were in hiding; but this is a wild goose chase. They're dead as dead."

"P'r'aps so, sir; but I think they're in hiding somewhere. P'r'aps here."

"Humph! No. Poor fellows, they were drowned."

"No, sir, I don't think it," said Ramsden. "Those niggers looked as if they knew something, and that tattooed fellow who has run away from Norfolk Island has encouraged them to desert. As like as not they may be in here listening to all I say."

"Well then, go in and fetch them out," said the boatswain. "You can go in while I have a rest."

Don's heart beat fast at those words, for he heard a loud hissing sound beside him, caused by Jem drawing in his breath; and the next moment, as he held his arm, he felt a thrill, for it seemed as if Jem's muscles had tightened up suddenly.

Then there was a hot breath upon his cheek, and a tickling sensation in his ear beyond; Jem's lips seemed to settle themselves against it, and the tickling sensation was renewed, as Jem whispered,—

"I've cleared my decks for action, Mas' Don. It was that beggar as told on us. You stand aside when he comes on."

Don twisted his head round, caught Jem by the shoulder, and favoured him with the same buzzing sensation as he whispered,—

"What are you going to do?'

Jem re-applied his lips to Don's ear.

"I'm going to make him very sorry he ever come to sea. Once I gets hold of him I'll make him feel like a walnut in a door."

"Don't look a very cheerful place, Mr. Jones," came from the mouth of the cavern.

"Afraid to go in?"

"Afraid, sir? You never knew me afraid."

"Well, in you go and fetch them out," said the boatswain with a laugh. "If you don't come back I shall know that the Maoris have got you, and are saving you for the pot."

From where Don and Jem stood in the darkness they could see their spying sinister friend give quite a start; but he laughed off the impression the boatswain's words had made, and began to come cautiously on, feeling his way as a man does who has just left the bright sunshine to enter a dark place.

Jem uttered a loud hiss as he drew his breath, and Ramsden heard it and stopped.

"Mr. Jones," he said sharply.

"Well?"

"Think there's any big snakes here? I heard a hiss."

"Only steam from a hot spring. No snakes in this country."

"Oh!" ejaculated Ramsden: and he came cautiously on.

Don felt Jem's arm begin to twitch, and discovery seemed imminent. For a few moments he was irresolute, but, knowing that if they were to escape they must remain unseen, he let his hand slide down to Jem's wrist, caught it firmly, and began to back farther into the cave.

For a few moments he had to drag hard at his companion but, as if yielding to silently communicated superior orders Jem followed him slowly, step by step, with the greatest of caution, and in utter silence.

The floor of the cave was wonderfully smooth, the rock feeling as if it had been worn by the constant passage over it of water, and using their bare feet as guides, and feeling with them every step, they backed in as fast as Ramsden approached, being as it were between two dangers, that of recapture, and the hidden perils, whatever they might be, of the cave.

It was nerve-stirring work, for all beyond was intense darkness, out of which, as they backed farther and farther in, came strange whisperings, guttural gurglings, which sounded to Don as if the inhabitants of the place were retiring angrily before their disturbers, till, driven to bay in some corner, they turned and attacked.

But still Don held tightly by Jem's wrist, and mastering his dread of the unknown, crept softly in, turning from time to time to watch Ramsden, who came on as if some instinct told him that those he sought for were there.

"Found 'em?" shouted the boatswain; and his voice taught the hiding pair that the cave went far in beyond them, for the sound went muttering by, and seemed to die away as if far down a long passage.

"Not yet, but I think I can hear 'em," replied Ramsden.

"You can hear a self-satisfied fool talking," said the boatswain, ill-humouredly.

"So can Mr. Jones," muttered the man. "Hear you. That's what I can hear."

"What are you muttering about?"

"I think I can hear 'em, sir. Now then, you two, give up. It'll be the worse for you if you don't."

Don's hand tightened on his companion's wrist, and they stood fast, for Ramsden was stopping in a bent attitude, listening.

There was nothing to be heard but the whisperings and gurglings, and then they saw him draw his cutlass and come on.

Jem's muscles gave another jerk, but he suffered himself to be drawn farther and farther into the cave, till they must have been quite two hundred yards from the mouth; and now, for the first time, the almost straight line which it had formed, changed, and they lost sight of the entrance, but could see the shadow of their enemy cast upon the glistening wall of the place, down which the water seemed to drip, giving it the look of glass.

All at once Don, as he crept back, felt his left foot, instead of encountering the smooth rock floor, go down, and as he quickly withdrew it and felt nearer to him, it was to touch the edge of what seemed a great crack crossing the floor diagonally.

As he paused, he felt that it might be a "fault" of a few inches in width or depth, or a vast chasm going right down into the bowels of the mountain!

"There's a hole here," he whispered to Jem. "Hold my hand."

Jem gripped him firmly, and he reached out with one leg, and felt over the side outward and downward; and, just as he was coming to the conclusion that the place was terribly deep, and a shudder at the danger was running through him, he found that he could touch bottom.

He was in the act of recovering himself, so as to try how

wide the crack or fault might be, when a peculiar strangling sensation attacked him, and he felt that he was falling.

The next thing he felt was Jem's lips to his ear, and feeling his whisper,—

"Hold on, lad. What's the matter?"

He panted and drew his breath in a catching way for a few minutes before whispering back,—

"Nothing. Only a sudden giddiness."

Jem made no comment, but gripped his hand tightly, and they stood listening, for the shadow cast faintly on the walls was motionless, and it was evident that their enemy was listening.

"I'm going on, Ramsden," said the boatswain. "Come along!"

"All right, sir. Join you as soon as I've got my prisoners.'

"Hold 'em tight," shouted the boatswain, and then there was a loud rustling sound, followed by the words faintly heard, "Look sharp. It's of no use fooling there."

Don could hear Ramsden mutter something, but he did not seem to be coming on; and mastering the dull, sluggish feeling, accompanied by a throbbing headache, the lad stole cautiously back to where he could look round and see their approaching enemy between them and the light.

To his intense surprise he found the man had his back to them, and was retiring; but as he watched, Ramsden made an angry gesticulation, turned sharply and came on again, but seemed to catch his foot against a projecting piece of rock, stumble and fall forward, his cutlass flying two or three yards on before him with a loud jingling noise.

What followed riveted Don to the spot.

CHAPTER XXXI.

GOOD FOR EVIL.

RAMSDEN struggled to his feet as if with an effort, and stood holding his hand to his head, evidently hurt. The next moment he stepped forward, staggering slightly, stooped to pick up his cutlass, and fell forward, uttered a groan, rose up again, and fell down once more, this time to lie without motion.

"Jem," whispered Don, "look at that!"

"Was looking," whispered back Jem. "Hit his head; sarve him right."

Ramsden did not move, and the two fugitives stood anxiously watching.

"What shall we do?"

"Wait! He'll soon come round and go. May as well sit down."

Jem lowered himself to a sitting position, and was in the act of trying to rest on his elbow when he gasped quickly two or three times, and caught at Don, who helped him to a kneeling position, from which he struggled up.

"Hah!" he ejaculated; "just as if some one caught me by the throat. Oh, how poorly I do feel. Just you put your head down there, Mas' Don."

Don stood thinking and trying to grasp what it meant. Then, with some hazy recollection of dangers encountered in old wells, he bent down cautiously and started up again, for it gradually dawned upon both that for about two feet above the floor there was a heavy stratum of poisonous gas, so potent that it overcame them directly; and it was into this they had plunged as soon as they had stooped down.

"Why, Jem," panted Don; "it stops your breath!"

"Stops your breath? It's just as if a man got hold of you by the throat. Why, if I'd stopped in that a minute I should never have got up again."

"But—but, that man?" whispered Don.

"What, old Ramsden? Phew! I'd forgot all about him. He's quiet enough."

"Jem, he must be dying."

"I won't say, 'Good job, too,' 'cause it wouldn't be nice," said Jem, with a chuckle. "What shall us do?"

"Do?" cried Don. "We must help him."

"What, get him out? If we do, he'll be down on us."

"We can't help that, Jem. We must not leave a fellow-creature to die," replied Don; and hurrying forward, he gave a glance toward the mouth of the cave, to satisfy himself that the good-natured boatswain was not there, and then, holding his breath, he stooped down and raised Ramsden into a sitting posture, Jem coming forward at once to help him.

"Goes ag'in the grain, Mas' Don," he muttered; "but I s'pose we must."

"Must? Yes! Now, what shall we do?"

"Dunno," said Jem; "s'pose fresh air 'd be best for him."

"Let's get him to the mouth, then," said Don.

"But the boatswain 'll see us, and we shall be took."

"I can't help that, Jem; the man will die here."

"Well, we don't want him. He's a hennymee."

"Jem!"

"Oh, all right, Mas' Don. I'll do as you say, but as I says, and I says it again, it goes ag'in the grain."

They each took one hand and placed their arms beneath those of the prostrate man; and, little as they stooped, they inhaled sufficient of the powerful gas to make them wince and cough; but, rising upright, taking a full breath and starting off, they dragged Ramsden backwards as rapidly as they could to where the fresh air blew into the mouth of the cave, and there they laid the man down.

But before doing so, Don went upon his knees, and placing his face close to the rocky floor, inhaled the air several times.

"It seems all right here," he said. "Try it, Jem."

"Oh! I'll try it," said Jem, grumpily; "only I don't see why we should take so much trouble about such a thing as this."

"Yes; it's all right," he said, after puffing and blowing down by the ground. "Rum, arn't it, that the air should be bad yonder and not close in here!"

"The cave goes downward," said Don; "and the foul air lies in the bottom, just as it does in a well. Do you think he's dead?"

"Him dead!" said Jem, contemptuously; "I don't believe you could kill a thing like that. Here, let's roll up one of these here blanket things and make him a pillow, and cover him up with the other, poor fellow, so as he may get better and go and tell 'em we're here."

"Don't talk like that, Jem!" cried Don.

"Why not? Soon as he gets better he'll try and do us all the harm he can."

"Poor fellow! I'm afraid he's dead," whispered Don.

"Then he won't want no more cutlashes and pistols," said Jem, coolly appropriating the arms; "these here will be useful to us."

"But they are the king's property, Jem."

"Ah! well, I dessay if the king knew how bad we wanted 'em, he'd lend 'em to us. He shall have 'em again when we've done with them."

As he spoke Jem helped himself to the ammunition, and then stood looking on as Don dragged Ramsden's head round, so that the wind blew in his face.

"How I should like to jump on him!" growled Jem. "I hate him like poison, and I would if I'd got on a pair o' boots. Shouldn't hurt him a bit like this."

"Don't talk nonsense, Jem. Mr. Jones might hear us. Let's hail; he can't be very far off."

"I say, Mas' Don, did our ugly swim last night send you half mad?"

"Mad? No!"

"Then, p'r'aps it's because you had no sleep. Here's a chap comes hunting of us down with a cutlash, ready to do anything; and now he's floored and we're all right, you want to make a pet on him. Why, it's my belief that if you met a tiger with the toothache you'd want to take out his tusk."

"Very likely, Jem," said Don, laughing.

"Ah, and as soon as you'd done it, 'Thankye, my lad,' says the tiger, 'that tooth's been so bad that I haven't made a comf'table meal for days, so here goes.'"

"And then he'd eat me, Jem."

"That's so, my lad."

"Ah, well, this isn't a tiger, Jem."

"Why, he's wuss than a tiger, Mas' Don; because he do know better, and tigers don't."

"Ramsden, ahoy!" came from below them in the ravine.

"Oh, crumpets!" exclaimed Jem. "Now we're done for. All that long swim for nothing."

"Back into the cave," whispered Don. "Perhaps they have not seen us."

He gave Jem a thrust, they backed in a few yards, and then stood watching and listening.

CHAPTER XXXII.

CLOSE SHAVING.

"THINK he's insensible, or only shamming?" said Jem.
"Insensible—quite! I'm afraid he's dead."

"I arn't," muttered Jem. "You might cut him up like a heel; legs and arms and body, and every bit of him would try and do you a mischief."

"I'm afraid, though, that he knew we were in here, and that as soon as he comes to, he'll tell the others."

"Not he. It was only his gammon to frighten us into speaking if we were there."

"Ramsden, ahoy!" came again from below; and then from a distance came another hail, which the same voice answered —evidently from some distance below the mouth of the cave.

"Ramsden! Here, my man; come along, they're not in there."

"Hear that, Jem? Mr. Jones."

"Oh yes, I hear," growled Jem. "He don't know yet; but wait a bit till old Ram tells him."

"We couldn't slip out yet, Jem?"

"No; o' course not. They'd see us now. Look!"

Jem was about to draw back, but feeling that a movement might betray them, Don held him fast, and they stood there in the shadow of the cave, looking on, for the boatswain's head appeared as he drew himself up the precipitous place, and then stepped on the shelf.

"Here, come out, sir! Are you asleep? Hah!"

He caught sight of the prostrate sailor, and bent down over him.

"Why, Ramsden, man!" he cried, as he tore open his sailor's shirt and placed his hand upon his throat.

"'COME ON HERE! QUICK!' HE SHOUTED, WITH HIS HANDS TO HIS MOUTH" (*p.* 250).

Then, starting up, he sent forth a tremendous hail.

"Ahoy!"

"Ahoy!" came back from several places, like the echoes of his call.

"Come on here! Quick!" he shouted, with his hands to his mouth.

"Ahoy!" came from a distance; and from nearer at hand, "Ay, ay, sir; ay, ay!"

From where Don and Jem stood they could see the boatswain's every movement, as, after once more feeling the sailor's throat and wrist, he bent over him and poured water from his bottle between his lips, bathed his forehead and eyes, and then fanned him with his hat, but without effect.

Then he looked out anxiously and hailed again, the replies coming from close by; and soon after first one and then another sailor, whose faces were quite familiar, climbed up to the shelf, when the boatswain explained hastily how he had left his companion.

"Some one knocked him down?" said one of his men.

"No; he's not hurt. I should say it's a fit. More water. Don't be afraid!"

Each of the men who had climbed up carried a supply, and a quantity was dashed over Ramsden's face with the effect that he began to display signs of returning consciousness, and at last sat up and stared.

"What's matter, mate?" said one of the men, as Don prepared to hurry back into the darkness, but longed to hear what Ramsden would say.

It was a painful moment, for upon his words seemed to depend their safety.

"Matter? I don't know—I——"

He put his hand to his head.

"Here, take a drink o' this, mate," said one of the men, and Ramsden swallowed some water with avidity.

"Arn't seen a ghost, have you?"

"I recollect now, Mr. Jones. You left me in that hole."

"And called to you to come out."

"Yes, but——"

Don's heart beat furiously. They were discovered, and now the betrayal was to come.

"Well, what happened?" said the boatswain.

"I felt sure that those two were in this place, and I went on farther into the darkness till I kicked against something and fell down."

"Out here and stunned yourself."

"No, no; in there! I'd got up and picked up my cutlash, and then something seemed to choke me, and I went down again."

Jem squeezed Don's arm, for they both felt more hopeful.

"And then one of they chaps came and give you a crack o' the head?" said a sailor.

Don's heart sank again.

"Nonsense!" said his old friend, the boatswain. "Foul air. He must have staggered out and fallen down insensible."

Jem gripped Don's arm with painful force here.

"How do you feel? Can you walk?"

Ramsden rose slowly, and staggered, but one of the men caught his arm.

"I—I think I can."

"Well, we must get you down to the boat as soon as we can. Walk, if you are able. If you can't, we must carry you."

"But them chaps," said one of the party, just as Don and Jem were beginning to breathe freely. "Think they're in yonder, mate?"

"I—I think so," said Ramsden faintly. "You had better search."

"What! a place full of foul air?" said the boatswain, greatly to Don's relief. "Absurd! If Ramsden could not live in there, how could the escaped men? Here, let's get him down."

"Ay, ay, sir. But I say, mate, where's your fighting tools? What yer done with them?"

Don made an angry gesticulation, and turned to Jem, who had the pistols and cutlass in his hand and waistbelt, and felt as if he should like to hurl them away.

"He must have dropped them inside. Here, one of you come with me and get them."

Don shrank back into the stony passage as a man volunteered, but the boatswain hesitated.

"No," he said, to Don's great relief; "I can't afford to run risks for the sake of a pair of pistols."

"Let me go in," said the man.

"I'm not going to send men where I'm afraid to go myself," said the boatswain bluntly. "Come on down."

The boatswain led the way, and Ramsden was helped down, the man who had volunteered to go in the cavern to fetch the pistols manœuvring so as to be last, and as soon as the party had disappeared over the shelf he gave a glance after them, and turned sharply.

"Foul air won't hurt me," he said; and he dived right in rapidly to regain the pistols and cutlass, so as to have the laugh of his messmates when they returned on board.

CHAPTER XXXIII.

ANOTHER ALARM.

"IT'S all over," thought Don, as the man came on, with discovery inevitable if he continued at his present rate. They were about fifty feet from the entrance, and they felt that if they moved they would be heard; and, as if urged by the same impulse, they stood fast, save that Jem doubled his fist and drew back his arm ready to strike.

All at once the man stopped short.

"He sees us," said Don, mentally.

But he was wrong, for the sailor thrust his fingers into his mouth and gave a shrill whistle, which ran echoing through the place in a curiously hollow way.

"That's a rum un," he said, with a laugh. "Blow some o' the foul air out. Wonder how far he went in?"

He walked on slowly, and then stopped short as if he saw the hiding pair; but there was no gesture made, and of course his face was invisible to the fugitives, to whom he seemed to be nothing but a black figure.

"Plaguey dark!" ejaculated the man aloud.

Hiss-s-s-s!

A tremendously loud sibillation came out of the darkness—such a noise as a mythical dragon might have made when a stranger had invaded his home. The effect was instantaneous. The young sailor spun round and darted back to the mouth of the cave, where he half lowered himself down over the shelf facing toward the entry, and supporting himself with one hand, shook his fist.

"You wait till I come back with a lanthorn!" he cried. "I'll just show you. Don't you think I'm scared."

Whos-s-s-s-s came that hissing again, in a loud deep tone this time, and the sailor's head disappeared, for he dropped down and hastily descended after his messmates, flushed and excited, but trying hard to look perfectly unconcerned, and thoroughly determined to keep his own counsel as to what he had heard, from a perfect faith in the effect of the disclosure—to wit, that his companions would laugh at him.

Inside the cave Jem was leaning up against the wall, making strange noises and lifting up first one foot and then the other. He seemed to be suffering agonies, for he puffed and gasped.

"Jem, be quiet!" whispered Don, shaking him sharply.

"Oh, dear! oh, dear!" groaned Jem, lifting up his bare feet alternately, and setting them down again with a loud pat on the rock.

"Be quiet! they may hear you."

"Hit me then! Give it me. Ho, ho, ho!"

"Jem, we are safe now, and you'll undo it all if you're not quiet."

"Knock me then, Mas' Don. Oh, dear! oh, dear! Hit me; a good un, dear lad. Ho, ho, ho, ho!"

"Oh, do be quiet! How can you be such an ass?"

"I dunno! Oh, dear! oh, dear! Did you see him run, Mas' Don? I—oh dear, I can't help it. Do knock me down and sit on me, dear lad—I never—oh dear me!"

Jem laughed till Don grew angry, and then the sturdy little fellow stopped short and stood wiping his eyes with the back of his hands.

"I couldn't help it, Mas' Don," he said. "I don't think I ever laughed so much before. There, I'm better now. Shan't have any more laugh in me for a twelvemonth. Hiss! Whoss-s-s!"

He made the two sounds again, and burst into another uncontrollable fit of laughter at the success of his ruse; but this time Don caught him by the throat, and he stopped at once.

"Hah!" he ejaculated, and wiped his eyes again. "Thank-ye, Mas' Don; that's just what you ought to ha' done before. There, it's all over now. What are you going to do?"

"Watch them," said Don, laconically; and he crept to the mouth of the cave, and peered cautiously over the edge of the shelf, but all was quiet; and beyond a distant hail or two, heard after listening for some minutes, there was nothing to indicate that the search party had been there.

"We must be well on the look-out, Jem. Your stupid trick may bring them back."

"Stoopid? Well, I do like that, Mas' Don, after saving us both as I did."

"I'd say let's go on at once, only we might meet some of them."

"And old 'My pakeha' wouldn't know where to find us. I say, Mas' Don, what are we going to do? Stop here with these people, and old Tomati, or go on at once and shift for ourselves?"

"We cannot shift for ourselves in a country like this without some way of getting food."

"Hush!" exclaimed Jem sharply.

"What's the matter?" cried Don, making for the inner part of their hiding-place.

"No, no; don't do that. It's all right, Mas' Don, only don't say anything more about food. I feel just now as if I could eat you. It's horrid how hungry I am."

"You see then," said Don, "how helpless we are."

"Yes; if it was only a biscuit I wouldn't mind just now, for there don't seem to be nothing to eat here, nor nothing to drink."

They stood leaning against the rocky wall, not caring to risk sitting down on account of the foul air, and not daring to go to the mouth of the cave for fear of being seen, till Don suggested that they should steal there cautiously, and lie down with their faces beyond the cavern floor.

This they did, glad of the restful change; but hours passed and no sounds met their ears, save the hissing and gurgling from the interior of the cave, and the harsh screech of some parrot or cockatoo.

Every time a louder hiss than usual came from the interior, Jem became convulsed, and threatened another explosion of laughter, in spite of Don's severely reproachful looks; but in every case Jem's mirthful looks and his comic ways of trying to suppress his hilarity proved to be too much for Don, who was fain to join in, and they both laughed heartily and well.

It is a curious fact, one perhaps which doctors can explain, and it seems paradoxical. For it might be supposed that when any one was hungry he would feel low-spirited, but all the same there is a stage in hunger when everything around the sufferer seems to wear a comic aspect, and the least thing sets him off laughing.

This was the stage now with Jem and Don, for, the danger being past, they lay there at the mouth of the hole, now laughing at the recollection of the sailor's fright, now at the cries of some parrot or the antics of a cockatoo which kept sailing round a large tree, whose hold on the steep rocky side of the ravine was precarious in the extreme.

The presence of white people seemed to cause the bird the greatest of wonder, and to pique his curiosity, and after a flit here and a flit there, he invariably came near and sat upon a bare branch, from which he could study the aspect of the two intruders.

He was a lovely-looking bird as far as the tints of the plumage went; but his short hooked beak, with a tuft of feathers each side, and forward curved crest, gave him a droll aspect which delighted Jem, as the bird came and sat upon a twig, shrieking and chattering at them in a state of the greatest excitement.

"Look at his starshers, Mas' Don," said Jem, as the bird's side tufts half covered the beak and then left it bare. "Look at his hair, too. Hasn't he brushed it up in a point? There, he heared what I said, and has laid it down again. Look at him! look at him! Did you ever see such a rum one in your life?"

For at that minute, after turning its head on one side for a good look, and then on the other, so as to inspect them again, the bird seemed to have an idea that it might gain a little more knowledge from a fresh point of view, and to effect this turned itself completely upside down, hanging by its soft yoke toes, and playing what Jem called a game of *peep-bo!*

This lasted for some minutes, and then the bird squatted upon the bough in a normal position, set up its feathers all over, and began to chatter.

"Hark at him, Mas' Don. He's calling names. There, hit me if he didn't. Did you hear him?"

"I heard him chatter."

"Yes; but I mean calling us that 'My pakeha—my pakeha!' that he did."

"Nonsense!"

"Ah, you may say nonsense, but parrots and cockatoos is werry strange birds. Wonderful what they knows and what they says."

"I don't believe they know what they say, Jem."

"Ah! that's because you're so young, Mas' Don. You'll know better some day. Parrots is as cunning as cunning. Well, now, did you ever see the likes of that? He's laughing and jeering at us."

For at that moment the bird began to bob its head up and down rapidly, gradually growing more excited, and chattering all the while, as it ended by dancing first on one leg and then on the other, in the most eccentric fashion.

"I should like to have that bird, Jem," said Don at last.

"Should you? Then you wouldn't have me along with you. I don't like him. I like a bird as can behave itself and whistle and sing and perch; but I don't like one as goes through all them monkey tricks. Wish I'd got a stone, I'd try and knock him off his perch."

Chur-r-r-r! shrieked the bird, and it let itself fall over backwards, dropping down head over heels like a tumbler pigeon, or an unfortunate which had been shot, and disappearing among the leaves far below.

"There!" cried Jem, triumphantly; "now, what do you say to that? Heard what I said, he did, and thought I was going to throw."

"Nonsense, Jem!"

"Ah! you may call it nonsense, Mas' Don, because you don't know better, but you didn't see him fall."

"Yes, I saw him fall, and—hist! Creep back; there's some one coming!"

The secret of the bird's sudden disappearance was explained for there was a rustling among the ferns far behind, as if some large body was forcing its way along the ravine; and as Jem backed slowly into the cavern, Don cautiously peered from behind a mass of stone into the hollow, to see that some one or something was approaching rapidly, as if with the intention of scaling the rock, and climbing to where they lay.

CHAPTER XXXIV.

AMONG FRIENDS AGAIN.

"IT'S all over with us, Mas' Don," whispered Jem, as soon as they were some little distance in the retreat. "That blackguard Ramsden's sure, after all, that we're in here, and that Tom Hoppers has come to his senses, and felt it was me as hissed at him, and they're coming to hunt us out."

"Let's hope not, Jem."

"Yah! What's the good o' hoping."

Churr-r-r! shrieked the cockatoo from far below.

"There now," said Jem. "Hark at that! He's telling 'em we're in here, and coming on before to show 'em the way."

"What nonsense, Jem!"

Churr-r! shrieked the cockatoo, ever so much nearer.

"Well, do you call that nonsense?" whispered Jem.

"The bird's being cheered on; some one coming."

Churr—churr—churr-r-r! shrieked the cockatoo nearer, nearer, and then right in front of the cave, as it flew by.

"All right, Mas' Don; I arn't going to hargue. You think your way, and I'll think mine; but if that wasn't saying in New Zealandee as those two misfortunate chaps is hiding in this here hole, I never lived in Bristol city, and I don't know sugar from tobacker."

"Hist!" whispered Don.

Hiss-s-s-s came from far in the depths of the cave.

Gurgle-urgle-gugg-pap! went something of a liquid kind.

"Here, I can't stand this here, Mas' Don," whispered Jem; "let's make a rush of it; and get right away in the woods."

"Hush! There's some one coming," whispered Don, drawing his companion farther back into the darkness.

"All right, Mas' Don! Take me in again where the bad air is; poison us both. Good-bye, Sally, my gal. It's all over now; but I forgives you. Shake hands, Mas' Don. I don't bear you no ill-will, nor nobody else. Here they come."

There was a rustling and panting noise, and they were on the tip-toe of expectation, when there was a heavy concussion, a deep-toned roar, and then an echoing rumble as the sound reverberated among the mountains. Then utter silence.

Jem gripped Don's arm with force, and stared at him wildly.

"Well!" whispered Don. "It was only a gun from the ship to recall the boats."

Jem stooped down and gave his leg a slap.

"You are a clever one, Mas' Don, and no mistake. Why, o' course it is. I never thought it was that."

"What did you think it was, then?"

"Some o' them hot water-works gone off, *bang!* and blown up the mountain.—There!'

He pointed to a hideous-looking head appearing above the edge of the shelf, and seen by the evening light as it fell athwart it, the countenance with its blue lines and scrolls ending in curls on either side of the nose was startling enough to make any one fear danger.

The owner of the face climbed up to the shelf, followed by another bronzed figure, when Don recognised the second as the tattooed Englishman, while there was no mistake about the first, for he made Jem give an angry grunt as a human voice shouted,—

"My pakeha."

"Somebody calling you, Mas' Don?"

"My pakeha!" shouted the New Zealander again. "Jem-meree Wimbee."

"Eh! Here, I say, call a fellow by his right name!' cried Jem, stepping forward.

The chief met him with advancing step, and caught him by the shoulders, and before Jem could realise what he was going to do, placed his blue nose against that which was coppery white, and gave it a peculiar rub.

"Here, I say, don't!" cried Jem, struggling to free himself, when the chief seized Don in turn, and bent down and served him the same.

"Don't you stand it, Mas' Don. Hit out.'

"Don't you, youngster," said the Englishman. "It's only his friendly way."

"Yes, that's what they say at home when a big dog goes at you, and nearly rolls you over," grumbled Jem. "I say, have you got anything to eat?"

"Not here, but plenty at Ngati's place. I'm glad to see you both safe, my lads. It gave me quite a turn when he told me he'd hidden you in here."

"Why?" said Don sharply.

"Well, I'll tell you, my lad. There's a kind o' bad steam lies along the bottom farther in, and if a man was to lie down on the floor and go to sleep, I don't s'pose he'd ever wake again. Come along!"

"Where are the men from the ship?"

"Gone off with their mates. Didn't you hear the gun?"

Don nodded.

"They've been searching all over for you. Can't make out whether you two got to shore, or were chopped up by the sharks out yonder. They won't come again till to-morrow, and you'll be safe till then. You must be hungry."

"Hungry?" said Jem, with a mocking laugh. "Hungry? Lookye here: you'd better take me where there's something, or it won't be safe. I heard tell as people ate one another out here, and I didn't believe it, but I do now. I'm ready for anything or anybody; so come along."

Ngati took possession of Don, and led the way, evidently very proud of his young companion; whilst Jem followed with the Englishman down the gully slope, and then in and out among the trees, ferns, and bushes, till the dangerous hot and mud springs were passed, and the *whare* was reached. Then the weary fugitives were seated before what seemed to them a banquet of well-cooked fish, fruits, and roots, with a kind of hasty pudding preparation, which was far from bad.

"Feel better, now?" said the Englishman, after he had sat and smoked till they had done.

"Better? Yes, I'm better," said Jem; "but I should like to know one thing."

"Well, what is it?"

"Will they go on feeding us like this?"

"Yes; and if they don't, I will."

"But—it don't—it don't mean any games, does it?" said Jem, in a doubting tone.

"You mean making game of you?" said the Englishman with a broad grin.

"Yes, hare or fezzun," said Jem.

The Englishman laughed, and turned to Don.

"I'll see if you can't have a better hiding-place to-night. That was very dangerous, and I may as well tell you to mind where you go about here, for more than one poor fellow has been smothered in the hot mud holes, and scalded to death."

"Is the water so hot as that?" said Don.

"Hot? Why, those vegetables and things you ate were cooked in one of the boiling springs."

"Phew!" whistled Jem.

They sat talking in the moonlight afterwards, listening to the tattooed Englishman, who spoke about what he had heard from the ship's crew. Among other things the news that they might sail at any time.

Don started, and the tattooed Englishman noticed it.

"Yes," he said; "that means going away and leaving you two behind. You don t seemed pleased."

Don looked up at him earnestly.

"No," he said; "I didn't at first. Don't think me ungrateful after what you've done."

"I don't, my lad," said the man, kindly; "I know what you feel. It's like being shut away from every one you know; and you feel as if you were going to be a savage, and never see England again. I felt something like that once; but I didn't come out like you did. Ah, well, that's neither here nor there. You're only a boy yet, with plenty o' time before you. Make yourself as happy as you can; these chaps are not so very bad when they don't want to get fighting, and I daresay you and me will be good enough friends. Eh? Hullo! what's the matter?"

He leaped to his feet, and Don, Jem, and the New Zealand savages about them did the same, for half-a-dozen of Ngati's followers came running up with news, which they communicated with plenty of gesticulations.

"What are they a-saying on, Mas' Don? I wish I could speak New Zealandee."

"Two boats' crews are coming ashore from the ship. I wish you two was brown and tattooed."

Jem glanced wildly at Don.

"Come on," said the Englishman. "I must see if I can't hide you before they come. What?"

This last was to a fresh man, who ran up and said something.

"Quick, my lads," said the Englishman. "Your people are close at hand."

CHAPTER XXXV.

LEFT BEHIND.

TOMATI hurried out, followed by Don, but the latter was thrust back into the hut directly, Tomati stretching out his arms so as to spread his blanket wide to act as a screen, under cover of which Don and Jem were half pushed, half backed into the large gathering hut of the tribe, Ngati giving some orders quickly, the result of which was that Don and Jem were hustled down into a sitting position and then thrown upon their faces.

"Here, I'm not going to——"

"Hush, Jem. You'll be heard," whispered Don.

"Yes, but—lookye here."

There was no time to say more. The first lieutenant of the ship, with a middy, Bosun Jones, and about twenty men came marching up, to find a group of Ngati's men seated in a close circle, their blankets spread about them and their heads bent forward, grunting together, and not so much as looking round.

The men were halted, and the lieutenant addressed the tattooed Englishman.

"Well!" he said; "where are our two men?"

"Ask the sharks," said the renegade, shortly.

"Humph! yes. I suppose we shall have to. Poor wretches! The captain thought we'd have a last look round. But mind this, if they turn up here, you and your men will detain them till we come back. I shall hold you responsible."

The Englishman grunted after the fashion of one of the savages.

"I suppose you don't want to come home, eh?"

"No; I'm comfortable enough here as an emigrant."

"An emigrant, eh? Look here, Master Tomati, if I did my duty, I suppose I should take you aboard, and hand you over to the authorities."

"What for?" said the Englishman, surlily.

"THE FIRST LIEUTENANT, BOSUN JONES, AND ABOUT TWENTY MEN CAME MARCHING UP."

"Escaping from Norfolk Island. That's right, isn't it?"

"Look here!" said the Englishman; "do you know, sir, that this is one of the worst parts of the coast, and that the people here think nothing of attacking boats' crews and plundering them, and making them prisoners, and often enough killing and eating 'em?"

"Threatening, eh?" said the lieutenant.

"Not I. But I'm a chief, and the people here would do everything I told them, and fight for me to a man."

"Then you are threatening."

"No, sir; I only wanted to remind you that your boats' crews have come and gone in peace; that you have been allowed to go about ashore, and been supplied with fruit and vegetables, and never a thing missed"

"That's true enough," said the lieutenant. "Well, what of that? A king's ship well armed would keep a larger tribe than yours quiet!"

"Oh! oh!" came from the group of natives.

"Yes, I repeat it," said the lieutenant sharply. "They can understand English, then?"

"Of course they do," said the tattooed man calmly, though he looked uneasily at the group; "and as to your ship, sir, what's the good of that if we were to fight you ashore?"

"Do you want to fight, then?" said the lieutenant sharply.

"It doesn't seem like it, when I've kept my tribe peaceful toward all your crew, and made them trade honestly."

"Out of respect to our guns."

"Can you bring your guns along the valleys and up into the mountains?"

"No; but we can bring plenty of well-drilled fighting men."

"Oh! oh!" came in quite a long-drawn groan.

"Yes," said the lieutenant looking toward the group, "well-drilled, well-armed fighting men, who would drive your people like leaves before the wind. But I don't want to quarrel. I am right, though; you are an escaped convict from Norfolk Island?"

"Yes, I am," said the man boldly; "but I've given up civilisation, and I'm a Maori now, and the English Government had better leave me alone."

"Well, I've no orders to take you."

"Oh! oh!" came again from the group: and Tomati turned sharply round, and said a few words indignantly in the Maori tongue, whose result was a huddling closer together of the men in the group and utter silence.

"They'll be quiet now," said Tomati. "They understand an English word now and then."

"Well, I've no more to say, only this—If those two men do come ashore, or you find that they have come ashore, you've got to seize them and make them prisoners. Make slaves of them if you like till we come again, and then you can give them up and receive a good reward."

"I shall never get any reward," said Tomati, grimly.

"Poor lads! No," said the boatswain; "I'm afraid not."

Just then there was a sharp movement among the Maoris, who set up a loud grunting noise, which drew the attention of the lieutenant, and made the men laugh.

"It's only their way," said the Englishman gruffly.

"Ah, a queer lot. Better come back to civilisation, my man," said the lieutenant.

"At Norfolk Island, sir?"

"Humph!" muttered the lieutenant; and facing his men round, he marched them back to the boats, after which they spent about four hours making soundings, and then returned to the ship.

Almost before the sailors were out of hearing, there was a scuffle and agitation in the group, and Jem struggled from among the Maoris, his face hot and nearly purple, Don's not being very much better.

"I won't stand it. Nearly smothered. I won't have it," cried Jem furiously.

"Don't be so foolish, Jem. It was to save us," said Don, trying to pacify him.

"Save us! Well they might ha' saved us gently. Look at me. I'm nearly flat."

"Nonsense! I found it unpleasant; but they hid us, and we're all right."

"But I arn't all right, Mas' Don; I feel like a pancake," cried Jem, rubbing and patting himself as if he were so much paste or clay which he wanted to get back into shape.

"Don't be so stupid, Jem!"

"Stoopid? 'Nough to make any man feel stoopid. I was 'most stuffocated."

"So was I."

"Yes, but you hadn't got that big, 'my pakeha chap sitting on you all the time."

"No, Jem, I hadn't," said Don, laughing.

"Well, I had, and he weighs 'bout as much as a sugar-hogshead at home, and that arn't light."

"But it was to hide us, Jem."

"Hide us, indeed! Bother me if it didn't seem as if they was all hens wanting to sit on one egg, and that egg was me. I know I shall never get right again."

"Oh yes, you will," laughed Don.

"Ah, it's all werry well for you to laugh, Mas' Don; but if my ribs hadn't been made o' the best o' bone, they'd ha' cracked like carrots, and where should I ha' been then?"

"Hurt, mate?" said Tomati, coming up and laughing at Jem, who was rubbing himself angrily.

"Just you go and be sat upon all that time, and see if you won't feel hurt," grumbled Jem. "Why, it hurts your feelings as much as it does your body."

"Ah, well, never mind. You're quite safe now."

Tomati walked away to speak to one of his men.

"Quite safe now, he says, Mas' Don. Well, I don't feel it. Hear what he said to the fust lufftenant; this was the worst part of the coast, and the people were ready to rob and murder and eat you?"

"I didn't hear all that, Jem," said Don quietly. "I heard him say that they were a warlike, fighting people; but that doesn't matter if they are kind to us."

"But that's what I'm feared on," said Jem, giving himself a jerk.

"Afraid of them being kind?"

"Ay, feared of them liking us too well. Pot."

"Pot?"

"Yes, Pot. Don't you understand?"

"No."

"Pot. P—O—T, Pot."

"Well, of course, I know that; but what does it mean?"

"Why, they've sat upon you, Mas' Don, till your head won't work; that's what's the matter with you, my lad. I mean treat us as if we was chyce fat sheep."

"Nonsense, Jem!"

"Oh, is it? Well, you'll see."

"I hope not," said Don, laughing.

"Ah, you may laugh, my lad, but you won't grin that day when it comes to the worst."

News was brought in soon after of the boats being busy taking soundings, and that night Don and Jem sat screened by the ferns high up on the mountain side, and saw the sloop of war with her sails set, and looking golden in the setting sun, gliding slowly away toward the north-east, careening slightly over before a brisk breeze, which grew stronger as they reached out farther beyond the shelter of the land; and in spite of hints from Tomati, and calls from Ngati, neither could be coaxed down till, just as it was growing dusk, Don rose and turned to his companion.

"Have we done right, Jem?"

"What, in getting away from being slaves aboard ship? Why, o' course."

Don shook his head.

"I don't know," he said, sadly. "We are here right away on the other side of the world amongst savages, and I see no chance of getting away back home."

"Oh, but we arn't tried yet, my lad."

"No, we haven't tried, Jem."

"My pakeha! my pakeha!" came from below.

"There he goes again!" growled Jem. "Do tell Tomati to ask him to call you something else. I know I shall get in a row if you don't."

"You must not get into any quarrel, Jem," said Don, thoughtfully; "for we ought to keep the best of friends with these people. Ahoy!"

An answering cry came back, and they began to descend with the darkness coming on and a strange depression of spirit troubling Don, as he felt more and more as if for the first time in their lives he and Jem Wimble were thoroughly alone in the world.

CHAPTER XXXVI.

SOMETHING TO DO.

"'TARN'T so bad, Mas' Don," said Jem, about a month later. "Never felt so clean before in my life. Them hot baths is lovely, and if we could get some tea and coffee, and a bit o' new bread and fresh butter now and then, and I could get my Sally out here, I don't know as I should much mind stopping."

"And what about the pot, Jem?"

"Tchah! That was all gammon. I don't b'lieve they ever did anything o' the sort. When's Tomati coming back? Tomati, Jemmaree, Donni-Donni. Pretty sort of a language. Why, any one could talk New Zealandee."

"I wish I could, Jem."

"Well, so you could if you tried. All you've got to do is to riddle-me-ree the words a bit. I'm getting on first rate; and what I like in these people is that they never laughs at you when you makes a mistake."

They had been furnished with a snug hut, close to one of the roughly made hot water baths, and were fairly well supplied with food, which they augmented by going out in Ngati's canoe, and catching abundance of fish, to the Maori's great delight; for he gazed with admiration at the skilful methods adopted by Jem, who was no mean angler.

"And the best of the fun is, Mas' Don, that the fishes out here are so stupid. They take any bait a'most, and taken altogether they're not such bad eating. Wonder what shark would be like?"

Don shuddered, and they both decided that they would not care to try.

Ngati of the fiercely savage face and huge size proved to be one of the most amiable of men, and was after them every morning, to go out in the forest collecting fruit, or to dam up some stream to catch the fresh-water fish, or to snare birds.

"He do cap me," Jem would say. "Just look at him, Mas' Don. That there chap's six foot four at least, half as broad again across the chest as I am, and he's got arms like a hele- phant, while to look at him with his blue face you'd say he was 'bout the fiercest-looking fighting man you ever see; and yet, when you come to know him inside, he's just like a big boy, and so good-tempered I could do anything with him."

"And only the other day you looked upon him as quite an enemy."

"Ay, I did, Mas' Don, but I don't now. Them there artful birds is my mortal enemies. They parrots and cockatoos is cunning and wicked enough, but them little birds is imps, that's what they are."

Jem shook his head and frowned, and no more was said then, for they were packing up a basket, and going up into the mountains to get fruit, taking provisions enough to last them for the day.

Their hut was right in the middle of the little village, and the Maoris treated them in the most friendly manner, smiling at them in an indolent fashion as they lolled about the place, doing very little except a little gardening; for their wants were few, and nature was kind in the abundance she gave for a little toil. This life soon had its effects upon Jem, who began to display a disposition to idle too.

"Seems so nat'ral, Mas' Don," he would say. "I don't see why a man should be always letting sugar hogsheads down out of waggons, and rolling 'em about and getting them into ware- houses. Why can't we take it coolly, same as they do?"

"Because we don't want to stand still, Jem," said Don quietly. "You and I are not savages."

"Well, no, Mas' Don, that's true; but it's very pleasant to take it as coolly as they do. Why, these chaps, the whole lot of 'em, live just as if it was always holidays, and a hot water bath thrown in."

"Uncle Josiah used to say that people soon got tired of having holidays."

"Your Uncle Josiah soon got tired o' giving holidays, Mas' Don. I never, as you know, wanted many, but he always looked rat-traps at me if I asked for a day. Here you can have as many as you like."

"Well, let's take one to-day, Jem," said Don. "Fill another basket with something to eat, take a couple of bags, and we'll go right away into the forest, and bring back as much fruit as we can."

"I'll be all ready in no time," said Jem, cheerily; and at the end of three minutes he was equipped, and they started off together, to find Ngati half lying on the sands in company with about a dozen more of his tribe, all of whom gave the pair a friendly smile and a wondering look at the trouble they seemed to take to obtain fruit, when some of the women or girls could have done the task just as well.

"They are about the idlest set of chaps I ever did see, Mas' Don," said Jem, as they trudged cautiously along through the ferny woodlands, where traces of volcanic action were wonderfully plentiful.

"But they work when there's any need for it, I daresay," said Don. "See how vigorously they can row, and how energetic they are when they go through the war-dance."

"Oh! any stoopid could jump about and make faces." replied Jem. "I wonder whether they really could fight if there was a row?"

"They look as if they could, Jem."

"Looks arn't much good in fighting, Mas' Don. Well, anyhow, they're big and strong enough. Look! What a pity we haven't got a gun. Might have shot a pig and had some pork."

He pointed to about half-a-dozen good-sized pigs, which had scurried across the path they followed, and then disappeared among the ferns.

"Rum thing, it always seems to me that there's nothing here except pigs. There must be, farther in the woods. Mind that hole, my lad."

Don carefully avoided stepping into a bubbling patch of hot mud right in their path, and, wondering what would be the consequences of a step in, he went on, in and out, among dangerous water holes and mud springs. Cockatoos whistled overhead, and parrots shrieked, while every now and then they came upon a curious-looking bird, whose covering resembled hair more than feathers, as it cocked its curved bill towards them, and then hurriedly disappeared by diving in amongst the dense low growth.

"Look at that!" said Jem. "Ostrich?"

"Ostrich!" cried Don contemptuously. "Why, an ostrich is eight feet high."

"Not when he's young," said Jem. "That's a little one. Shouldn't wonder if there's some more."

"You may be right, Jem, but I don't think there are ostriches here."

"Well, I like that," said Jem, "when we've just seen one. I knew it directly. There used to be a picture of one in my old reading-book when I was at school."

They trudged on for some distance in silence.

"What yer thinking 'bout, Mas' Don?"

"Home," said Don, quietly.

"Oh! I say, don't think about home, Mas' Don, because if you do, I shall too; it do make me so unked."

"I can't help it, Jem. It doesn't seem natural to settle down here, and go on week after week. I get asking myself, what we are doing it for."

"To catch fish, and find fruit and keep ourselves alive. Say, Mas' Don, it's under them trees they digs up the big lumps of gum that they burn. Ah, there's a bit."

Jem stooped and picked out from among the rotten pine

needles a piece of pale yellowish-looking gum of the size of his fist.

"That'll do for a light for us," Don said. "Take it back."

"Going to," said Jem laconically. "We may want it 'fore long."

"Here's another bit," said Don, finding a similar sized piece, and thrusting it into the basket. "Couldn't we make some matches, Jem?"

"Couldn't we make some matches? Why, of course we could. There's plenty of brimstone, I'm going to try and manage a tinder-box after a time."

They again walked on in silence, climbing higher and higher, till, coming to an opening, they both paused in silent admiration of the view spread out before them, of river, lake, and mountain, whose top glistened like silver, where glacier and snow lay unmelted in spite of the summer heat.

"Wouldn't you like to go up there, Mas' Don?" said Jem, after a few moments' silence.

"Go? I'd give anything to climb up there, Jem. What a view it must be."

"Ah, it must, Mas' Don; but we won't try it to-day; and now, as we've been on the tramp a good two hours, I vote we sit down and have a bit of a peck."

Don agreed, and they sat down at the edge of the wood to partake of the rather scanty fare which they spread on the ground between them.

"Yes, it would be fine," said Jem, with his mouth and hands full. "We ought to go up that mountain some day. I've never been up a mountain. Hi! woa!"

This was shouted at another of the peculiar-looking little birds which ran swiftly out of the undergrowth, gave each in turn a comical look, and then seized a good-sized piece of their provender and ran off.

"Well, I call that sarce," said Jem; "that's what I calls that. Ah, if I'd had a stone I'd soon have made him drop that."

"Now," said Don laughing, "do you call that an ostrich?"

"To be sure I do!" cried Jem. "That proves it. I've read

in a book as ostriches do steal and swallow anything—nails, pocket-knives, and bits o' stone. Well! I never did!"

Jem snatched off his cap and sent it spinning after another rail which had run up and seized a fruit from their basket, and skimmed off with its legs forming a misty appearance like the spokes of a rapidly turning wheel.

"Sarce is nothing to it, Mas' Don. Why, that little beggar's ten times worse than the old mag we used to have in the yard. They're so quick, too. Now, just look at that."

Either the same or another of the little birds came out of the undergrowth, peering about in the most eccentric manner, and without displaying the least alarm.

"Just look at him, Jem."

"Look at him, Mas' Don? I am a-looking at him with all my eyes. He's a beauty, he is. Why, if I was a bird like that with such a shabby, dingy looking, sooty suit o' clothes, I know what I'd do."

"What would you do?"

"Why, I'd moult at once. Look at the rum little beggar. Arn't he comic? Why, he arn't got no wings and no tail. Hi! cocky, how did you get your beak bent that way? Look as if you'd had it caught in a gate. Have another?"

Jem took up a large raspberry-like fruit that he had picked some time before, and held it out to the bird, which stopped short, and held its head down comically, looking first at Jem, and then at the berry. With a rapid twist it turned its head on the other side, and performed the same operation with the left eye.

"Well, he is a rum un!" cried Jem, laughing. "Look! Mas' Don, look!"

Don was watching the eccentric-looking little creature, which ran forward rapidly, and then paused.

"Why, 'tarn't a wild bird at all!" cried Jem. 'It's one of the 'my pakeha' chap's cocks an' hens. Well, I ham blessed!"

For rapid almost as thought, and before Jem could recover from his surprise, the bird had darted forward, seized the fruit, and was off a dozen yards before he had darted out his hand after it.

"Too late, Jem."

"Yes, Mas' Don, too late that time; but I mean to ketch that chap, just to show him he arn't so clever as he thinks. You sit still, and go on eating, and don't take no notice, and look out—look out."

"Oh!" ejaculated Don. For at that moment one of the birds had come up behind him, and almost before he had heard Jem's warning cry, he was made aware of the bird's presence by a sharp dig of its beak in the hand holding a portion of his dinner, which was carried rapidly away.

"Magpies is nothing to 'em," cried Jem. "But wait a bit, my fine fellows, and you shall see what you shall see. Pass that there basket, Mas' Don. Ah! that's a good bait for my gentleman. Look at 'em. I can see three peeping out of the bushes. They're a-watching to see what I'm going to do."

"Three! I can see four, Jem."

"More for me to ketch, Mas' Don. Wonder whether they're good to eat? I say, do you think they can understand English?"

Don laughed, and went on with his dinner, as Jem began to play fox, by putting a tempting-looking berry in his hand, stretching it out to the full extent of his arm, and then lying back among the ferns.

"Now then, don't take no notice, Mas' Don. Let you an' me keep on feeding, and that'll 'tract 'em out."

Don was already quietly "feeding," and he rested his back against a piece of stone, watching intently all the while.

Two of the birds began to approach directly, while the others looked on as if deeply interested.

The approach of the advance force was particularly curious, for they came on picking here and picking there, as if they had not the slightest intention of going near the fruit in Jem's hand; but in spite of several feints of going right away, always getting nearer, while Jem munched away, using his left hand, and keeping his eyes half shut.

They had not long to wait, for one of the birds manœuvred until it was a few feet away, then made a rush, caught the berry from Jem's hand, which closed with a snap, the second bird made a dart and caught the berry from the first bird's beak, and Jem sat up holding a few feathers, staring after the birds, one of which cried out in a shrill piping tone.

"Yes, I'll give you pepper next time, my fine fellow!" cried Jem. "Nearly had you. My word, Mas' Don, they are quick. Give's another berry."

Jem baited his natural trap again, and went on with his meal; but he had scared away the birds for the time being, and they came no more.

"The worst of eating, Jem, is that it makes you lazy."

"And not want to move, Mas' Don. Yes, it do. But it's my 'pinion as this was meant for a lazy country, else the water wouldn't be always on the bile, ready for use."

"Think that's fire?" said Don, after a dreamy pause, during which he had lain back gazing at the brilliant silver-tipped mountain, above which floated a cloud.

"No," said Jem. "I should say as there's a big hot water place up yonder, and that there's steam. Yes, one do feel lazy here; but it don't matter, Mas' Don; there's no bosun, and no master and lufftenant and captain to order you about. I rather likes it, only I seem to want my Sally here. Wonder what she'd say to it?"

"We must get away from it, Jem."

"But we arn't got no boat, and it takes pretty nigh a hunderd men to row one of them canoes."

"We must make a long journey through the country, Jem, right beyond those mountains, and sooner or later we shall come to a place where there are Englishmen, who will help us to get a passage in a ship."

Jem shook his head.

"I don't believe there's any Englishmen here, Mas' Don."

"I do. I think I've read that there are; and if we do not find any, we shall have seen the place, and can come back here."

"He talks just like as if he was going for a ride to Exeter by the Bristol waggon! Ah, well, just as you like, Mas' Don, only don't let's go this afternoon, it's all too nice and comfortable. I don't want to move. Say, wonder whether there's any fish in that lake?"

"Sure to be, Jem, and hundreds of wonders to see if we journey on."

"Dessay, my lad, dessay; but it's werry wonderful here. Look along that hollow place where the big fir trees is growing."

"Lovely, Jem. What a beautiful home it would make."

"Say, Mas' Don, let's make our fortunes."

"How?"

"Let's set up in trade, and deal in wood. Lookye yonder, there's fir trees there, that if we cut 'em down and trimmed 'em, they'd be worth no end o' money in Bristol, for ships' masts."

"Yes, Jem," said Don drily; "and how are you going to get them there?"

"Ah!" said Jem, scratching his head. "Never thought of that."

There was half an hour's drowsy silence. The sun shone down with glorious power, and the lizards rustled among the large stones. From the forest behind there came the buzz of insects, and the occasional cry of some parrot. Save for these sounds all was wonderfully still.

And they sat there gazing before them at the hundreds of acres of uncultivated land, rich in its wild beauty, unwilling to move, till Don said suddenly,—

"Yes, Jem; this is a lazy land. Let's be up and doing."

"Yes, Mas' Don. What?"

"I don't know, Jem; something useful."

"But there arn't nothing useful to do. I couldn't make a boat, but I think I could make a hogshead after a fashion; but if I did, there arn't no sugar to put in it, and——"

"Look, Jem!"

"What at, Mas' Don? Eh?" he continued as he followed

his companion's pointing hand. "Why, I thought you said there was no beasts here."

"And there are none."

"Well, if that arn't a drove o' cattle coming down that mountain side, I'm a Dutchman."

"It does look like it, Jem," said Don. "It seems strange."

"Look like it, Mas' Don? Why, it is. Brown cattle, and you can see if you look at the sun shining on their horns."

"Horns! Jem!" cried Don, excitedly; "they're spears!"

"What?"

"And those are savages."

"So they are!" cried Jem. "Why, Mas' Don, that there don't mean a fight, do it?"

"I don't know, Jem. But they can't see us, can they?"

"No. These here bushes shades us. Let's creep back through the wood, and go and tell 'em down below. They don't know, p'r'aps, and we may get there first."

"We must," said Don quickly. "Jem, I'm sure of it. You can see the spears quite plainly, and perhaps it's a war-party out from some other tribe. Quick, lad, quick! We can get there first."

"And if it's a false alarm, they'll laugh at us, Mas' Don."

"Let them. They won't laugh if there's danger in the way."

Don caught up the basket and backed into the shelter of the trees, keeping in a stooping position, while Jem followed, and now, with all the sensation of indolence gone, they hurried along the rugged and dangerous path, to spread the alarm in the village far below, where they had left the inmates dreaming away their existence in happy ignorance of the danger so close at hand.

CHAPTER XXXVII.

A PERILOUS DESCENT.

THE heat was terrible, and it seemed to Don as if the difficulties met with in their outward journey had been intensified on their return. Thorns caught in their garments, and, failing these, in their flesh. Twice over Jem stepped a little too much off the faint track, and had narrow escapes of plunging into pools of hot mud, whose presence was marked by films of strange green vegetation.

Then they mistook their way, and after struggling along some distance they came out suddenly on a portion of the mountain side, where to continue their course meant that they must clamber up, descend a sheer precipice of at least a hundred feet by hanging on to the vine-like growths and ferns, or return.

They stopped and stared at each other in dismay.

"Know where we went wrong, Mas' Don?" said Jem.

"No; do you?"

"Not I, my lad. Think it must ha' been where I had that last slip into the black hasty pudding."

"What shall we do, Jem? If we go back we shall lose an hour."

"Yes! quite that; and 'tarn't no good to climb up here. I could do it; but it's waste o' time."

"Could we get down here?"

"Oh, yes," said Jem drily; "we could get down easy enough; only the thing is, how should we be when we did get down?"

"You mean we should fall to the bottom?"

"Well, you see, Mas' Don," said Jem, rubbing one ear as he peered down; "it wouldn't be a clean fall, 'cause we should scrittle and scruttle from bush to bush, and ketch here and snatch there. We should go right down to the bottom, sure enough, but we might be broke by the time we got there."

"Jem, Jem, don't talk like that!" cried Don angrily. "Do you think it possible to go down?"

"Well, Mas' Don, I think the best way down would be with our old crane and the windlass tackle."

"Do you dare climb down?"

"Ye—es, I think so, Mas' Don; only arn't there no other way?"

"Not if we want to save them down at the village."

"Well, but do we want to save 'em Mas' Don? They're all werry well, but——"

"And have been very kind to us, Jem. We must warn them of danger."

"But, lookye here, Mas' Don, s'pose it arn't danger. Pretty pair o' Bristol noodles we shall look, lying down at the bottom here, with all our legs and arms broke for nothing at all."

Don stood gazing at his companion, full of perplexity.

"Think it is real danger, Mas' Don?"

"I'm afraid so. You heard Tomati say that there were desperate fights sometimes."

"Don't call him Tomati; I 'ates it," growled Jem. "Well, I s'pose it is danger, then."

"And we must look the matter in the face, Jem. If we go back those people will be at the village before us. Perhaps we shall meet them, and be made prisoners; but if we go on here, we shall save an hour, perhaps two. Yes, I shall climb down."

"No, no; let me go first, Mas' Don."

"Why?"

"Because I shall do to tumble on if you do let go, or any bush breaks."

"Here seems to be about the best place, Jem," said Don, without heeding his companion's last remark; and, setting his teeth, he lowered himself down, holding on by the bushes and

"'I'M GETTING ON SPLEN——'" (*p*. 284).

aërial roots of the various tough, stunted pieces of vegetation, which clung to the decomposing volcanic rock.

Jem's face puckered up as he set his teeth, and watched Don descend a few feet. Then, stooping over, he said cheerily,—

"That's the way, Mas' Don; take it cool, stick tight, and never think about the bottom. Are you getting on all right?"

"Yes."

"That's your sort. I'm coming now."

Jem began to whistle as he lowered himself over the edge of the precipice, a few feet to Don's right; and directly after he began to sing merrily,—

> "'There was a man in Bristol city,
> Fol de rol de riddle-lol-de-ri.
> And that's the first o' this here ditty,
> Fol de rol de-riddle-lol-de-ri.'

Say, Mas' Don, 'tarn't so bad, after all."

"It's terrible, Jem!" panted Don, "Can we do it?"

"Can we do it? Ha, ha, ha!" cried Jem. "Can we do it? Hark at him! We're just the boys as can do it. Why, it arn't half so bad as being up on the main-top gallant yard.

> 'Fol de rol de-riddle-lol-de-ri.'"

"Don't make that noise, Jem, pray."

"Why not, my lad? That's your sort; try all the roots before you trust 'em. I'm getting on splen——"

Rush!

"Jem!"

"All right, Mas' Don! Only slipped ten foot of an easy bit to save tumbles."

"It isn't true. I was looking at you, and I saw that root you were holding come out of the rock."

"Did you, Mas' Don? Oh, I thought I did that o' purpose," came from below.

"Where are you?"

"Sitting straddling on a big bit o' bush."

"Where? I can't see you."

"Here, all right. 'Tarn't ten foot, it's about five and twenty—

> De-riddle-lol-de-ri.'"

"Jem, we must climb back. It is too risky."

"No, we mustn't, Mas' Don; and it arn't a bit too risky. Come along, and I'll wait for you."

Don hesitated for a minute, and then continued his descent, which seemed to grow more perilous each moment.

"Say, Mas' Don," cried Jem cheerily, "what a chance for them birds. Couldn't they dig their bills into us now!"

"Don't talk so, Jem. I can't answer you."

"Must talk, my lad. Them fern things is as rotten as mud. Don't you hold on by them. Steady! steady!"

"Yes. Slipped a little."

"Well, then, don't slip a little. What's your hands for?

> 'There was a man in Bristol city,
> Fol de rol de——'

Say, Mas' Don, think there's any monkeys here?"

"No, no."

"'Cause how one o' they would scramble down this precipit. Rather pricky, arn't it?"

"Yes; don't talk so."

"All right!

> 'De-riddle-liddle-lol.

I'm getting on first rate now, Mas' Don—I say."

"Yes!"

"No press-gang waiting for us down at the bottom here, Mas' Don?"

"Can you manage it, Jem?"

"Can I manage it? Why, in course I can. How are you getting on?"

Don did not reply, but drew a long breath, as he slowly descended the perilous natural ladder, which seemed interminable.

They were now going down pretty close together, and nearly on a level, presence and example giving to each nerve and endurance to perform the task.

"Steady, dear lad, steady!" cried Jem suddenly, as there was a sharp crack and a slip.

"Piece I was resting on gave way," said Don hoarsely, as he hung at the full length of his arms, vainly trying to get a resting-place for his feet.

Jem grasped the position in an instant, but remained perfectly cool.

"Don't kick, Mas' Don."

"But I can't hang here long, Jem."

"Nobody wants you to, my lad. Wait a minute, and I'll be under you, and set you right.

'There was a man in Bristol city,'"

he sang cheerily, as he struggled sidewise. "'Fol de——' I say, Mas' Don, he was a clever one, but I believe this here would ha' bothered him. It's hold on by your eyelids one minute, and wish you was a fly next."

"Jem."

"Hullo, lad?"

"If I let go and dropped, how far should I fall?"

"'Bout two foot ten," said Jem, after a glance below them at the sheer precipice.

"Then I had better drop."

"If you do you will knock me to the bottom, so just you hold on till I tells you."

Jem kept up his jocular way of speaking; but if any one could have looked on, he would have seen that his face was curiously mottled with sallow, while his hands were trembling when at liberty, and that there was a curiously wild, set look in his eyes.

"There, Mas' Don," he said cheerily, as he finished climbing sidewise till he was exactly beneath. "Now, one moment. That's it."

As he spoke he drew himself up a little, taking fast hold of the stem of a bush, and of a projecting stone, while he found foot-hold in a wide crevice.

"Now then, rest your foot on my shoulders. There you are. That's the way. Two heads is better than one."

"Can you bear my weight, Jem?"

"Can I bear your weight? Why, you may stand there for a week. Now just you rest your wristies a bit, and then go on climbing down, just as if I warn't here."

The minute before Don had felt that he could bear the strain no longer. Now the despairing sensation which came over him had gone, his heart felt lighter as he stood on Jem's shoulders, and sought another hold for his hands lower down. The wild, fluttering pulsation ceased, and he grew composed.

"I'm rested now, Jem," said Don.

"Of course you are, my lad. Well, then, now you can climb down aside me. 'Tarn't so much farther to the bottom."

"Can you reach out far enough for me to come between you and the rock?"

"Just you try, Mas' Don."

By this time Don had found a fresh hold for his feet; and nerving himself, he descended slowly, Jem forcing himself out, so that there was enough room for any one to pass; but as Don cleared him, and got right below, the bush to which Jem clung with one hand came slowly out of the interstices of the stones, and but for the exercise of a large amount of muscular power and rigidity of will, he would have swung round and fallen headlong.

"I'm all right now, Jem!" cried Don from below.

"Glad of it, my lad," muttered Jem, "because I arn't."

"Come along down now."

"How, Mas' Don?" said Jem grimly.

"The same way as I did."

"Oh! All right; but the bush I held on by is gone."

"Well take hold of another."

"Just you get from under me, Mas' Don."

"Why? What do you mean?"

"I'm too heavy to ketch like a cricket ball. That s all, my lad."

"Oh, Jem, don't say you are in danger."

"Not I, my lad, if you don't want me to; but it is awk'ard. Stand clear," he shouted. "I'm coming down. No, I arn't," he said directly after, as he made a tremendous effort to reach a tough stem below, failed, and then dropped and caught it, and swung first by one hand and then by two.

"I say, Mas' Don, I thought I was gone."

"You made my heart seem to jump into my mouth."

"Did I, lad? Well, it was awk'ard. I was scared lest I should knock you off. Felt just as I did when the chain broke, and you could see the link opening, and a big sugar hogshead threatening to come down. All right now, my lad. Let's get on down. Think we're birds' nesting, Mas' Don, and it'll be all right."

Don had to nerve himself once more, and they steadily lowered themselves from tuft to tuft, and from stone to stone, with more confidence, till they were about thirty feet from the foot, when farther progress became impossible, for, in place of being perpendicular, the cliff face sloped inward for some distance before becoming perpendicular once more.

"Well, I do call that stoopid," said Jem, as he stared helplessly at Don. "What are we going to do now?"

"I don't know, Jem. If we had a bit of rope we could easily descend."

"And if we'd got wings, Mas' Don, we might fly."

"We must climb back, Jem, as—— Look here, would these trees bear us?"

"Not likely," said Jem, staring hard at a couple of young kauri pines, which grew up at the foot of the precipice, and whose fine pointed tops were within a few feet of where they clung.

"But if we could reach them and get fast hold, they would bend and let us down."

"They'd let us down," said Jem drily; "but I don't know 'bout bending."

Don clung to the face of the rock, hesitating, and wondering whether by any possibility they could get down another way, and finding that it was absolutely hopeless, he made up his mind to act.

"It is next to impossible to climb up, Jem," he said.

"Yes, Mas' Don."

"And we can't get down."

"No, Mas' Don. We shall have to live here for a bit, only I don't know how we're going to eat and sleep."

"Jem."

"Yes, Mas' Don."

"I'm going to jump into that tree."

"No, Mas' Don, you mustn't risk it."

"And if it breaks——"

"Never mind about the tree breaking. What I don't like is, s'pose you break."

"I shall go first, and you can try afterwards."

"No, no, Mas' Don; let me try first."

Don paid no heed to his words, but turned himself completely round, so that he held on, with his back to the stony wall, and his heels upon a couple of rough projections, in so perilous a position that Jem looked on aghast, afraid now to speak. In front of Don, about nine feet away, and the top level with his feet, was the tree of which he had spoken.

As far as support was concerned, it was about as reasonable to trust to a tall fishing-rod; but it appeared to be the only chance, and Don hesitated no longer than was necessary to calculate his chances.

"Don't do it, Mas' Don. It's impossible, and like chucking yourself away. Let's climb up again; it's the only chance;

and if we can't get to the village in time, why, it arn't our fault. No, my lad, don't!"

As the last words left his lips, Don stood perfectly upright, balancing himself for a few moments, and then, almost as if he were going to dive into the water, he extended his hands and sprang outward into space.

Jem Wimble uttered a low groan.

CHAPTER XXXVIII.

DON'S REPORT.

IN the case of a leap like that made by Don, there was no suspense for the looker on, for the whole affair seemed to be momentary. Jem saw him pass through the air and disappear in the mass of greenery with a loud rushing sound, which continued for a few moments, and then all was still.

"He's killed; he's killed!" groaned Jem to himself; "and my Sally will say it was all my fault."

He listened eagerly.

"Mas' Don!" he shouted.

"Hullo, Jem! I say, would you drop if you were me?"

"Drop? Then you arn't killed?"

"No, not yet. Would you drop?"

"I don't know what you mean."

"I'm hanging on to the end of that young tree, and it keeps going up and down like a spring, and it won't go any nearer than about twelve feet from the ground. Would you drop?"

Whish! Rush! Crash! Thud!

The young tree sprang up again, cleaving a way for itself through the thick growth, and standing nearly erect once more, ragged and sadly deprived of its elegant proportions, just as a dull sound announced Don's arrival on *terra firma*.

"All right, Jem!" he cried. "Not hurt. Look here; spread your arms out well and catch tight round the tree as you jump at it. You'll slip down some distance and scratch yourself, but you can't hurt much."

"I hear, Mas' Don," said Jem, drawing a long breath full of

relief. "I'm a-coming. It's like taking physic," he added to himself; "but the sooner you takes it, the sooner it's down. Here goes! Say, Mas' Don, do you ketch hold o' the tree with your hands, or your arms and legs?"

"All of them. Aim straight at the stem, and leap out boldly."

"Oh, yes," grumbled Jem; "it's all very well, but I was never 'prenticed to this sort o' fun.—Below!"

"A good bold jump, Jem. I'm out of the way."

"Below then," said Jem again.

"Yes, jump away. Quick!"

But Jem did not jump. He distrusted the ability of the tree to bear his weight.

"Why don't you jump?"

"'Cause it seems like breaking my neck, which is white, to save those of them people in the village, which is black, Mas' Don."

"But you will not break your neck if you are careful."

"Oh, yes! I'll be careful, Mas' Don; don't you be 'fraid of that."

"Well, come along. You're not nervous, are you, Jem?"

"Yes, Mas' Don, reg'lar scared; but, below, once more. Here goes! Don't tell my Sally I was afraid if I do get broke."

Possibly Jem would have hesitated longer, but the stump of the bush upon which he stood gave such plain intimation of coming out by the roots, that he thought it better to leap than fall, and gathering himself up, he plunged right into the second kauri pine, and went headlong down with a tremendous crash.

For he had been right in his doubts. The pine was not so able to bear his weight as its fellow had been to carry Don. He caught it tightly, and the tree bent right down, carrying him nearly to the earth, where he would have done well to have let go; but he clung to it fast, and the tree sprang up again, bent once more, and broke short off, Jem falling at least twenty feet into the bushes below.

"Hurt, Jem?" cried Don, forcing his way to his side.

"Hurt? Now is it likely, Mas' Don? Hurt? no. I feel just like a babby that's been lifted gently down and laid on a feather cushion. That's 'bout how I feel. Oh, dear! oh, dear! Here, give's a hand. Gently, dear lad; I'm like a skin full o' broken bones. Help me out o' this tangle, and let's see how much of me's good, and how much 'll have to be throwed away. Eggs and bacon! what a state I'm in!"

Don helped him as tenderly as he could out into an open space, and softly assisted him to lie down, which Jem did, groaning, and was perfectly still for a few moments flat there on his back.

"Are you in much pain, Jem?" said Don, anxiously.

"Horrid, lad, horrid. I think you'd better go on and warn 'em, and come and fetch me arterwards; only don't forget where I am, and not find me. Look! there's two o' them birds coming to see what's the matter."

"I can't leave you, Jem. You're of more consequence to me than all the New Zealanders in the place."

"Am I, Mas' Don? Come, that's kindly spoke of you. But bother that tree! Might ha' behaved as well to me as t'other did to you."

"Where do you feel in pain, Jem?"

"Where? It's one big solid slapping pain all over me, but it's worst where there's a big thorn stuck in my arm."

"Let me see."

"No; wait a bit. I don't mean to be left alone out here if I can help it. Now, Mas' Don, you lift that there left leg, and see if it's broke."

Don raised it tenderly, and replaced it gently.

"I don't think it's broken, Jem."

"Arn't it? Well, it feels like it. P'r'aps it's t'other one. Try."

Don raised and replaced Jem's right leg.

"That isn't broken either, Jem."

"P'r'aps they're only crushed. Try my arms, my lad."

These were tried in turn, and laid down.

"No, Jem."

"Seems stoopid," said Jem. "I thought I was broke all over. It must be my back, and when a man's back's broke, he feels it all over. Here, lend us a hand, my lad; and I'll try and walk. Soon see whether a man's back's broke."

Don offered his arm, and Jem, after a good deal of grunting and groaning, rose to his feet, gave himself a wrench, and then stamped with first one leg and then with the other.

"Why, I seems all right, Mas' Don," he said, eagerly.

"Yes, Jem."

"Think it's my ribs? I've heared say that a man don't always know when his ribs is broke."

"Do you feel as if they were, Jem?"

"Oh, yes; just exactly. All down one side, and up the other."

"Could you manage to walk as far as the village? I don't like to leave you."

"Oh, yes; I think I can walk. Anyhow I'm going to try. I say, if you hear me squeak or crack anywhere, you'll stop me, won't you?"

"Of course."

"Come on then, and let's get there. Oh, crumpets! what a pain."

"Lean on me."

"No; I'm going to lean on myself," said Jem, stoutly. "I'm pretty sure I arn't broke, Mas' Don; but feel just as if I was cracked all over like an old pot, and that's werry bad, you know, arn't it? Now then, which way is it?"

"This way, Jem, to the right of the mountain."

"Ah, I suppose you're right, Mas' Don. I say, I can walk."

"Does it hurt you very much?"

"Oh, yes; it hurts me horrid. But I say, Mas' Don, there arn't many chaps in Bristol as could have fallen down like that without breaking theirselves, is there?"

"I think it's wonderful, Jem."

"'That's what I think, Mas' Don, and I'm as proud of it as can be. Here, step out, sir; works is beginning to go better every minute. Tidy stiff; but, I say, Mas' Don, I don't believe I'm even cracked."

"I am glad, Jem," cried Don. "I felt a little while ago as if I would rather it had been me."

"Did you, though, Mas' Don? Well, that's kind of you, that it is. I do like that. Come along. Don't you be afraid. I can walk as fast as you can. Never fear! Think we shall be in time?"

"I don't know, Jem. I was in such trouble about you that I had almost forgotten the people at the village."

'So had I. Pain always makes me forget everything, 'speshly toothache. Why, that's the right way," he cried, as they turned the corner of a steep bluff.

"Yes, and in a quarter of an hour we can be there; that is, if you can walk fast?"

"I can walk fast, my lad: look. But what's quarter of a hour? I got muddled enough over the bells board ship—three bells, and four bells, and the rest of it; but out here there don't seem to be no time at all. Wonder how near those fellows are as we see. I *am* glad I arn't broke."

In about the time Don had said, they came to the path leading to the ravine, where the cave pierced the mountain side. A few minutes later they were by the hot bath spring, and directly after, to Don's great delight, they came upon Tomati.

"I was coming to look for you two," he said. "You had better not go far from the *whare*. Two of the tribes have turned savage, and are talking about war."

Don interrupted him, and told him what they had seen.

"So soon!" he said hurriedly.

"Is it bad news, then?" asked Don, anxiously.

"Bad, my lads! bad as it can be."

"Then that was a war-party we saw?"

"Yes; come on."

He then put his hands to his mouth and uttered a wildly

savage yell, whose effect was instantaneous. It was answered in all directions, and followed by a shrieking and wailing chorus from the women and children, who came trooping out of their huts, laden with household treasures, and hurrying up one particular path at the back of the village, one which neither Don nor Jem had intruded upon, from the belief that it led to some temple or place connected with the Maoris' religion.

A few minutes before the men were idling about, lying on the black sand, sleeping, or eating and drinking in the most careless, indolent way. Now all were in a state of the wildest excitement, and as Don saw the great stalwart fellows come running here and there, armed with spear and stone axe, he felt that he had misjudged them, and thought that they looked like so many grand bronze figures, suddenly come to life. Their faces and nearly naked bodies were made hideous with tattooing marks; but their skins shone and the muscles stood out, and as they all grouped together under the orders of Tomati and Ngati, both Don and Jem thought that if the party they had seen were coming on to the attack, the fighting might be desperate after all.

In less time than it takes to tell, men had been sent out as scouts; and pending their return, Tomati led the way up the path, after the women and children, to where, to Don's astonishment, there was a strong blockaded enclosure, or *pah*, made by binding great stakes together at the tops, after they had been driven into the ground.

There was but one entrance to the enclosure, which was on the summit of a rock with exceedingly steep sides, save where the path zigzagged to the top; and here every one was soon busy trying to strengthen the place, the spears of the men being laid against the stockade.

"May as well help," said Jem, sturdily. "I'm not going to fight, but I don't mind helping them to take care of themselves."

They set to and aided in every way they could, Ngati smiling approval, patting Don on the back, and then hurrying away to return with two spears, which he handed to the two young men.

"My pakeha!" he said; and Jem gave an angry stamp, and was about to refuse to take the weapon, when there was a yell of excitement from all in the *pah*, for one of the scouts came running in, and as he came nearer, it could be seen that he was bleeding from a wound in the shoulder, and that he had lost his spear.

As if nerved by this sight, Don and Jem seized the spears offered for their defence.

"Yes, Mas' Don," said Jem; "we shall have to try and fight; seems to me as if the war's begun!"

A wild shriek followed his words, and Don saw that they were but too true.

CHAPTER XXXIX.

WAR.

TOMATI soon showed the reason for his elevation to the position of chief among the Maoris, for, in addition to being a man of commanding presence and great strength, his adventurous life had given him quickness and decision in his actions, which told with a savage race none too ready to discriminate.

He rushed out of the *pah*, and caught the man by the shoulder, questioned him, turned him over to a couple of his friends to be doctored, and then in a loud voice informed the excited crowd that the danger was not imminent, following up this announcement with orders to go on strengthening the stockade.

He was instantly obeyed, his cool manner giving his followers confidence; and they went on working hard at securing certain spots and strengthening the entrance, but always with their spears close at hand.

There was another shout from a sentry, and again the whole tribe was electrified, women and children huddling under shelter, and the warriors seizing their weapons.

This time a scout came running in uninjured and with his spear to announce the nearer approach of the enemy.

Tomati received his news coolly enough, and then, after a word or two with Ngati, signed to the man to join the defenders, while two fresh scouts were sent out to spy the neighbourhood, and keep the chiefs well informed of the coming danger.

Ngati's eyes seemed to flash, and there was a savage rigidity in his countenance that suggested hard times for the man who attacked him; but he seemed to place the most implicit confidence in Tomati, obeying his slightest suggestion, and evidently settling himself into the place of lieutenant to the white captain.

After the first wailing and tears, the women and children settled down in their shelter quite as a matter of course, and as if such an event as this were no novelty in their social history. Once within the *pah*, and surrounded by stout fighting men on whom they could depend, they seemed quite satisfied, and full of confidence in the result of an attack, and this took Jem's notice.

"Can't be much danger," he said, half contemptuously, "or these here wouldn't take it so coolly."

"But it looks as if there was going to be a desperate fight."

"Tchah! Not that, Mas' Don."

"But look at that scout who ran in. He was hurt."

"So is a boy who has had his head punched, and whose nose bleeds. There won't be no real fighting, my lad. I mean men being killed, and that sort o' thing."

"Think not, Jem?"

"Sure of it, my lad. T'other side 'll come up and dance a war-dance, and shake their spears at our lot. Then our lot 'll dance up and down like jack-jumpers, and make faces, and put out their tongues at 'em, and call 'em names. I know their ways; and then they'll all yell out, and shout; and then the others 'll dance another war-dance, and shout in Noo Zealandee that they'll kill and eat us all, and our lot 'll say they'd like to see 'em do it, and that'll be all."

Don shook his head. The preparations looked too genuine.

"Ah, you'll see," continued Jem. "Then one lot 'll laugh, and say you're obliged to go, and t'other lot 'll come back again, and they'll call one another more names, and finish off with killing pigs, and eating till they can't eat no more."

"You seem to know all about it, Jem."

"Well, anybody could know as much as that," said Jem,

going to the side and taking up a bundle formed with one of the native blankets, which he began to undo.

"What have you got there?"

"You just wait a minute," said Jem, with a dry look. "There! Didn't know that was the arm chest, did you?"

He unrolled and took out a cutlass and two pistols, with the ammunition, and looked up smilingly at Don.

"There!" he said, "what do you think o' them?"

"I'd forgotten all about them, Jem."

"I hadn't, my lad. There you are. Buckle on that cutlash."

"No; you had better have that, Jem. I should never use it."

"Oh, yes, you would, my lad, if it was wanted. On with it."

Don reluctantly buckled on the weapon, and Jem solemnly charged the pistols, giving Don one, and taking the other to stick in his own waistbelt.

"There," he said, retaking the spear given to him. "Don't you feel like fighting now?"

"No, Jem; not a bit."

"You don't?"

"No. Do you?"

"Well, if you put it in that way," said Jem, rubbing his ear, "I can't say as I do. You can't feel to want to do much in that way till some one hurts you. Then it's different."

"It's horrible, Jem!"

"Well, I suppose it is; but don't you get looking like that. There'll be no fighting here. I say, Mas' Don, it would be a bit of a game, though, to stick the pynte of this here spear a little way into one of the savages. Wonder what he'd say."

"Ah! My pakeha!" cried a voice just behind them; and they turned sharply, to find themselves face to face with Ngati, who patted Don on the shoulder, and then pointed to his cutlass and pistol.

"Hah!" he ejaculated, with a deep breath; and then, without warning, snatched Don's spear from his hand, threw himself into a series of wild attitudes, and went through the action of one engaged in an encounter with an enemy, stabbing, parrying, dodging, and darting here and there in a way that suggested instant immolation for the unfortunate he encountered.

"Look at him, Mas' Don," whispered Jem. "Look at him pretending. That's the way they fight. By-an'-by, you'll see lots o' that, but you mark my words, none on 'em won't go nigh enough to hurt one another."

Ngati ceased as suddenly as he had begun, returned the spear to Don, and seemed to intimate that he should go through the same performance

"You wait a bit, old chap!" cried Jem. "We don't fight that way."

"Hah!" ejaculated Ngati, and he ran across to a portion of the *pah* where several of his warriors were busily binding some of the posts more securely.

"It do make me laugh," said Jem; "but I s'pose all that bouncing helps 'em. Poor things. Mas' Don, you and I ought to be werry thankful as we was born in Bristol, and that Bristol's in old England. Say, shall you give any one a chop if it does come to a fight?"

Don shook his head.

Jem laughed.

"If it warn't for wasting the powder, I tell you what we'd do. Get up atop yonder where we could lean over the palings, wait till the other chaps comes up, and then shoot over their heads with the pistols. That'd make some of 'em run."

There was another shout here, for two of the scouts came running in, and every man seized his spear, and darted to the spot he was expected to defend.

"Why, Mas' Don, how they can run! Look at 'em. An Englishman wouldn't run like that from a dozen men. Here, let's chuck these spears away. We sha'n't want 'em. An Englishman as has got fists don't want no spears. Look! look!"

The two scouts had come running in very swiftly till they

were about a hundred yards from the gateway of the *pah*, when they stopped short and faced about as two of the enemy, who were in chase, dashed at them, spear in hand.

Then, to Jem's astonishment, a sharp passage of arms occurred; the spears clashed together, there was a wonderful display of thrusting and parrying, and the two enemies fell back, and the scouts continued their retreat to the shelter of the fort.

"What do you think of that, Jem?" said Don excitedly. "That was real fighting."

"Real?" cried Jem; "it was wonderful!" and he spoke huskily. "Why, both those chaps was wounded, and these here's got it, too."

The two scouts were both gashed about the arms by their enemies' spears, but they came bravely in, without making any display, and were received by cheers, Tomati going up to each in turn, and gripping his hand.

Just then the Englishman caught sight of his compatriots, and came across to them quickly.

"Hullo!" he said, with a grim smile, "cleared for action, and guns run out?"

"Yes, we're ready," said Jem.

"Going to fight on our side?"

"Well, I don't know," said Jem, in a dubious kind of way. "Fighting arn't much in my line."

"Not in yours neither, youngster. There, I daresay we shall soon beat them off. You two keep under shelter, and if things go against us, you both get away, and make for the mountain. Go right into that cave, and wait till I join you."

"But there will not be much fighting, will there—I mean real fighting?" said Jem.

"I don't know what you mean by real fighting, squire; but I suppose we shall keep on till half of us on both sides are killed and wounded."

"So bad as that?"

"P'r'aps worse," said the man grimly. "Here, shake hands

young un, in case we don't have another chance. If you have to run for it, keep along the east coast for about a hundred miles; there's white men settled down yonder. Good-bye."

Tomati shook hands heartily, and went off to his fighting men, who were excitedly watching the level below the *pah*, to which part it was expected the enemy would first come.

Don joined them, eager to see how matters were going, and hopeful still, in spite of Tomati's words, that matters would not assume so serious an aspect; but just then a hand was laid upon his arm.

"I was out of it, Mas' Don," whispered Jem. "They do bounce a deal. But there s going to be real fighting on. One o' those poor fellows who came running in, and stood up as if nothing was wrong, is dead."

"Dead?"

"Yes, my lad. Spear went right through his chest. Hark at 'em!"

There was a low wailing noise from the corner of the *pah*, where the two men were sheltered, and Don felt a chill of horror run through him.

"Then it is going to be quite a savage battle, Jem?"

"'Fraid so, my lad—no, I don't mean 'fraid—think so. Now, look here, Mas' Don, it won't be long first, so you'd better go and lie down behind them high palings, where you'll be safe."

"And what are you going to do?"

"Stop here and see what there is to see."

"But you may be hurt."

"Well, Mas' Don," said Jem bitterly; "it don't much matter if I am. Run along, my lad."

"I'm going to stop with you, Jem."

"And suppose you're hurt; what am I to say to your mother? Why, she'd never forgive me."

"Nor me either, Jem, if I were to go and hide, while you stood out here."

"But it's going to be real dangerous, Mas' Don."

"It will be just as dangerous for you, Jem. What should I say to your wife if you were hurt?"

"Don't know, Mas' Don," said Jem sadly. "I don't think she'd mind a deal."

"You don't mean it, Jem!" cried Don sharply. "Now, are you coming into shelter?"

"No," said Jem, with a peculiarly hard, stern look in his face. "I'm going to fight."

"Then I shall stay too, Jem."

"Won't you feel frightened, Mas' Don?"

"Yes, I suppose so. It seems very horrible."

"Yes, so it is, but it's them others as makes it horrible. I'm going to give one on 'em something for spearing that poor chap. Look out, Mas' Don; here they come!"

There was a fierce shout of defiance as the scouts came running in now as hard as they could, followed by a body of about two hundred naked warriors, whose bronzed bodies glistened in the sunshine. They came on in a regular body, running swiftly, and not keeping step, but with wonderful regularity, till they were about fifty yards from the *pah*, when, after opening out into a solid oblong mass to show a broader front, they stopped suddenly as one man, dropped into a half-kneeling position, and remained perfectly motionless, every savage with his head bent round, as if he were looking over his left shoulder, and then turning his eyes to the ground, and holding his weapon diagonally across his body.

The whole business was as correctly gone through as if it was a manœuvre of some well-drilled European regiment, and then there was an utter silence for a few minutes.

Not a sound arose from either side; enemies and friends resembled statues, and it was as if the earth had some great attraction for them, for every eye looked down instead of at a foe.

Don's heart beat heavily. As the band of heavy warriors came on, the air seemed to throb, and the earth resound. It was exciting enough then; but this was, in its utter stillness, horribly intense, and with breathless interest the two adventurers scanned the fierce-looking band.

All at once Jem placed his lips close to Don's ear, and whispered,—

"Dunno what to say to it all, Mas' Don. P'r'aps it's flam after all."

"No, Jem; they look too fierce," whispered back Don.

"Ay, my lad, that's it; they look so fierce. If they didn't look so precious ugly, I should believe in 'em a bit more. Looks to me as if they were going to pretend to bite, and then run off."

A sudden yell rose from the attacking party just then, and three of the enemy rushed forward to the front, armed with short-handled stone tomahawks. They seemed to be chiefs, and were men of great height and bulk, but none the less active; and as they advanced, a low murmur of dismay was started by such of the women as could command a view of what was going on outside. This seemed to be communicated to all the rest, women and children taking up the murmur, which rose to a piteous wail. This started the pigs and dogs which had been driven into the protection of the *pah*, and the discord was terrible.

But meanwhile, partly to encourage their followers, partly to dismay those they had come to attack, the three leaders rushed wildly to and fro before the opening to the fort, brandishing their stone axes, grimacing horribly, putting out their tongues, and turning up their eyes, till only the whites were visible.

"It's that 'ere which makes me think they won't fight," said Jem, as he and Don watched the scene intently.

"Don't talk, Jem. See what they are going to do. Are we to shoot if they do attack?"

"If you don't they'll give it to us," replied Jem. "Oh, what a row!"

For at that moment there was a terrible and peculiar cry given from somewhere behind the little army, and the three men gave place to one who rushed from behind. The cry was given out three times as the man indulged in a similar set of wild evolutions to those which had been displayed by the three leaders, and with his eyes showing only the whites, he too thrust out his tongue derisively.

"If I was only near enough to give you a chop under the chin!" grumbled Jem.

Then he grasped and cocked the pistol he held, for the chief in front suddenly began to stamp on the ground, and shouted forth the beginning of his war-song.

Up leaped the whole of the enemy, to shake their spears as they yelled out the chorus, leaping and stamping with regular movement, till the earth seemed to quiver. The acts of the chief were imitated, every man seeming to strive to outdo his fellows in the contortions of their countenances, the protrusion of their tongues, and the way in which they rolled and displayed the whites of their eyes.

There was quite a military precision in the stamping and bounding, while the rhythm of the wild war-song was kept with wonderful accuracy.

"Feel scared, Mas' Don?" whispered Jem.

"I did at first, Jem," replied Don; "but they seem such a set of ridiculous idiots, that I am more disposed to laugh at them."

"That's just how I feel, my lad, only aggravated like, too. I should like to go among 'em with a big stick. I never see such faces as they make. It is all flam; they won't fight."

The war-song went on as if the enemy were exciting themselves for the affray, and all the time the men of Tomati and Ngati stood firm, and as watchful as could be of their foes, who leaped, and stamped, and sang till Jem turned to Don, and said in a low voice,—

"Look here, Mas' Don, it's my opinion that these here chaps never grew inside their heads after they was six or seven. They've got bodies big enough, but no more brains than a little child. Look at that six-foot-four chap making faces at us; why, it's like a little boy. They won't fight."

It seemed so to Don, and that it was all going to be an attempt to frighten the tribe he was with. But all the same, the enemy came by degrees nearer and nearer, as they yelled and leaped; and a suspicion suddenly crossed Don's mind that there might be a motive in all this.

"Jem, they mean to make a rush."

"'Think so, Mas' Don?"

"Yes, and our people know it. Look out!"

The followers of Tomati had thoroughly grasped the meaning of the indirect approach, just as a man who has practised a certain manœuvre is prepared for the same on the part of his enemy, and they had gradually edged towards the entrance to the *pah*, which was closed, but which naturally presented the most accessible way to the interior.

The howling chorus and the dancing continued, till, at a signal, the rush was made, and the fight began.

Jem Wimble's doubts disappeared in an instant; for, childish as the actions of the enemy had been previously, they were now those of desperate savage men, who made no account of their lives in carrying out the attack upon the weaker tribe.

With a daring that would have done credit to the best disciplined forces, they darted up to the stout fence, some of them attacking the defenders, by thrusting through their spears, while others strove to climb up and cut the lashings of the *toro-toro*, the stout fibrous creeper with which the palings were bound together.

One minute the enemy were dancing and singing, the next wildly engaged in the fight; while hard above the din, in a mournful booming bleat, rang out the notes of a long wooden horn.

The tumult increased, and was made more terrible by the screaming of the women and the crying of the children, which were increased as some unfortunate defender of the *pah* went down before the spear-thrusts of the enemy.

The attack was as daring and brave as could be; but the defence was no less gallant, and was supplemented by a desperate valour, which seemed to be roused to the pitch of madness as the women's cries arose over some fallen warrior. A spear was thrust through at the defenders; answering thrusts were given, but with the disadvantage that the enemy were about two to one. Tomati fought with the solid energy of his race, always on the look-out to lead half-a-dozen men to points which were most fiercely assailed; and his efforts in this way were so successful that over and over again the enemy were driven back in spots where they had made the most energetic efforts to break through.

As Don and Jem looked on they saw Tomati's spear darted through the great fence at some savage who had climbed up, and was hacking the lashings; and so sure as that thrust was made, the stone tomahawk ceased to hack, and its user fell back with a yell of pain or despair.

Ngati, too, made no grotesque contortions of his face; there was no lolling out of the tongue, or turning up of the eyes, for his countenance was set in one fixed stare, and his white teeth clenched as he fought with the valour of some knight of old.

"I would not ha' thought it, Mas' Don," said Jem excitedly. "Look at him; and I say—oh, poor chap!"

This last was as Jem saw a fine-looking young Maori, who was defending a rather open portion of the stockade, deliver a thrust, and then draw back, drop his spear, throw up his arms, and then reel and stagger forward, to fall upon his face—dead.

"They'll be through there directly, Mas' Don!" cried Jem, hoarsely, as Don stooped upon one knee to raise the poor fellow's head, and lay it gently down again, for there was a look upon it that even he could understand.

"Through there, Jem?" said Don, rising slowly, and looking half stunned with horror.

"Yes, my lad; and Tomati's busy over the other side, and can't come. Arn't it time us two did something?"

"Yes," said Don, with his face flushing, as he gave a final look at the dead Maori. "Ah!"

Both he and Jem stopped short then, for there was a yell of dismay as Ngati was seen now to stagger away from the fence, and fall headlong, bleeding from half-a-dozen wounds.

An answering yell came from outside, and the clatter of spear and tomahawk seemed to increase, while the posts were beginning to yield in the weak spot near where the two companions stood.

"Come on, Jem!" cried Don, who seemed to be moved by

a spirit of excitement, which made him forget to feel afraid; and together they ran to where two men, supported by their companions outside, were hacking at the *toro-toro*, while others were fiercely thrusting their spears through whenever the defenders tried to force the axe-men down.

"Pistols, Jem, and together, before those two fellows cut the lashings."

"That's your sort!" cried Jem; and there was a sharp *click, click*, as they cocked their pistols.

"Now, Jem, we mustn't miss," said Don. "Do as I do."

He walked to within three or four yards of the great fence, and rested the butt of the spear he carried on the ground. Then, holding the pistol-barrel against the spear-shaft with his left hand, thus turning the spear into a support, he took a long and careful aim at a great bulky savage, holding on the top of the fence.

Jem followed his example, and covered the other; while the enemy yelled, and thrust at them with their spears, yelling the more excitedly as it was found impossible to reach them.

"Let me give the word, Mas' Don!" cried Jem, whose voice shook with excitement. "Mind and don't miss, dear lad, or they'll be down upon us. Ready?"

"Yes," said Don.

"Here goes, then," cried Jem. "Fire! Stop your vents."

The two pistols went off simultaneously, and for a few moments the smoke concealed the results. Then there was a tremendous yelling outside, one that was answered from within by the defenders, who seemed to have become inspirited by the shots; for either from fright, or from the effects of the bullets, the two great Maoris who were cutting the lashings were down, and the defenders were once more at the fence, keeping the enemy back.

"Load quickly, Jem," said Don.

"That's just what I was a-going to say to you, Mas' Don."

"Well done, my lads! That's good!" cried a hoarse voice; and Tomati was close to them. "Keep that up; but hold your fire till you see them trying to get over, and wherever you see that, run there and give 'em a couple of shots. Ha, ha! Ha, ha!" he roared, as he rushed away to encourage his followers, just as Jem had rammed home his charge, and examined the priming in the pistol pan.

"That's just what we will do," said Jem; "only I should like to keep at it while my blood's warm. If I cool down I can't fight. Say, Mas' Don, I hope we didn't kill those two chaps."

"I hope they're wounded, Jem, so that they can't fight," replied Don, as he finished his priming. "Quick! they're getting up yonder."

They ran across to the other side of the *pah*, and repeated their previous act of defence with equally good result; while the defenders, who had seemed to be flagging, yelled with delight at the two young Englishmen, and began fighting with renewed vigour.

"Load away, Mas' Don!" cried Jem; "make your ramrod hop. Never mind the pistol kicking; it kicks much harder with the other end. Four men down. What would my Sally say?"

"Hi! quick, my lads!" shouted Tomati; and as Don looked up he saw the tattooed Englishman, who looked a very savage now, pointing with his spear at one corner of the place.

Don nodded, and ran with Jem in the required direction, finishing the loading as they went.

It was none too soon, for three of the enemy were on the top of the fence, and, spear in hand, were about to drop down among the defenders.

Bang! went Jem's pistol, and one of the savages fell back.

Bang! Don's shot followed, and the man at whom he aimed fell too, but right among the spears of the defenders; while the third leaped into the *pah*, and the next moment lay transfixed by half-a-dozen weapons.

"I don't like this, Jem," muttered Don, as he loaded again.

"More don't I, my lad; but it's shoot them or spear us; so load away."

Jem words were so much to the point, that they swept away Don's compunction, and they hastily reloaded.

All around were the yelling and clashing of spears; and how many of the attacking party fell could not be seen, but there was constantly the depressing sight of some brave defender of the women and children staggering away from the fence, to fall dead, or to creep away out of the struggle to where the weeping women eagerly sought to staunch his wounds and give him water.

"That's splendid, my lads! that's splendid! ten times better than using a spear," cried Tomati, coming up to them again. "Plenty of powder and ball?"

"Not a very great deal," said Don.

"Be careful, then, and don't waste a shot. They can't stand that."

"Shall we beat them off?" said Don, after seeing that his pistol was charged.

"Beat them off? Why, of course. There you are again. Look sharp!"

Once more the two pistols cleared the attacking Maoris from the top of the fence, where they were vainly trying to cut through the lashings; and, cheered on by these successes, the defenders yelled with delight, and used their spears with terrible effect. But the attacking party, after a recoil, came on again as stubbornly as ever, and it was plain enough to those who handled the firearms that it was only a question of time before the besieged would be beaten by numbers; and Don shuddered as he thought of the massacre that must ensue.

He had been looking round, and then found that Jem was eyeing him fixedly.

"Just what I was a-thinking, Mas' Don. We've fought like men; but we can't do impossibles, as I says to your uncle, when he wanted me to move a molasses barrel. Sooner we cuts and runs, the better."

"I was not thinking of running, Jem."

"Then you ought to have been, my lad; for there's them at home as wouldn't like us two to be killed."

"Don't! Don't! Jem!" cried Don. "Come on. There's a man over! Two—three—four! Look!"

He ran toward the side, where a desperate attack was being made, and, as he said, four men were over, and others following, when once more the pistols sent down a couple who had mounted the fence, one of them being shot through the chest, the other dropping on seeing his companion fall, but with no further hurt than the fright caused by a bullet whistling by his ear.

The four who were over made a desperate stand, but Tomati joined in the attack, and the daring fellows soon lay weltering in their blood; while, as Don rapidly loaded once more, he saw that Tomati was leaning on his spear, and rocking himself slowly to and fro.

"Are you hurt?" said Don, running up, and loading as he went.

"Hurt, my lad? Yes: got it horrid. Look here, if you and him see a chance make for the mountain, and then go south'ard."

"But shall we be beaten?"

"We are beaten, my lad, only we can't show it. I'm about done."

"Oh!"

"Hush! Don't show the white feather, boy. Keep on firing, and the beggars outside may get tired first. If not—— There, fire away!"

He made a brave effort to seem unhurt, and went to assist his men; while once more Don and Jem ran to the side, and fired just in time to save the lashings of the fence; but Jem's pistol went off with quite a roar, and he flung the stock away, and stood shaking his bleeding fingers.

"Are you hurt, Jem?"

"Hurt! He says, 'Am I hurt?' Why, the precious thing bursted all to shivers; and, oh, crumpets, don't it sting!"

"Let me bind it up."

"You go on and load; never mind me. Pretty sort o' soldier you'd make. D'yer hear? Load, I say; load!"

"Can't, Jem," said Don sadly; "that was my last charge."

"So it was mine, and I rammed in half-a-dozen stones as well to give 'em an extra dose. Think that's what made her burst?"

"Of course it was, Jem."

"Bad job; but it's done, and we've got the cutlash and spears. Which are you going to use?"

"The spear. No; the cutlass, Jem."

"Bravo, my lad! Phew! how my hand bleeds."

"I'm afraid we shall be beaten, Jem."

"I'm sure of it, my lad. My right hand, too; I can't hit with it. Wish we was all going to run away now."

"Do you, Jem?"

"Ay, that I do; only we couldn't run away and leave the women and children, even if they are beaten."

A terrible yelling and shrieking arose at that moment from behind where they stood, and as they turned, it was to see the whole of the defenders, headed by Tomati, making a rush for one portion of the fence where some of the stout poles had given way. A breach had been made, and yelling like furies, the enemy were pouring through in a crowd.

CHAPTER XL.

DEFEATED.

TWO minutes at the outside must have been the lapse of time before the last spear held up in defence of the *pah* was lowered by its brave owner in weakness, despair, or death.

Tomati's men fought with desperate valour, but they were so reduced that the enemy were four to one; and as they were driven back step by step, till they were huddled together in one corner of the *pah*, the slaughter was frightful.

Stirred to fury at seeing the poor fellows drop, both Don and Jem had made unskilful use of their weapons, for they were unwillingly mingled with the crowd of defenders, and driven with them into the corner of the great enclosure.

One minute they were surrounded by panting, desperate men, using their spears valorously, as the Greeks might have used theirs in days of old; then there came a rush, a horrible crowding together, a sensation to Don as if some mountain had suddenly fallen on his head to crush out the hideous din of yelling and despairing shrieks, and then all was darkness.

* * * * * *

It was still darkness, but the stars were shining brightly overhead, when Don opened his eyes again to begin wondering why his head should ache so terribly, and he should feel so cold.

Those thoughts were only momentary, for a colder chill ran through him as on both sides of where he lay a low moaning sound arose, as of some one in pain.

"Where am I?" he thought. "What is the matter?"

Then he realised what had happened, for a familiar voice said almost in a whisper,—

"Poor little Sally! I wish she was here with a bit o' rag.'

"Jem!"

"Mas' Don! Oh! thank the Lord! Amen! I thought —I thought—— Oh! oh!"

A choking sensation rose in Don's throat, for he could hear close beside him the brave, true fellow sobbing like a woman.

"Jem! Jem, old chap!" whispered Don. "Don't, pray don't do that."

"I'm a-trying not to as hard as ever I can," whispered the poor fellow hoarsely; "but I've been bleeding like a pig, Mas' Don, and it's made me as weak as a great gal. You see I thought as you was dead."

"No, no, Jem; I'm here safe, only—only my head aches, and I can't get my hands free."

"No, my lad, more can't I. We're both tied up, hands and legs."

"But the others? Where is Tomati?"

"Don't ask me, my lad."

"Oh, Jem!"

There was a few minutes' awful silence, during which the low moaning sound went on from different places close at hand.

"Where is Ngati?" whispered Don at last.

"Half killed, or dead, Mas' Don," said Jem, sadly. "We're reg'lar beat. But, my word, Mas' Don, I am sorry."

"Sorry? Of course."

"Ah! but I mean for all I said about the poor fellows. I thought they couldn't fight."

"The women and children, Jem?"

"All prisoners, 'cept some as would fight, and they——"

"Yes—go on."

"They served them same as they did those poor chaps as wouldn't give in."

"How horrible!"

"Ah, 'tis horrid, my lad; and I've been wishing we hadn't cut and run. We was better off on board ship."

"It's of no use to talk like that, Jem. Are you much hurt?"

"Hand's all cut about with that pistol busting, and there's a hole through my left shoulder, as feels as if it had been bored with a red hot poker. But there, never mind. Worse disasters at sea, Mas' Don. Not much hurt, are you?"

"I don't know, Jem. I can remember nothing."

"Good job for you, my lad. One of 'em hit you over the head with the back of a stonechopper; and I thought he'd killed you, so I——"

Jem ceased speaking.

"Well, go on," whispered Don.

"That's all," said Jem, sullenly.

"But you were going to say what you did when the man struck me."

"Was I? Ah, well, I forget now."

Don was silent, for Jem had given him something terrible to dwell upon as he tried to think.

At last he spoke again.

"Where are the enemy, Jem?"

"Enemy, indeed!" growled Jem. "Savages like them don't deserve such a fine name. Brutes!"

"But where are they? Did you see what they did?"

"See? Yes. Don't ask me."

"But where are they?"

"Sleep. Drunk, I think. After they'd tied us prisoners all up and shut up all the women and children in the big *whare*, what do you think they did?"

"Kill them?"

"Killed 'em? No. Lit fires, and set to and had a reg'lar feast, and danced about—them as could!" added Jem with a chuckle. "Some on 'em had got too many holes in 'em to enjoy dancing much. But, Mas' Don."

"Yes, Jem."

"Don't ask me to tell you no more, my lad. I'm too badly, just now. Think you could go to sleep?"

"I don't know, Jem. I don't think so."

"I'd say, let's try and get ourselves loose, and set to and get away, for I don't think anybody's watching us; but I couldn't go two steps, I know. Could you run away by yourself?"

"I don't know," said Don. "I'm not going to try."

"Well, but that's stupid, Mas' Don, when you might go somewhere, p'r'aps, and get help."

"Where, Jem?"

"Ah!" said the poor fellow, after a pause, "I never thought about that."

They lay still under the blinking stars, with the wind blowing chill from the icy mountains; and the feeling of bitter despondency which hung over Don's spirit seemed to grow darker. His head throbbed violently, and a dull numbing pain was in his wrists and ankles. Then, too, as he opened his lips, he felt a cruel, parching, feverish thirst, which seemed by degrees to pass away as he listened to the low moaning, and then for a few minutes he lost consciousness.

But it was only to start into wakefulness again, and stare wildly at the faintly-seen fence of the great *pah*, right over his head, and through which he could see the twinkling of a star.

As he realised where he was once more, he whispered Jem's name again and again, but a heavy breathing was the only response, and he lay thinking of home and of his bedroom all those thousand miles away. And as he thought of Bristol, a curious feeling of thankfulness came over him that his mother was in ignorance of the fate that had befallen her son.

"What would she say—what would she think, if she knew that I was lying here on the ground, a prisoner, and wounded —here at the mercy of a set of savages—what would she say?"

A short time before Don had been thinking that fate had done its worst for him, and that his position could not possibly have been more grave. But he thought now that it might have been far worse, for his mother was spared his horror.

And then as he lay helpless there, and in pain, with his companion badly hurt, and the low moan of some wounded savage now and then making him shudder, the scene of the desperate fight seemed to come back, and he felt feverish and wild. But after a time that passed off, and the pain and chill troubled him, but only to pass off as well, and be succeeded by a drowsy sensation.

And then as he lay there, the words of the old, old prayers he had repeated at his mother's knee rose to his lips, and he was repeating them as sleep fell upon his weary eyes ; and the agony and horrors of that terrible time were as nothing to him then.

CHAPTER XLI.

PRISONERS OF WAR.

"I WISH our old ship was here, and I was at one of the guns to help give these beggars a broadside."

"It is very, very horrible, Jem."

"Ten times as horrid as that, Mas' Don. Here was we all as quiet and comf'table as could be—taking our warm baths. I say, shouldn't I like one now! I'm that stiff and sore I can hardly move."

"Yes, it would be a comfort, Jem."

"Yes, and as I was saying, here was we going on as quiet as could be, and interfering with nobody, when these warmints came; and look at things now."

"Yes," said Don, sadly, as he looked round; "half the men dead, the others wounded and prisoners, with the women and children."

"And the village—I s'pose they calls this a village; I don't, for there arn't no church—all racked and ruined."

They sat together, with their hands tightly bound behind them, gazing at the desolation. The prisoners were all huddled together, perfectly silent, and with a dull, sullen, despairing look in their countenances, which seemed to suggest that they were accepting their fate as a matter of course.

It was a horrible scene, so many of the warriors being badly wounded, but they made no complaint; and, truth to tell, most of those who were now helpless prisoners had taken part in raids to inflict the pain they now suffered themselves.

The dead had been dragged away before Don woke that morning, but there were hideous traces on the trampled ground, with broken weapons scattered here and there, while the wounded were lying together perfectly untended, many of them bound, to prevent escape—hardly possible even to an uninjured man, for a guard was keeping watch over them ready to advance threateningly, spear in hand, if a prisoner attempted to move.

Where Don and Jem were sitting a portion of the great fence was broken, and they could see through it down to the shore.

"What a shame it seems on such a glorious morning, Jem!"

"Shame! Mas' Don? I should just like to shame 'em. Head hurt much?"

"Not so very much, Jem. How is your shoulder?"

"Rather pickly."

"Rather what?"

"Pickly, as if there was vinegar and pepper and salt being rubbed into it. But my old mother used to say that it was a good sign when a cut smarted a lot. So I s'pose my wound's first rate, for it smarts like a furze bush in a fit."

"I wish I could bathe it for you, Jem."

"Thank ye, Mas' Don. I wish my Sally could do it. More in her way."

"We must try and bear it all, I suppose, Jem. How hot the sun is; and, ill as I am, I should be so glad of something to eat and drink."

"I'm that hungry, Mas' Don," growled Jem, "that I could eat one o' these here savages. Not all at once, of course."

"Look, Jem. What are they doing there?"

Don nodded his head in the direction of the broken fence; and together they looked down from the eminence on which the *pah* was formed, right upon the black volcanic sand, over which the sea ran foaming like so much glistening silver.

"THEY SAT TOGETHER, WITH THEIR HANDS TIGHTLY BOUND BEHIND THEM" (p. 319).

There were about fifty of the enemy busy there running to and fro, and the spectators were not long left in doubt as to what they were doing, for amid a great deal of shouting one of the huge war canoes was run down over the sand and launched, a couple of men being left to keep her by the shore, while their comrades busied themselves in launching others, till every canoe belonging to the conquered tribe was in the water.

"That's it, is it?" said Jem. "They came over land, and now they're going back by water. Well, I s'pose, they'll do as they like."

"Isn't this nearest one Ngati's canoe, Jem?"

"Yes, my lad; that's she. I know her by that handsome face cut in the front. I s'pose poor Ngati's dead."

"I'm afraid so," said Don, sadly. "I've been trying to make out his face and Tomati's among the prisoners, but I can't see either."

"More can't I, Mas' Don. It's a werry bad job. Lookye yonder now."

Don was already looking, for a great deal of excited business was going on below, where the victorious tribe was at work, going and coming, and bringing down loads of plunder taken from the various huts. One man bore a bundle of spears, another some stone tomahawks, which were rattled into the bottom of the canoes. Then paddles, and bundles of hempen garments were carried down, with other objects of value in the savage eye.

This went on for hours amidst a great deal of shouting and laughter, till a large amount of spoil was loaded into the canoes, one being filled up and deep in the water.

Then there seemed to be a pause, the canoes being secured to trees growing close down to the shore, and the party busy there a short time before absent.

"Coming to fetch us now, I suppose, Mas' Don," said Jem. "Wonder whether they've got your pistol and cutlash."

But no one but the guards came in sight, and a couple of

weary hours passed, during which the other prisoners sat crouched together, talking in a low tone, apparently quite indifferent to their fate; and this indifference seemed so great that some of the thoughtless children began to laugh and talk aloud.

For some time this was passed over unnoticed; but at last one of the guards, a tall Maori, whose face was so lined in curves that it seemed to be absolutely blue, walked slowly over to the merry group, spear in hand, to give one child a poke with the butt, another a sharp blow over the head, evidently with the intention of producing silence; but in the case of the younger children his movements had the opposite effect, and this roused the ire of some of the women, who spoke out angrily enough to make the tall, blue-faced savage give a threatening gesture with his spear.

Just at that moment, however, a loud shouting and singing arose, which took the man's attention, and he and his fellows mounted on a stage at one corner of the *pah* to stand leaning upon their spears, gazing down at the festivities being carried on at the edge of the sands below.

For some time past it had seemed to Don that the plundering party had fired the village, for a tall column of smoke had risen up, and this had died down and risen again as combustible matter had caught.

The fire was too far below to be seen, but the smoke rose in clouds as the work of destruction seemed to be going on.

The singing and shouting increased, and once or twice the other prisoners appeared to take an excited interest in the sounds that came up to them; but they only sank directly after into a state of moody apathy, letting their chins go down upon their chests, and many of them dropping off to sleep.

The noise and shouting had been going on for some time, and then ceased, to be succeeded by a low, busy murmur, as of a vast swarm of bees; and now, after sitting very silent and thoughtful, watching the faint smoke which came up from the fire, and eagerly drinking in the various sounds, Don turned his eyes in a curiously furtive manner to steal a look at Jem.

He did not move his head, but proceeded with the greatest caution, so as to try and read his companion's countenance, when, to his surprise, he found that Jem was stealing a look at him, and both, as it were, snatched their eyes away, and began looking at the prisoners.

But at that time it was as if the eyes of both were filled with some strange attractive force, which made them turn and gaze in a peculiarly hard, wild way.

Don seemed to be reading Jem's thoughts as his sight plunged deeply into the eyes of his companion, and as he gazed, he shuddered, and tried to look elsewhere.

But he could not look elsewhere, only hard at Jem, who also shuddered, and looked shame-faced and horrified.

For they were reading each other's thoughts only too correctly, and the effect of that perusal was to make big drops of perspiration roll down Jem's face, and to turn Don deadly pale.

At last each snatched his eyes away, Jem to watch the prisoners, Don to close his, and sit trembling and listening to the bursts of merriment which came up.

At such times, in spite of their efforts, they could not imitate the apathy of the New Zealanders, but gazed wildly at each other, trying to make themselves believe that what they imagined was false, or else the prisoners would have shown some sign of excitement.

At last Jem ceased to make any pretence about the matter. He stared speechlessly and full of misery at Don, who let his eyes rest wildly on Jem's for a time before dropping his head upon his chest, and sitting motionless.

All through the rest of that hour, and hour after hour, till towards evening, did the wretched prisoners sit in despair and misery without food or water ; and the sounds of merriment and feasting came loudly to where they were.

The sun was descending rapidly when about half-a-dozen

of the conquering tribe came up to the *pah*, with the result that those who were on guard suddenly grew wildly excited, and giving up their duties to the new comers, uttered eager shouts and rushed off in a way that was frantic in the extreme.

Don and Jem again exchanged looks full of misery and despair, and then gazed with wonder and loathing at the new comers, who walked slowly about for a few minutes, and then went and leaned their backs against the palisading of the *pah*, and partially supported themselves upon their spears.

"Ugh!" ejaculated Jem with a shudder as he turned away. "You wretches! Mas' Don, I felt as I lay here last night, all dull and miserable and sick, and hardly able to bear myself— I felt so miserable because I knew I must have shot some of those chaps."

"So did I, Jem," sighed Don; "so did I."

"Well, just now, Mas' Don, I'm just 'tother way; ay, for I wish with all my heart I'd shot the lot. Hark, there!"

They listened, and could hear a burst of shouting and laughing.

"That's them sentries gone down now to the feast. I say, Mas' Don, look at these here fellows."

"Yes, Jem, I've been looking at them. It's horrible, and we must escape."

They sat gazing at their guards again, to see that they were flushed, their eyes full, heavy, and starting, and that they were absolutely stupefied and torpid as some huge serpent which has finished a meal.

"They must be all drunk, Jem," whispered Don, with a fresh shudder of horror and loathing.

"No, Mas' Don, 'tarn't that," said Jem, with a look of disgust. "Old Mike used to tell us stories, and most of 'em was yarns as I didn't believe; but he told us one thing as I do believe now. He said as some of the blacks in Africa would go with the hunters who killed the hippipperpothymouses, and when they'd killed one, they'd light a fire, and then cut off long strips of the big beast, hold 'em in the flame for a bit, and then eat 'em, and cut off more strips and eat them, and go on eating all day till they could hardly see or move."

"Yes, I remember, Jem; and he said the men ate till they were drunk; and you said it was all nonsense, for a man couldn't get drunk without drink."

"Yes, Mas' Don; but I was all wrong, and Mike was right. Those wretches there are as much like Mike Bannock was when he bored a hole in the rum puncheon as can be. Eating too much makes people as stupid as drinking; and knowing what I do, I wishes I was in Africa and not here."

"Knowing what you do, Jem?"

"Yes, Mas' Don, knowing what I do. It's what you know too. I can see you do."

Don shuddered.

"Don't, Jem, don't; it's too horrid even to think about."

"Yes, dear lad, but we must think about it. These here people's used to it, and done it theirselves, I daresay; and they don't seem to mind; but we do. Ah, Mas' Don, I'd rather ha' been a sailor all my life, or been had by the sharks when we was swimming ashore; for I feel as if I can't stand this. There, listen!"

There was a sound of shouting and singing from the beach below, and one of the guards tossed up his spear in a sleepy way, and shouted too, but only to subside again into a sluggish state of torpidity.

"Why, Mas' Don, by-and-by they'll all be asleep, and if we tried, you and me might get our arms and legs undone, and take a spear apiece, and kill the lot. What do you say?"

"The same as you will, if you think, Jem," replied Don. "No."

"No, it is, Mas' Don, of course. Englishmen couldn't do such a thing as that."

"But only let us have a fair chance at them again, Jem, and I don't think we shall feel very sorry if we slay a few."

"Sorry?" said Jem, between his teeth. 'I mean a hundred

of 'em at least, as soon as we can get away; and get away we will."

They sat listening till the horrible feast below was at an end, and everything became so silent that they concluded that the enemy must be asleep, and began to wonder that the prisoners should all crouch together in so apathetic a state. But all at once, when everything seemed most still, and half the prisoners were dozing, there came the heavy trampling of feet; the guards roused up, and in the dim light of the late evening, the bonds which secured the captives' feet were loosened, and, like a herd of cattle, they were driven down from the platform upon which the *pah* was constructed, and along the slope to the sands, where the canoes rode lightly on the swell.

Into these they were forced to climb, some getting in with alacrity, others slowly and painfully; two or three falling helplessly in the water, and then, half drowned, being dragged in over the side.

"Not a bit sorry I killed some of 'em," muttered Jem. "They arn't men, Mas' Don, but savage beasts."

It did not take long, for there was plenty of room in the little fleet of canoes. The prisoners were divided, some being placed in the canoes with the plunder, and treated as if they were spoil. Others were divided among the long canoes, manned by the enemy, whose own wounded men, even to the worst, did not hesitate to take to a paddle, and fill their places. Some of the children whimpered, but an apathetic state of misery and dejection seemed to have affected even them, while in one or two cases, a blow from a paddle was sufficient to awe the poor little unfortunates into silence.

As soon as the last man was in his place, a herculean chief waved his hands; one of his followers raised a great wooden trumpet, and blew a long, bellowing note; the paddles dipped almost as one into the water, and the men burst into a triumphal chorus, as, for a few hundred yards, the great war canoes which they had captured swept with their freight of spoil at a rapid rate southward along the shore.

Then the sudden burst of energy ceased, the song broke off,

the speed diminished; and the men slowly dipped their paddles in a heavy, drowsy way. Every now and then one of the warriors ceased paddling, or contented himself with going through the motion; but still the great serpent-like vessels glided on, though slowly, while the darkness came on rapidly, and the water flashed as its phosphorescent inhabitants were disturbed.

The darkness grew intense, but not for long. Soon a gradual lightening became visible in the east, and suddenly a flash of light glanced along the surface of the sea, as the moon slowly rose to give a weird aspect to the long row of dusky warriors sluggishly urging the great canoes onward.

Don and Jem had the good fortune to be together in the largest and leading canoe; and as they sat there in silence, the strangeness of the scene appeared awful. The shore looked almost black, save where the moon illumined the mountainous background; but the sea seemed to have been turned into a pale greenish metal, flowing easily in a molten state. No one spoke, not a sigh was heard from the prisoners, who must have been suffering keenly as they cowered down in the boat.

Don sat watching the weird panorama as they went along, asking himself at times if it was all real, or only the effect of some vivid dream. For it appeared to be impossible that he could have gone through what he had on the previous night, and be there now, borne who could say whither, by the successful raiders, who were moving their oars mechanically as the canoe glided on.

"It must be a dream," he said to himself. "I shall awake soon, and——"

"What a chance, Mas' Don!" said a low voice at his side, to prove to him that he was awake.

"Chance? What chance?" said Don, starting.

"I don't mean to get away, but for any other tribe to give it to them, and serve 'em as they served our poor friends; for they was friends to us, Mas' Don."

"I wish the wretches could be punished," said Don sadly; "but I see no chance of that."

"Ah! wait a bit, my lad; you don't know. But what a chance it would be with them all in this state. If it wasn't that I don't care about being drowned, I should like to set to work with my pocket knife, and make a hole in the bottom of the canoe."

"It would drown the innocent and the guilty, Jem."

"Ay, that's so, my lad. I say, Mas' Don, arn't you hungry?"

"Yes, I suppose so, Jem. Not hungry; but I feel as if I have had no food. I am *too* miserable to be hungry."

"So am I sometimes when my shoulder burns; at other times I feel as if I could eat wood."

They sat in silence as the moon rose higher, and the long lines of paddles in the different boats looked more weird and strange, while in the distance a mountain top that stood above the long black line of trees flashed in the moonlight as if emitting silver fire.

"Wonder where they'll take us?" said Jem, at last.

"To their *pah*, I suppose," replied Don, dreamily.

"I s'pose they'll give us something to eat when we get there, eh?

"I suppose so, Jem. I don't know, and I feel too miserable even to try and think."

"Ah," said Jem; "that's how those poor women and the wounded prisoners feel, Mas' Don; but they're only copper-coloured blacks, and we're whites. We can't afford to feel as they do. Look here, my lad, how soon do you think you'll be strong enough to try and escape?"

"I don't know, Jem."

"I say to-morrow."

"Shall you be fit?"

Jem was silent for a few minutes.

"I'm like you, Mas' Don," he said. "I dunno; but I tell you what, we will not say to-morrow or next day, but make up our minds to go first chance. What do you say to that?"

"Anything is better than being in the power of such wretches as these, Jem; so let's do as you say."

Jem nodded his head as he sat in the bottom of the canoe in the broad moonlight, and Don watched the soft silver sea, the black velvet-looking shore, and the brilliant stars; and then, just as in his faintness, hunger, and misery, he had determined in his own mind that he would be obliged to sit there and suffer the long night through, and began wondering how long it would be before morning, he became aware of the fact that Nature is bounteously good to those who suffer, for he saw that Jem kept on nodding his head, as if in acquiescence with that which he had said; and then he seemed to subside slowly with his brow against the side.

"He's asleep!" said Don to himself. "Poor Jem! he always could go to sleep directly."

This turned Don's thoughts to the times when, after a hard morning's work, and a hasty dinner, he had seen Jem sit down in a corner with his back against a tub, and drop off apparently in an instant.

"I wish I could go to sleep and forget all this," Don said to himself with a sigh—"all this horror and weariness and misery."

He shook his head: it was impossible; and he looked again at the dark shore that they were passing, at the shimmering sea, and then at the bronzed backs of the warriors as they paddled on in their drowsy, mechanical way.

The movement looked more and more strange as he gazed. The men's bodies swayed very little, and their arms all along the line looked misty, and seemed to stretch right away into infinity, so far away was the last rower from the prow. The water flashed with the moonlight on one side, and gleamed pallidly on the other as the blades stirred it; and then they grew more misty and more misty, but kept on *plash—plash—plash*, and the paddles of the line of canoes behind echoed the sound, or seemed to, as they beat the water, and Jem whispered softly in his ear,—

"Don't move, Mas' Don, my lad, I'm not tired!"

But he did move, for he started up from where his head had

been lying on Jem's knees, and the poor fellow smiled at him in the broad morning sunshine.

Sunshine, and not moonshine; and Don stared.

"Why, Jem," he said, "have I been asleep?"

"S'pose so, Mas' Don. I know I have, and when I woke a bit ago, you'd got your head in my lap, and you was smiling just as if you was enjoying your bit of rest."

CHAPTER XLII.

TOMATI ESCAPES.

"HAVE they been rowing—I mean paddling—all night, Jem?" said Don, as he looked back and saw the long line of canoes following the one he was in.

"S'pose so, my lad. Seems to me they can go to sleep and keep on, just as old Rumble's mare used to doze away in the carrier's cart, all but her legs, which used to keep on going. Them chaps, p'r'aps, goes to sleep all but their arms."

A terrible gnawing sensation was troubling Don now, as he looked eagerly about to see that they were going swiftly along the coast line; for their captors had roused themselves with the coming of day, and sent the canoes forward at a rapid rate for about an hour, until they ran their long narrow vessels in upon the beach and landed, making their prisoners do the same, close by the mouth of a swift rocky stream, whose bright waters came tumbling down over a series of cascades.

Here it seemed as if a halt was to be made for resting, and after satisfying their own thirst, leave was given to the unhappy prisoners to assuage theirs, and then a certain amount of the food found in the various huts was served round.

"Better than nothing, Mas' Don," said Jem, attacking his portion with the same avidity as was displayed by his fellow-prisoners. "'Tarn't good, but it'll fill up."

"Look, Jem!" whispered Don; "isn't that Tomati?"

Jem ceased eating, and stared in the direction indicated by Don.

"Why, 'tis," he whispered. "Don't take no notice, lad, or they'll stop us, but let's keep on edging along till we get to him. Will you go first, or follow me?"

"I'll follow you," whispered Don; and Jem began at once by changing his position a little as he went on eating. Then a little more, Don following, till they had placed a group of the miserable, apathetic-looking women between them and the warriors.

These women looked at them sadly, but made no effort to speak, only sat watching them as they crept on and on till they were close upon the recumbent figure which they had taken to be the tattooed Englishman.

"Why, if this is so easy, Mas' Don," said Jem, "why couldn't we get right among the trees and make for the woods?"

"Hush! some one may understand English, and then our chance would be gone. Go on."

Another half-dozen yards placed them close beside the figure they had sought to reach, and as he lay beside him, Don touched the poor fellow on the breast.

"Tomati!" he whispered, "is that you?"

The man turned his head feebly round and stared vacantly —so changed that for a moment they were in doubt.

But the doubt was soon solved, for the poor wounded fellow said with a smile,—

"Ay, my lad; I was—afraid—you were—done for."

"No, no; not much hurt," said Don. "Are you badly wounded?"

Tomati nodded.

"Can I do anything for you?"

"No," was the reply, feebly given. "It's all over with me at last; they will fight—and kill one another. I've tried—to stop it—no use."

Jem exchanged glances with Don, for there was something terrible in the English chief's aspect.

"Where are they taking us?" said Don, after a pause.

"Down to Werigna—their place. But look here, don't stop

to be taken there. Go off into the woods and journey south—farther than they go. Don't stay."

"Will they kill us if we stay?" whispered Don.

"Yes," said Tomati, with a curious look. "Run for it—both."

"But we can't leave you."

Tomati smiled, and was silent for a few minutes.

"You will not—leave me," he whispered, as he smiled sadly. "I—shall escape."

"I am glad," whispered Don. "But Ngati?—where is Ngati?"

"Crawled away up the mountain. Badly wounded, but he got away."

"Then he has escaped," whispered Don joyfully.

"Yes. So must you," said Tomati, shivering painfully. 'Good lads, both."

"I don't like to leave you," said Don again.

"Ah! that's right. Don, my lad, can you take hold—of my hand—and say—a prayer or two. I'm going—to escape."

A thrill of horror ran through Don as he caught hold of the Englishman's icy hand, and the tears started to his eyes as in a broken voice he repeated the old, old words of supplication; but before his lips had formed half the beautiful old prayer and breathed it into the poor fellow's ear, Don felt his hand twitched spasmodically, and one of the chiefs shouted some order.

"Down, Mas' Don! lie still!" whispered Jem. "They're ordering 'em into the boat again. Think we could crawl into the bush from here?"

"No, Jem; it would be impossible."

"So it would, lad, so it would; but as he said, poor chap, we must take to the woods. Think any of these would come with us?"

Don shook his head despairingly, as he longed to look in Tomati's face again, but he dared not stir.

A few minutes later they were once more in the leading canoe, which was being urged rapidly over the smooth sea, and it was a long time before Don could frame the words he wished to say. For whenever he tried to speak there was a strange choking sensation in his throat, and he ended by asking the question mutely as he gazed wildly in his companion's face.

"Tomati, Mas' Don?" said Jem sadly.

Don nodded.

"Ah, I thought that was what you meant, my lad. Didn't you understand him when he spoke?"

"No—yes—I'm afraid I did," whispered back Don.

"Yes, you did, my lad. He meant it, and he knew it. He has got away."

Don gazed wildly in Jem's eyes, and then bent his head low down to hide the emotion he felt, for it was nothing to him then that the English chief was an escaped convict from Norfolk Island. He had been a true friend and defender to them both; and Don in his misery, pain, and starvation could only ask himself whether that was the way that he must escape —the only open road.

It was quite an hour before he spoke again, and then hardly above his breath.

"Jem," he said, "shall we ever see our dear old home again?"

Jem looked at him wistfully, and tried to answer cheerily, but the paddles were flashing in the sun, and the canoe was bearing them farther and farther away to a life of slavery, perhaps to a death of such horror that he dared not even think of it, much less speak.

CHAPTER XLIII.

A SEARCH IN THE DARK.

TWO days' more water journey within easy reach of the verdant shore, past inlet, gulf, bay, and island, round jagged points, about which the waves beat and foamed; and then, amidst shouting, singing, and endless barbaric triumphal clamour, the captured canoes with their loads of prisoners and spoil were run up to a black beach, where a crowd of warriors with their women and children and those of the little conquering army eagerly awaited their coming.

Utterly worn out, the two English prisoners hardly had the spirit to scan the beautiful nook, through which a foaming stream of water dashed, at whose mouth lay several large war canoes, and close by which was the large open *whare* with its carven posts and grotesque heads, quite a village of huts being scattered around.

Similarly placed to that which he had helped to defend, Don could see upon a shoulder of the hill which ran up behind the *whare*, a great strongly made *pah*, ready for the tribe to enter should they be besieged by some enemy.

But the whole scene with its natural beauty, seemed accursed to Don, as he was half dragged out of the canoe, to stagger and fall upon the sands—the fate of many of the wounded prisoners, who made no resistance, but resigned themselves to their fate.

A scene of rejoicing ensued, in the midst of which fires which had been lighted as soon as the canoes came in sight, were well used by the women who cooked, and before long a banquet was prepared, in which three pigs and a vast number of potatoes formed the principal dishes.

But there was an abundance of fruit, and bowls of a peculiar gruel-like food, quantities of which were served out to the wretched prisoners, where they squatted together, as dismal a group as could be imagined, and compared their own state with that of the victors, whose reception was almost frantic, and whose spoil was passed from hand to hand, to be marvelled at, or laughed at with contempt.

At another time Don would have turned with disgust from the unattractive mess offered to him, but hunger and thirst made him swallow it eagerly, and the effect was wonderful.

A short time before he had felt ready to lay down and die; but, after partaking of the food, he was ready to accept Jem's suggestion that they should bathe their hands and faces in the rushing water that foamed by close at hand, the conquerors being too much occupied with their singing and feasting to pay much heed to them. So they crept to the rocky edge of the clear, sparkling water, and to their surprise found that it was quite warm.

But it was none the less refreshing, and as they half lay afterwards on the sun-warmed rock at the side, watching suspiciously every act of their new masters, in dread of that horror which sent a chill through both, they felt the refreshing glow send new life and strength through them, and as if their vigour were returning with every breath they drew.

"Feel better, Mas' Don?"

"Yes, much."

"So 'm I. If it wasn't for the hole in my shoulder, and it being so stiff, I shouldn't be long before I was all right."

"Does it pain you very much?"

"Come, that's better, Mas' Don," said Jem.

"Better?"

"Yes; you're looking up again, and taking a bit o' interest

in things. You quite frightened me, you seemed so down. My shoulder? Well, it do give it me pretty tidy. I thought I should have had to squeal when I was washing just now. But my legs are all right, Mas' Don. How's yourn?"

"My legs?"

"Yes. How soon shall we be ready to cut away?"

"Hush!"

"Oh! there's no one here understands English. When shall it be—to-night?"

"First time there is an opportunity, Jem," said Don, softly.

"That's so, my lad; so every time you get a 'chance, you eat; and when you don't eat you drink, and lie down all you can."

"Do you think any of the men here would try to escape with us?"

Jem shook his head.

"I don't understand 'em, Mas' Don. Seems to me that these chaps are all fight till they're beaten; but as soon as they're beaten, they're like some horses over a job: they won't try again. No, they're no good to help us, and I suppose they mean to take it as it comes."

The two lay in silence now, watching the proceedings of their captors, who were being feasted, till there was a sudden movement, and about a dozen men approached them, spear in hand.

At a shouted order the prisoners, wounded and sound, rose up with the women and children; and as patiently and apathetically as possible, allowed themselves to be driven up the hill-side to the strongly-built *pah*, through whose gateway they entered, and then threw themselves wearily down in the shadow of the great fence, while their captors secured the entrance, and a couple of them remained on guard.

"Do I look like a sheep, Mas' Don?" said Jem, as he threw himself on the earth.

"Sheep? No, Jem. Why?"

"Because I feels like one, my lad. Driven in here like one of a flock, and this place just like a great pen; and here we are to be kept till we're wanted for—— Oh, don't look like that, Mas' Don. It was only my fun. I say, you look as white as a wax image."

"Then don't talk that way," said Don, hoarsely. "It is too horrible."

"So it is, dear lad; but it seems to me that they only want to keep us now for slaves or servants. They're not going to, eh?"

"No, Jem," said Don looking at the great fence.

"Yes, that's just what I think, my lad. Posts like this may keep in Noo Zealanders, but they won't keep in two English chaps, will they?"

"Do you think if we got away in the woods, we could manage to live, Jem?"

"I think, my lad, if we stop in this here *pah*, we can't manage to at all, so we'll try that other way as soon as we can."

"Do you think it will be cowardly to leave these poor creatures in the power of the enemy?"

"If we could do 'em any good by staying it would be cowardly; but we can't do 'em any good. So as soon as you like, as I said before, I'm ready for a start. Why, there's fern roots, and fruit, and rivers, and the sea—— Oh, yes, Mas' Don, I think we could pick up a living somehow, till we reached a settlement, or friendly tribe."

Night began to fall soon afterward, and half-a-dozen women came in, bearing more bowls of the gruel-like food, and a couple of baskets of potatoes, which were set down near the prisoners, along with a couple of great vessels of water.

"Didn't think I wanted any more yet," said Jem, after eating heartily, for there was an abundance. "Go on, Mas Don; 'tarn't so bad when you're used to it, but a shovel full of our best West Indy plarntation sugar wouldn't ha' done it any harm to my thinking."

"I have eaten all I care for, Jem," said Don, wearily; and he sat gazing at the great fence which kept them in.

"No," said Jem, softly; "not there, Mas' Don. Just cast your eyes a bit more to the left. There's quite a rough bit, and if we couldn't climb it, I'm not here."

"But what about your shoulder?"

"I'll climb it with one hand, Mas' Don, or know the reason why."

"But the men on sentry?"

"Tchah! They think we're all too done up and cowardly to try to get away. I've been thinking it all over, and if you're the same mind as me, off we go to-night."

Don's heart beat fast, and a curious feeling of timidity came over him, consequent upon his weakness, but he mastered it, and, laying his hand on his companion's arm, responded,—

"I am ready."

"Then we'll make our hay while the sun shines, and as soon as it's dark," said Jem, earnestly, and unconscious of the peculiarity of his use of the proverb. "Let's lie still just as the others do, and then, I'm sorry for 'em; but this here's a case where we must help ourselves."

Jem lay there on his back as if asleep, when three stalwart Maoris came round soon after dusk, and took out the bowls which had held the food. They were laughing and talking together, as if in high glee, and it was apparently about the success of the festival, for they looked at their prisoners, whom they then seemed to count over, each in turn touching the poor creatures with the butt ends of their long spears.

Don felt the hot blood surge through his veins as one of the three guards gave him a harsh thrust with his spear, but he did not wince, only lay back patiently and waited till the men had gone. They secured the way into the *pah*, after which they squatted down, and began talking together in a low voice.

Don listened to them for a time, and then turned over to where Jem lay as if asleep.

"Is it dark enough?" he whispered.

"Plenty. I'm ready."

"Can you manage to get over?"

"I will get over," said Jem, almost fiercely. "Wait a little while, Mas' Don."

"I can't wait, Jem," he whispered. "I feel now as if I must act. But one minute: I don't like leaving these poor creatures in their helplessness."

"More do I; but what can we do? They won't stir to help themselves. Only thing seems to me is to get away, and try and find some one who will come and punish the brutes as brought us here."

Don's heart sank, but he knew that his companion's words were those of truth, and after a little hesitation he touched Jem with his hand, and then began to crawl slowly across the open space toward the fence.

He looked back to make sure that Jem was following, but the darkness was so thick now, that even at that short distance he could not see him. Just then a touch on his foot set him at rest, and he crept softly on, listening to the low muttering of the men at the gate, and wondering whether he could find the rough part of the fence to which Jem had directed his attention.

As he crept on he began to wonder next whether the prisoners would miss them, and do or say anything to call the attention of the guard; but all remained still, save that the Maoris laughed aloud at something one of them had said.

This gave him confidence, and ceasing his crawling movement, he rose to his hands and feet, and crept on all fours to the fence, where he rose now to an erect position, and began to feel about for the rough post.

Jem was up and by him directly after. Don placed his lips to his ear.

"Whereabouts was it?"

"Somewhere 'bout here. You try one way, and I'll try the other," whispered Jem; and then Don gripped his arm, and they stood listening, for a faint rustling sound seemed to come from outside.

The noise was not repeated; but for quite half an hour they remained listening, till, gaining courage from the silence —the Maori guard only speaking from time to time, and then in a low, drowsy voice—Don began to follow Jem's suggestion, feeling post after post, and sometimes passing his arm through. But every one of the stout pales he touched was smooth and unclimbable without some help; and thinking that perhaps he had missed the place, he began to move back in the darkness, straining his ears the while to catch any sound made by his companion.

But all was perfectly still, and every pale he touched was smooth and regular, set, too, so close to the next that there was not the slightest chance of even a child creeping through.

All at once there was a rustling sound on his left.

"Jem has found it," he thought; and he pressed forward toward where he had parted from Jem, passing one hand along the pales, the other extended so as to touch his companion as soon as they were near.

The rustling sound again close at hand; but he dare not speak, only creep on in the dense blackness, straining his eyes to see; and his ears to catch his companion's breath.

"Ah!"

Don uttered a sigh of satisfaction, for it was painful to be alone at such a time, and he had at last touched the strong sturdy arm which was slightly withdrawn, and then the hand gripped him firmly.

Don remained motionless, listening for the danger which must be threatening, or else Jem would have spoken; but at last the silence became so irksome that the prisoner raised his left hand to grasp Jem's wrist.

But it was not Jem's wrist. It was bigger and stouter; and quick as thought Don ran his hand along the arm to force back the holder of his arm, when to his horror, he found that the limb had been thrust through one of the openings of the fence, and he was a prisoner to some fierce chief who had suspected the design to escape, held in so strong a grip, that had he dared to struggle to free himself, it would not have been possible to drag the fettered arm away.

"Jem! Help!" was on his lips, but he uttered no cry, only breathlessly listened to a deep panting from the outer side of the *pah*.

CHAPTER XLIV.

AFTER SUSPENSE.

WHAT would happen? A powerful savage had hold of him firmly, had caught him just as he was about to escape; and the next thing would be that he would feel a spear driven through the opening between the pales, and that spear would run him through and through.

His first idea was to give warning of the danger, but he dared not call, and Jem was apparently beyond hearing of the rustling and panting noise which could still be heard.

Directly after Don determined to wrest his arm away, and dart back into the darkness.

But the hand which held him still gripped with a force which made this impossible; and in despair and dread he was about to fling himself down, when Jem came gliding up out of the darkness, and touched his cold, wet face.

"I've found the post, Mas' Don!" he whispered.

Don caught him with his disengaged hand, and placed Jem's against the arm which held him.

For a few moments Jem seemed unable to grasp the situation, for nothing was visible. Then he placed his lips once more close to Don's ear.

"Wait a moment till I've opened my knife."

"No, no," whispered Don in a horrified tone. "It is too dreadful."

"Then let's both try together, and wrench your arm away."

A peculiar hissing sound came at that moment from the outside of the *pah*, and Don felt his arm jerked.

"My pakeha! My pakeha!"

"Why, it's Ngati!" whispered Don joyfully; and he laid his disengaged hand on the massive fist which held him.

The grasp relaxed on the instant, and Don's hand was seized, and held firmly.

"It's Ngati, Jem," whispered Don, "come to help us."

"Good luck to him!" said Jem eagerly; and he felt for the chief's great hand, to pat it, and grasp it in a friendly way.

His grasp was returned, and then they listened as Ngati put his face to the opening, and whispered a few words, the only part of which they could understand being,—

"My pakeha. Come."

"Yes; we want to come," whispered Don.

"Tomati. Gone," came back, and then the chief said something rapidly in his own tongue.

Don sighed, for he could not comprehend a word.

"It's no good trying, Mas' Don," whispered Jem; "and if we don't try to get away, we mayn't have a chance to-morrow. Let's—— Here it is. Quick! I've got it. You climb up first, get over the top, and hang by your hands, and wait till I come. We must both drop together, and then be off. Oh, if we could only make him understand. What a fool of a language his is."

Don could not even then help thinking that Ngati might have said the same, but he did not lose a moment. Loosening his hold of the chief's hand, he whispered,—

"Pakeha. Come." Then giving himself up to the guidance of Jem, his hands were placed upon a rough post, and he began to climb, Jem helping him, somewhat after the fashion in which he had once assisted him to reach the window.

Then, almost noiselessly, he reached the top, climbed over with ease by the aid of the lashings, and getting a tight hold of the strong fibrous bands, he lowered himself down to await Jem's coming.

Ngati was more intelligent than Don had expected, for directly after he felt two great warm hands placed under to support his bare feet. These were raised and lowered a little; and, seizing the opportunity, he let himself sink down, till Ngati placed his feet upon two broad shoulders, and then Don felt himself seized by the hips, and lifted to the ground.

As this went on Don could feel the post he had climbed vibrating, and though he could not see, he could tell that Jem had mounted to the top.

"Where are you?" whispered Jem.

"Look out! Ngati will help you."

Jem grasped the situation, and the chief caught his feet, lowering him slowly, when all at once something seemed to spring out of the darkness, knocking Don right over, and seizing Ngati.

That it was one of the guards there could be no doubt, for the man raised the alarm, and held on to the prisoner he had made, Jem going down awkwardly in turn.

He and Don could have fled at once, but they could not leave their New Zealand friend in the lurch; and as the struggle went on, Jem had literally to feel his way to Ngati's help, no easy task in the darkness when two men are struggling.

At last he was successful, and got a grip of one of the combatants' throat; but a hoarse, "No, pakeha!" told him of his mistake.

He rectified it directly, getting his arm round the neck of the guard, tightening his grasp, and with such good effect, that Ngati wrenched himself free, and directly after Don heard one heavy blow, followed by a groan.

"My pakeha!"

"Here!" whispered Don, as they heard the rapid beating of feet, shouts below, in the *pah*, and close at hand.

Ngati seized Don's hand, and after stooping down, thrust a spear into it. Then, uttering a grunt, he placed another spear in Jem's hand, the spoils of their fallen enemy, and leaving him for a moment, he felt along the fence for his own weapon.

He spoke no more, but by means of action made Don understand that he would go first, holding his spear at the trail, he grasping one end, Don the other. Jem was to do likewise, and thus linked together they would not be separated.

All this took time, and during the brief moments that elapsed it was evident that the whole tribe was alarmed, and coming up to the *pah*.

"All right, Mas' Don! I understand. It's follow my leader, and old ' my pakeha to lead."

Ngati did not hesitate a moment, but went rapidly down the steep descent, straight for the river, apparently right for where some of the yelling tribe were advancing.

All at once the New Zealand chief stopped short, turned quickly, and pressed his hands firmly on Don's shoulder; for voices were heard just in front, and so near, that the lad feared that they must be seen.

But he grasped the chief's idea, and lay flat down, Jem following his example; and almost as they crouched to the ground, a group of the enemy ran up so close, that one of them caught his foot against Jem, and fell headlong.

Fortunately Jem was too much startled to move, and, muttering angrily, the man sprang up, not—as Don expected— to let drive with a spear at his companion, but attributing his fall to some stone, or the trunk of a tree, he ran on after his companions. Then Ngati rose, uttered a few words, whose import they grasped, and once more they hurried on straight for the river.

It was their only chance of escape, unless they made for the sea, and chanced finding a small canoe on the sands.

But that was evidently not Ngati's intention. Over the river seemed to be the only way not likely to be watched; and, going straight for it, he only paused again close to its brink, listening to the shouting going on but a very short distance from where they stood.

While Don listened, it sounded to him as if the Maoris were literally hunting them down, the men spreading out like a pack of dogs, and covering every inch of ground so closely that, unless they escaped from where they were, capture was absolutely certain.

As they stood panting there, Ngati caught Don's hand, and tightened it round the spear, following this up by the same action with Jem.

"He means we are to hold tight, Jem."

"Is he going to take us across this tumbling river, Mas' Don?"

"It seems so."

"Then I shall hold tight."

Before them they could faintly make out the foaming water, and though the distance was not above twenty or thirty yards, the water ran roaring over great stones in so fierce a torrent, that Don felt his heart sink, and shrank from the venture.

But on the other side of the torrent was freedom from a death so horrible that the boy shuddered at the thought, and without hesitation he tightened his hold on the spear, and followed the great Maori as he stepped boldly into the rushing stream.

It was a new sensation to Don as he moved on with the water over his waist, and pressing so hard against him, that but for the support of the spear-shaft, he must have been swept away. Sturdy even as Jem was, he, too, had a terribly hard task to keep his footing; for his short, broad figure offered a great deal of surface to the swift current, while the rugged stony bed of the river varied in depth at every step.

They had a tower of strength, though, in Ngati, who, in spite of the wounds he had received, seemed as vigorous as ever; and though Don twice lost his footing, he clung tightly to the spear, and soon fought his way back to a perpendicular position.

But even towers of strength are sometimes undermined and give way. It was so here. They were about half way across the river, whose white foam gave them sufficient light to enable them to see their way, when, just as Ngati came opposite to a huge block of lava, over which the water poured in tremendous volume, he stepped down into a hole of great

"DON TWICE LOST HIS FOOTING, BUT CLUNG TIGHTLY TO THE SPEAR."

depth, and, in spite of his vast strength and efforts to recover himself, he was whirled here and there for a few moments by the power of the fall.

Both Don and Jem stood firm, though having hard work to keep their footing, and drew upon the spear-shaft, to which Ngati still held. But all at once there was a sharp jerk, quite sufficient to disturb Don's balance, and the next moment Ngati shot along a swift current of water, that ran through a narrow trough-like channel, and Don and Jem followed.

Rushing water, a sensation of hot lead in the nostrils, a curious strangling and choking, with the thundering of strange noises in the ears. Next a confused feeling of being knocked about, turned over and beaten down, and then Don felt that he was in swift shallow water amongst stones.

He rose to his feet to find, as soon as he could get his breath regularly, that he had still hold of the spear-shaft, and that he had been swept down nearly to the sandy level, over which the river ran before joining the sea.

A minute later and he was walking over the soft, dry sand, following Ngati on the further shore, the great chief plodding on in and out among bushes and trees as if nothing had happened. The shouting of those in search was continued, but between them and the enemy the torrent ran, with its waters roaring, thundering, and plashing as they leaped in and out among the rocks toward the sea; and now that they were safely across, Don felt hopeful that the Maoris would look upon the torrent as impassable, and trust to their being still on the same side as the *pah*.

As they trudged on, dripping and feeling bruised and sore, Jem found opportunities for a word here and there.

"Thought I was going to be drownded after all, Mas' Don," he whispered. "I knocked my head against a rock, and if it wasn't that my skull's made o' the strongest stuff, it would ha' been broken."

"You had better not speak much, Jem," said Don softly.

"No, my lad; I won't. But what a ducking! All the time we were going across, it ran just as if some one on the left was shoving hard. I didn't know water could push like that."

"I expected to be swept away every moment."

"I expected as we was going to be drownded, and if I'm to be drownded, I don't want it to be like that. It was such a rough-and-tumble way."

Don was silent.

"Mas' Don."

"Yes."

"But, of course, I don't want to be drownded at all."

"No, Jem; of course not. I wonder whether they'll follow us across the river."

"They'll follow us anywhere, Mas' Don, and catch us if they can. Say, Mas' Don, though, I'm glad we've got old 'my pakeha.' He'll show us the way, and help us to get something to eat."

"I hope so, Jem."

"Say, Mas' Don, think we can trust him?"

"Trust him, Jem! Why, of course."

"That's all very well, Mas' Don. You're such a trusting chap. See how you used to trust Mike Bannock, and how he turned you over."

"Yes; but he was a scoundrel. Ngati is a simple-hearted savage."

"Hope he is, Mas' Don; but what I'm feared on is, that he may be a simple-stomached savage."

"Why, what do you mean, Jem?"

"Only as he may turn hungry some day, as 'tis his nature to."

"Of course."

"And then, 'spose he has us out in the woods at his mercy like, how then?"

"Jem, you're always thinking about cannibals. How car you be so absurd?"

"Come, I like that, Mas' Don; arn't I had enough to make me think of 'em?"

"Hssh!"

The warning came from Ngati; for just then the breeze seemed to sweep the faint roar of the torrent aside, and the shouting of the Maoris came loud and clear.

"They're over the river," said Jem excitedly. "Well, I've got a spear in my hand, and I mean to die fighting for the sake of old Bristol and my little wife."

CHAPTER XLV.

IN THE WOODS

"THEY'RE not over the river, Jem," said Don, impatiently. "I wish you wouldn't always look on the worst side of everything."

"That's what your Uncle Josiah allus does with the sugar, Mas' Don. If the foots was werry treacley when he had a hogshead turned up to look at the bottom first, he allus used to say as all the rest was poor quality."

"We're not dealing with sugar now."

"No, Mas' Don; this here arn't half so sweet. I wish it was."

"Hssh!" came from Ngati again. And for the rest of the night they followed him in silence along ravines, over rugged patches of mountain side, with the great fronds of the tree-ferns brushing their faces, and nocturnal birds rushing away from them as their steps invaded the solitudes where they indulged in their hunt for food.

When they encountered a stream, which came foaming and plunging down from the mountain, after carefully trying its depth, Ngati still led the way. Hour after hour they tramped wearily on through the darkness, Ngati rarely speaking, but pausing now and then to help them over some rugged place. Everything in the darkness was wild and strange, and there was an unreality in the journey that appeared dreamlike, the more so that, utterly worn out, Don from time to time tramped on in a state of drowsiness resembling sleep.

But all this passed away as the faint light of day gave place to the brilliant glow of the morning sunshine, and Ngati came to a standstill in a ferny gully, down which a tremendous torrent poured with a heavy thunderous sound.

And now, as Don and Jem were about to throw themselves down upon a bed of thick moss, Ngati held out his hand in English fashion to Don.

"My pakeha," he said softly, "morning."

There was something so quaint in his salutation that, in spite of weariness and trouble, Don laughed till he saw the great chief's countenance cloud.

But it cleared at once as Don caught his hand, pressed it warmly, and looked gratefully in his face.

"Hah!" cried Ngati, grasping the hand he held with painful energy. "My pakeha, morning. Want eat?"

"Yes, yes!" cried Jem, eagerly.

"Yes, yes," said Ngati; and then he stood, looking puzzled, as he tried to remember. At last, shaking his head sadly, he said, "No, no," in a helpless, dissatisfied tone. "Want Tomati. Tomati——"

He closed his eyes, and laid his head sidewise, to suggest that Tomati was dead, and his countenance, in spite of his grotesque tattooing, wore an aspect of sadness that touched Don.

"Tomati dead," he said slowly, and the chief's eyes brightened.

"Dead," he said; "Tomati dead—dead—all—dead."

"Yes, poor fellows, all but the prisoners," said Don, speaking slowly, in the hope that the chief might grasp some of his words.

But he did not understand a syllable, though he seemed to feel that Don was sympathising with him, and he shook hands again gravely.

"My pakeha," he said, pressing Don's hand. Then turning to Jem, he held out his other hand, and said slowly, "Jem-meree. Good boy."

"Well, that's very kind of you," said Jem, quietly. "We don't understand one another much, but I do think you a good fellow, Ngati; so I shake hands hearty; and I'll stand by you, mate, as you've stood by me."

"Good, good," said Ngati, smiling, as if he understood all. Then, looking grave and pained again, he pointed over the mountain. "Maori kill," he said. "Want eat?"

"Yes; eat, eat," said Jem, making signs with his mouth. "Pig—meat."

"No pig; no meat," said Ngati, grasping the meaning directly; and going to a palm-like tree, he broke out some of its tender growth and handed it to his companions.

"Eat," he said; and he began to munch some of it himself.

"Look at that now," said Jem. "I should ha' gone by that tree a hundred times without thinking it was good to eat. What's it like, Mas' Don?"

"Something like stalky celery, or nut, or pear, all mixed up together.'

"Yes; 'tarn't bad," said Jem. "What's he doing now?"

Ngati was busily hunting about for something, peering amongst the trees, but he did not seem to find that of which he was in search. He uttered a cry of satisfaction the next minute, though, as he stooped down and took a couple of eggs from a nest upon the ground.

"Good—good!" he exclaimed, eagerly; and he gave them to Don to carry, while he once more resumed his search, which this time was successful, for he found a young tree, and stripped from its branches a large number of its olive-like berries.

"There now," said Jem. "Why, it's all right, Mas' Don; 'tarn't tea and coffee, and bread and butter, but it's salad and eggs and fruit. Why, fighting cocks 'll be nothing to it. We shall live like princes, see if we don't. What's them things like?"

"Like very ripe apples, Jem, or medlars," replied Don, who had been tasting the fruit carefully.

"That'll do, then. Pity we can't find some more of them eggs, and don't light a fire to cook 'em. I say, Ngati."

The Maori looked at him inquiringly.

"More, more," said Jem, holding up one of the eggs, and pointing to the ferny thicket.

"No, no," said Ngati, shaking his head. "Moa, moa."

He stooped down and held his hands apart in different directions, as if he were describing the shape of a moderate-sized oval pumpkin. Then, rising erect, he raised one hand to the full extent of his arm, bending the fingers so as to imitate the shape of a bird's head, pressed his head against his arm, placed the left arm close to his body and a little forward, and then began to stalk about slowly.

"Moa, moa," he said, dropping his arm again, and pointing to the eggs, "Kiwi, kiwi."

"Kiwi, kiwi," said Jem. "Can't make out what he means, Mas' Don; but it don't matter. Shall we suck the eggs raw?"

He made a gesture as if to break one, but Ngati snatched it away.

"No, no!' he cried sharply, and snatched the other away.

"Pig!" ejaculated Jem. "Well, I do call that greedy."

But if the chief was greedy over the eggs, which he secured in a roughly-made bag of palm strips, ingeniously woven, he was generous enough over the fruit and palm, upon which they made a fair breakfast; after which Ngati examined Jem's wounds, and then signed to him to come down to the side of the stream, seizing him by the wrist, and half dragging him in his energetic way.

"Is he going to drown me, Mas' Don?"

"No, no, Jem. I know: he wants to bathe your wound."

So it proved, for Ngati made him lie down by a pool, and tenderly washed the injuries, ending by applying some cool bruised leaves to the places, and binding them up with wild flax.

This done, he examined Don's head, smiling with satisfaction because it was no worse.

"Say, Mas' Don, it do feel comftable. Why, he's quite a doctor, eh?"

"What?" continued Jem, staring, as Ngati made signs

"He wants you to bathe his wounds. Your arm's painful, Jem; I'll do it."

Ngati lay down by the pool, and, pulling up some moss, Don bathed a couple of ugly gashes and a stab, that was roughly plugged with fibre. The wounds were so bad that it was a wonder to both that the great fellow could keep about; but he appeared to bear them patiently enough, smiling with satisfaction as his attendant carefully washed them, and in imitation of what he had seen, applied bruised leaves and moss, and finally bound them up with native flax.

Don shuddered more than once as he performed his task, and was glad when it was over, Jem looking on calmly the while.

"Why, Mas' Don, a chap at home would want to go into hospital for less than that."

"Yes, Jem; but these men seem so healthy and well, they heal up quickly, and bear their hurts as if nothing was wrong."

"Sleep," said Ngati, suddenly; and he signed to Don to lie down and to Jem to keep watch, while he lay down at once in the mossy nook close to the river, and hidden by overhanging canopies of ferns.

"Oh, all right, Mas' Don, I don't mind," said Jem; "only I was just as tired as him."

"Let me take the first watch, Jem."

"No, no; it's all right, Mas' Don. I meant you to lie down and rest, only he might ha' offered to toss for first go."

"Call me then, at the end of an hour."

"All right, Mas' Don," said Jem, going through the business of taking out an imaginary watch, winding it up, and then looking at its face. "Five and twenty past seven, Mas' Don, but I'm afraid I'm a little slow. These here baths don't do one's watch any good."

"You'll keep a good look out, Jem."

"Just so, Mas' Don. Moment I hear or see anything I calls you up. What time would you like your shaving water, sir? Boots or shoes this morning?"

"Ah, Jem," said Don, smiling, "I'm too tired to laugh."

And he lay back and dropped off to sleep directly, Ngati's eyes having already closed.

"Too tired to laugh," said Jem to himself. "Poor dear lad, and him as brave as a young lion. Think of our coming to this. Shall we ever see old England again, and if we do, shall I be a cripple in this arm? Well, if I am, I won't grumble, but bear it all like a man; and," he added reverently, "please God save us and bring us back, if it's only for my poor Sally's sake, for I said I'd love her and cherish her, and keep her; and here am I one side o' the world, and she's t'other; and such is life."

CHAPTER XLVI.

AN UNTIRING ENEMY.

JEM kept careful watch and ward as he stood leaning on his spear.

He was very weary, and could not help feeling envious of those who were sleeping so well. But he heard no sound of pursuit, and after a time the wondrous beauty of the glen in which they had halted, with its rushing waters and green lacing ferns, had so composing an effect upon his spirits, that he began to take an interest in the flowers that hung here and there, while the song of a finch sounded pleasant and homelike. Then the delicious melody of the bell-bird fell upon his ear; and while he was listening to this, he became interested in a beautiful blackbird, which came and hopped about him.

Jem laughed, for his visitor had some white feathers just below the beak, and they suggested an idea to him as the bird bobbed and bowed and chattered.

"Well," he said, "if I was naming birds, I should call you the parson, for you look like one, with that white thing about your neck."

The bird looked at him knowingly, and flitted away. Directly after, as he turned his eyes in the direction where the uneaten fruit was lying, he saw that they had a visitor in the shape of one of the curious rails. The bird was already investigating the fruit, and after satisfying itself that the berries were of the kind that it could find for itself in the bush, it came running towards Jem, staring up at him, and as he extended the spear handle, instead of being frightened away, it pecked at the butt and then came nearer.

"Well, you are a rum little beggar," said Jem, stroking the bird's back with the end of the spear. "I should just like to have you at home to run in and out among the sugar barrels. I'd—— Hah!"

He turned round sharply, and levelled his spear at a great Maori, whose shadow had been cast across him, and who seemed to have sprung out of the bush.

"Why, I thought it was one o' they cannibals," said Jem, lowering the spear. "Good job it wasn't dark, old chap, or I should have given you a dig. What d'yer want?"

"Sleep," said Ngati laconically, and, taking Jem's spear, he pointed to where Don was lying.

"Me? What, already? Lie down?"

"Sleep," said Ngati again; and he patted Jem on the shoulder.

"All right, I'll go. Didn't think I'd been watching so long." He nodded and walked away. "Wish he wouldn't pat me on the back that way. It makes me feel suspicious. It's just as if he wanted to feel if I was getting fat enough."

Don was sleeping peacefully as Jem lay down and uttered a faint groan, for his left shoulder was very painful and stiff.

"Wonder how long wounds take to heal," he said softly. "Cuts arn't much more than a week. Heigh-ho-hum! I'm very tired, but I sha'n't be able to go to——"

He was asleep almost as soon as he lay down, and directly after, as it seemed to him, he started into wakefulness, to find Ngati standing a few yards away, shading his eyes and gazing down the gully, and Don poking him with his spear.

"All right, Sally, I'll get up. I—— Oh, it's you, Mas Don."

"Quick, Jem! The Maoris are coming.'

Jem sprang to his feet and seized the spear offered to him, as Ngati came forward, brushed the ferns about so as to destroy the traces of their bivouac, and then, holding up his hand for silence, he stood listening.

A faint shout was heard, followed by another, nearer; and signing them to follow, the Maori went along up the gully, with the stream on their right.

It was arduous work, for the ground was rapidly rising; but they were forced to hurry along, for every time they halted, they could hear the shouts of their pursuers, who seemed to be coming on with a pertinacity that there was no shaking off.

It was hot in the extreme, but a crisp, cool air was blowing to refresh them, and, of its kind, there was plenty of food, Ngati cautiously picking and breaking in places where the disarrangement was not likely to be seen. Every now and then, too, they saw him make quite an eager dash on one side and return with eggs, which he carefully placed in the woven bag he had made.

This went on till he had nearly a couple of dozen, at which, as he trudged along, Jem kept casting longing eyes.

In spite of the danger and weariness, Don could not help admiring the beauty of the scene, as, from time to time, the gully opened out sufficiently for him to see that they were steadily rising toward a fine cone, which stood up high above a cluster of mountains, the silvery cloud that floated from its summit telling plainly of its volcanic nature.

"*Tapu! tapu!*" Ngati said, every time he saw Don gazing at the mountain; but it was not till long after that he comprehended the meaning of the chief's words, that the place was "tapu," or sacred, and that it would act as a refuge for them, could they reach it, as the ordinary Maoris would not dare to follow them there.

Higher up the valley, where the waters were dashing furiously down in many a cascade, Don began to realise that they were following the bed of a river, whose source was somewhere high up the mountain he kept on seeing from time to time, while, after several hours' climbing, often over the most arduous, rocky ground, he saw that they were once more entering upon a volcanic district. Pillars of steam rose here and there, and all at once he started aside as a gurgling noise arose from beyond a patch of vivid green which covered the edges of a mud-pool, so hot that it was painful to the hand.

From time to time Ngati had stopped to listen, the shouts growing fainter each time, while, as they progressed, a heavy thunderous roar grew louder, died away, and grew louder again.

Don looked inquiringly at Jem.

"It's the big chimney of that mountain drawing, Mas' Don."

"Nonsense!"

"Nay, that's what it is; and what I say is this. It's all wery well getting away from them cannibals, but don't let's let old Ngati——"

The chief looked sharply round.

"Yes, I'm a-talking about you, old chap. I say, you're not to take us right up that mountain, and into a place where we shall tumble in."

"*Tapu! tapu!*" said Ngati, nodding his head, and pointing toward the steaming cloud above the mountain.

"Oh, you aggrawating savage!" cried Jem.

Ngati took it as a compliment, and smiled. Then, pointing to a cluster of rocks where a jet of steam was being forced out violently, he led the way there, when they had to pass over a tiny stream of hot water, and a few yards farther on, they came to its source, a beautiful bright fount of the loveliest sapphire blue, with an edge that looked like a marble bath of a roseate tint, fringed every here and there with crystals of sulphur.

"Let's have a bathe!" cried Jem eagerly. "Is there time?"

He stepped forward, and was about to plunge in his hand, when Ngati seized his shoulders and dragged him back.

"What yer doing that for?" cried Jem.

The Maori stepped forward, and made as if to dip in one of his feet, but snatched it back as if in pain. Then, smiling, he twisted some strands of grass into a band, fastened the end to the palm basket, and gently lowered it, full of eggs, into the sapphire depths, a jet of steam and a series of bubbles rising to the surface as the basket sank.

"Why, Jem," said Don laughing, "you wanted to bathe in the big copper."

"How was I to know that this was a foreign out-door kitchen?" replied Jem laughing.

"And the water's boiling hot," added Don. "You can see it bubbling just at this end."

"Think o' that now!" said Jem. "I say, what a big fire there must be somewhere down b'low. Strikes me, Mas' Don, that when I makes my fortun' and buys an estate I sha'n't settle here."

"No, Jem. 'There's no place like home.'"

"Well, home's where you settle, arn't it? But this won't do for me. It's dangerous to be safe."

Meanwhile, Ngati was listening intently, but, save the hissing of steam, the gurgling of boiling water, and the softened roar that seemed now distant, now close at hand, there was nothing to be heard, so he signed to them to sit down and rest.

He set the example, and Don followed, to lie upon his back, restfully gazing up at the blue sky above, when Jem, who had been more particular about the choice of a place, slowly sat down, remained stationary for a few moments, and then sprang up, uttering a cry of pain.

"Why, that stone's red hot!" he cried.

This was not the truth, but it was quite hot enough to make it a painful seat, and he chose another.

"Well, of all the rum places, Mas' Don!"

He said no more on the subject, for just then Ngati rose, and carefully drew the bag of eggs from the boiling pool.

"And I called him a pig!" said Jem, self-reproachfully.

"No: no pig," said Ngati, who caught the word.

"Well, I didn't say there was, obstinit," said Jem. "Here, give us an egg. Fruit and young wood's all werry well; but there's no spoons and no salt!"

In spite of these drawbacks, and amid a series of remarks on the convenience of cooking cauldrons all over the place, Jem made a hearty meal of new laid eggs, which they had just finished when Ngati looked up and seized his spear.

"What's the matter?" cried Don listening.

Ngati pointed, and bent down, holding his hand to his ear.

"I can hear nothing," said Jem.

Ngati pointed down the ravine again, his keen sense having detected the sound of voices inaudible to his companions. Then carefully gathering up the egg shells, so as to leave no traces, he took the bag with the rest of the eggs, and led the way onward at a rapid rate.

The path grew more wild and rugged, and the roar increased as they ascended, till, after turning an angle in the winding gully, the sound came continuously with a deep-toned, thunderous bellow.

"There, what did I tell you?" said Jem, as the top of the mountain was plainly in view, emitting steam, and about a mile distant. "That's the chimney roaring."

"It's a great waterfall somewhere on ahead," replied Don; and a few yards farther on they came once more upon the edge of the river, which here ran foaming along at the bottom of what was a mere jagged crack stretching down from high up the mountain, and with precipitous walls, a couple of hundred feet down.

Ngati seemed more satisfied after a while, and they sat down in a narrow valley they were ascending to finish the eggs, whose shells were thrown into the torrent.

"I should like to know where he's going to take us," said Jem, all at once.

"It does not matter, so long as it is into safety," said Don. "For my part, I—— Lie down, quick!"

Jem obeyed, and bending low, Don seized the Maori's arm, pointing the while down the way they had come at a couple of naked savages, leaping from stone to stone, spear armed, and each wearing the white-tipped tail feathers of a bird in his hair.

Ngati saw the danger instantly, fell flat on his breast, and signing to his companions to follow, began to crawl in and out among the rocks and bushes, making for every point likely to afford shelter, while, in an agony of apprehension as to whether they had been seen, Don and Jem followed painfully,

"DON POINTED TO A COUPLE OF SAVAGES, LEAPING FROM STONE TO STONE."

till the chief halted to reconnoitre and make some plan of escape.

It was quite time, for the Maoris had either seen them or some of the traces they had left behind; and, carefully examining every foot of the narrow valley shelf along which they had climbed, were coming rapidly on.

Don's heart sank, for it seemed to him that they were in a trap. On his right was the wall-like side of the gully they ascended; on his left the sheer precipice down to the awful torrent; before them the sound of a mighty cataract; and behind the enemy, coming quickly and stealthily on.

CHAPTER XLVII.

A DANGEROUS PHASE.

NGATI took all in at a glance, and signing to his companions to follow, he again lay down, creeping on for a short distance, trailing his spear, till they were well behind a pile of rocks.

Here he gave a sharp look round at the *cul de sac* into which they had been driven, and without hesitation crept to their left to where the rocky wall descended to the raging torrent.

To him the place seemed to have no danger, as he passed over the edge and disappeared, but to Don it was like seeking death.

"We can never do it, Jem," he said.

"Must, Mas' Don. Go on."

Don looked at him wildly, and then in a fit of desperation he lowered himself over the edge, felt a pair of great hands grasp him by the loins, and, as he loosened his hold, he was dropped upon a rough ledge of rock, where he stood giddy and confused, with the torrent rushing furiously along beneath his feet, and in front, dimly seen through a mist which rose from below, he caught a glimpse of a huge fall of water which came from high up, behind some projecting rocks, and disappeared below.

The noise of falling water now increased, reverberating from the walls of rock; the mist came cool and wet against his face, and, hurried and startled, Don stood upon the wet, rocky shelf, holding on tightly, till Ngati laid his hand upon his shoulder, passed round him, and then, signing to him to follow, went on.

Don's first thought was of Jem, and looking behind him, there was his companion close to where he stood.

Jem nodded to him to go on, just as a faint shout arose from somewhere above, and this seemed to nerve him to proceed over the slippery stones to where Ngati was passing round a corner, holding tightly by the rock, which he seemed to embrace.

The way was dangerous in the extreme—a narrow ledge of the most rugged kind with a perpendicular moss-covered wall on the right, and on the left, space, with far below the foaming torrent, a glance at which seemed to produce vertigo.

To stand still seemed to be worse than going on, and taking it to his comfort that what one man could do another might, Don reached the corner, but hesitated again, for there seemed to be no foothold whatever. But as he hesitated a great brown hand came round, ready to grasp his firmly; and with this help he made the venture, pressing himself close against the rock and creeping on.

He was just in the most perilous part, well out over the torrent, when his left foot slipped, and a horrible chill ran through him, as he felt that he was falling into the chasm below to instant death. He held on with his right hand, and strove to press his breast against the rock, but the effort was vain; his right hand slipped from the crevice in which it was thrust, his right foot glided over the wet moss, and he slipped down, hung for a moment or two over the foaming waters, and then felt himself swung up and on to a broad ledge, upon which Ngati was standing.

The Maori took it as a matter of course, signed to him to get up, and passed his hand round the rock once more to assist Jem.

A curious sensation ran through Don as he watched for Jem's coming, and trembling and unnerved, it seemed to him that watching another's peril was more painful than suffering oneself.

But in spite of his wounded shoulder Jem came round the point slowly and carefully, but with his brow rugged from the pain he suffered as Ngati held him firmly by his injured arm.

As soon as he was in safety Jem passed his hand across his wet forehead and bit his lip, whilst once more signing to them to follow, Ngati led on.

The way now was downward from rock to rock, and, terrible though it looked, the danger was less, for there was ample foothold and an abundance of bushy stems and fern fronds ready to their hands. The falls were again invisible, and they pressed on toward where another shoulder of the rocks jutted out, hiding the falling waters, whose noise was now so deafening that, had they wished to speak, a shout close to the ear would hardly have been heard.

Big as the Maori was, he seemed to be as active as a goat, and picking the easiest ways over the mist-moistened stones, he led his companions lower and lower down the rock wall till, when they reached the next projection, and on passing round, it was to find themselves in what was little more than a huge rock pit, facing a mass of water which fell from quite two hundred feet above them into a vast cauldron of white foam, which chafed and roared and cast up clouds of spray as it whirled round and then rushed out of the narrow opening along the jagged gash by whose side they had come.

The appearance of the vast body of water falling in one clear bound was bewildering, while the noise, as it reverberated from the rocky sides, produced a feeling of awe which made Don stand motionless till Ngati passed him, and sheltering his face behind a tuft of fern, peered round the corner they had just passed.

He withdrew his head, looking fierce and determined, signed once more to Don to follow, and went on climbing carefully along the sides of the huge pit.

"Where can he be going now?" thought Don, as he caught sight of a refulgent rainbow spanning the falls, and his eyes rested upon the brilliant, sun-illumined greens of fern, bush, and grass, with pendent mosses, all luxuriating in the heat and moisture of the wind-sheltered place.

These were but momentary glances, for his whole thoughts seemed to be taken up by the struggle for life imperilled in a hundred ways.

For still Ngati climbed on, turning every now and then to extend his hand or spear shaft to Don when the place was unusually difficult; and by this means they went on and on till first they were on a level with the side of the fall, then partially shielded by it, and at last, when the Maori paused, unable to proceed farther either up or down, they were standing upon a projecting mass of rock with the great veil of water between them and the daylight, one vast curve of hundreds of tons of greenish water falling, ever falling, into the chasm below.

It was dim with a greenish light where they stood, and the mist wetted them as they glanced sidewise along the way by which they had come, to see whether their enemies were in pursuit; but after watching for some time Ngati smiled and shook his head.

"No," he said, or seemed to say, for they could only judge by the movement of his lips. "No," and he shook his head, and seating himself, gazed calmly and placidly at the water, as if there were no such thing as danger.

In fact, to the great savage there was no such thing as peril in any of the objects of nature. Full of strength and calm matter-of-fact courage, climbing rocks or making his way into such a place as this was a very commonplace affair. His idea of danger was in the sight of enemies thirsting for his blood. Now that they were out of reach, and he believed that he had thrown them off the scent, he was perfectly content, and ready to smile at the perfection of the hiding-place he had sought.

"Can you hear me, Jem?" said Don at last, after they had

sat on the wet stones for some time, watching the falling water and listening to the thunderous roar.

"Yes, if you shout quite close?"

"Isn't it an awful place?"

"Ay, 'tis."

"Do you think we shall escape?"

"I was thinking what a good job it was that we had managed a good feed."

"How are we to get away again?"

"Dunno. P'r'aps there's another way out."

"I hope so. It will be horrible to have to go back as we came."

Jem nodded, and began to nibble the dry skin at the side of his finger nails, looking up thoughtfully at the translucent arch.

Then he nodded to Don as if he wished to speak, and Don put his ear close to Jem's lips.

"Think there's much more on it to come down?"

"More, Jem?"

"Yes. 'Cause when it's all run out, they'll be able to see us."

"I should think it is always falling like this, Jem."

"Oh!"

No more was said, and they sat patiently waiting for danger or freedom, whichever might be in store for them. Ngati held out his great fist from time to time to shake hands in a congratulatory way, and the hours glided on till it began to grow dark, and another horror assailed Don. It was evident that they must pass the night there in the cold and damp, for to attempt to escape in the dark would be madness, and how would it be if they dropped off to sleep and slipped?

He shuddered at the thought, and sat in silence gazing at Ngati, who waited calmly till the shadows of evening had quite filled the chasm, when he rose, and it was evident that he did not consider escape in the darkness impossible, for, grasping Don's arm, he uttered the one word "Come!" and led the way out from beneath the watery arch, to stand, as soon as they were quite clear, shading his eyes and gazing through the transparent gloom in search of their enemies.

Apparently satisfied, he tapped both on the shoulder, and with a shudder of dread Don followed him along the side of the gulf.

CHAPTER XLVIII.

NGATI'S DISGUISE.

THE return journey proved to be less perilous than the descent. The awful chaos of water was beneath them, but invisible, the darkness being so intense that everything was hidden but the mass of rock over and by which they climbed. In addition, the exertion and busy action after the long waiting seemed to keep them from thinking of anything but the task on which they were engaged. So that, to Don's surprise, he found himself on the outer side of the dangerous corner, with the gulf left behind, and then clambering on and on by the side of the torrent chasm, past the other perilous parts, and before he could realise the fact, they were all together on the shelf, crouching down. Here Ngati slowly raised his head, to stand gazing over the edge at the level above, watching for a long time before stooping again, and uttering a low grunt.

He mounted directly, bent down and extended a hand to each in turn, and then taking the lead, went cautiously onward to get out of the deep rift, and find a place that would enable them to reach the higher ground.

It was still dark, but not so dense but that they could pick their way, and they passed on till they reached the hot spring, a little beyond which Ngati believed that they could strike up to the left, and cross the mountain to reach the plains beyond.

Another half hour was devoted to retracing their steps, when Don stopped short, his ear being the first to detect danger.

They were passing the mud spring, whose gurgling had startled them in coming, and for a moment Don thought that a sound which he had heard came from the thin greyish-black mud; but it was repeated, and was evidently the laugh of some one not far away.

Ngati pressed their arms; and signing to them to lie down and wait, he crept onward, to be absent about a quarter of an hour, when he returned to say a few words in his native tongue, and then squat down and bury his face in his hands, as if in thought.

"They're just in front, Mas' Don. I keep hearing of 'em," whispered Jem. "Sometimes I hear 'em one way, sometimes the other."

"That is through the echoes, Jem. How are we to manage now?"

Ngati answered the question in silence, for, rising quickly, after being deep in thought, he silently picked some grass and moss, rolled it into a pear shape, and bound it on the end of his spear. Then holding the weapon up high, he bent his body in a peculiar way, and stalked off slowly, turning and gazing here and there, and from time to time lowering his spear, till, as he moved about in the shadowy light, he had all the appearance of some huge ostrich slowly feeding its way along the mountain slope.

"Moa! moa!" he whispered, as he returned. "Jemmeree moa; my pakeha moa."

"He wants us to imitate great birds, too, Jem," said Don, eagerly. "Can you do that?"

"Can I do it?" said Jem. "O' course; you shall see."

Ngati seemed delighted that his plan was understood, and he rapidly fashioned rough balls to resemble birds' heads for his companions' spears, and made them turn up their trousers above the knee, when, but for their white appearance, they both looked bird-like. But this difficulty was got over by Ngati, who took it as a matter of course that they would not object, and rapidly smeared their hands, legs, and faces with the slimy mud from the volcanic pool.

"Well, of all the nasty smells!" whispered Jem. "Oh, Mas' Don, are you going to stand this? He has filled my eyes with mud."

"Hush, Jem!" whispered Don.

"But shall we come across any hot baths by-and-by?"

"Silence, Jem!"

"All right, Mas' Don, you're master, but this is—oh, bad eggs!"

Ngati held up his hand for silence, and then whispering the word "Moa" again, he imitated the movements of a gigantic bird, signing to them to do likewise.

Don obeyed, and in spite of the peril they were in, could hardly help laughing, especially when Jem kept up an incessant growling, like that of some angry animal.

Ngati was evidently satisfied, for he paused, and then pointing forward, strode slowly through the low bushes, with Don and Jem following and imitating his movements as nearly as they could.

As they walked on they could hear the murmur of voices, and this sound increased as Ngati went slowly forward, bearing off to the left.

It seemed to Don that they were going straight into danger, and his heart beat with excitement as the talking suddenly stopped, and there was a rustling sound, as if several men had sprung to their feet.

But Ngati did not swerve from his course, going slowly on, and raising the spear from time to time, while a low excited whispering went on.

"What will they do?" thought Don; "try to spear us, or surround and seize us?"

The Maoris did neither. Ngati knew the dread his fellow-countrymen possessed for anything approaching the supernatural, and in the belief that they would be startled at the sight of the huge birds known only to them by tradition, he had boldly adopted the disguise—one possible only in the darkness; and so far his plan was successful.

To have attempted to pass in their ordinary shape meant

either capture or death; but there was the chance that they might succeed like this.

They went on in the most deliberate way, both Don and Jem following in Ngati's steps, but at every whisper on their right Don felt as if he must start off in a run; and over and over again he heard Jem utter a peculiar sigh.

A harder test of their endurance it would have been difficult to find, as in momentary expectation of a rush, they stalked slowly on, till the whispering grew more distant, and finally died away.

All at once Ngati paused to let them come up, and then pointed in the direction he intended to go, keeping up the imitation of the bird hour after hour, but not letting it interfere with their speed, till, feeling toward morning that they were safe, he once more halted, and was in the act of signing to his companions to cease their clumsy imitation, when a faint sound behind put him on his guard once more.

The task had been in vain. They had passed the Maoris, and were making for the farther side of the mountains, but their enemies had been tracking them all the night, and the moment day broke, they would see through the cunning disguise, and dash upon them at once.

They all knew this, and hastened on, as much to gain time as from any hope of escape, till just at daybreak, when, panting and exhausted, they were crossing a patch of brush, they became aware that the Maoris had overcome their alarm at the sight of the gigantic birds, and were coming on.

CHAPTER XLIX.

UNWELCOME ACQUAINTANCES.

"WE shall have to turn and fight, Mas' Don," whispered Jem, as they were labouring through the bushes. "They're close on to us. Here, why don't Ngati stop?"

There was a faint grey light beginning to steal in among the ferns as they struggled on, keeping up the imitation still, when a shout rose behind, and the Maoris made a rush to overtake them. At that moment from a dark patch of the bush in front three shots were fired in rapid succession.

Don stopped short in the faint grey light, half stunned by the echoing reverberations of the reports which rolled away like thunder, while there was a rushing noise as of people forcing their way in rapid flight through the bush. But he hardly heeded this, his attention being taken up by the way in which Ngati dropped heavily to the ground, and just behind him Jem fell as if struck by some large stone.

A terrible feeling of despair came over Don as, feeling himself between two parties of enemies, he obeyed the natural instinct which prompted him to concealment, and sank down among the ferns.

What should he do? Run for his life, or stay to help his wounded companions, and share their fate?

He stopped and listened to a peculiar sound which he knew was the forcing down of a wad in a gun-barrel. Then the strange hissing noise was continued, and he could tell by the sounds that three guns were being loaded.

The natives, as far as he knew, had no guns, therefore these must be a party of sailors sent to shoot them down; and in the horror of being seen and made the mark for a bullet, Don was about to creep cautiously into a denser part of the bush, when he stopped short, asking himself whether he was in a dream.

"All primed?" cried a hoarse voice, which made Don wonder whether he was back in his uncle's yard at Bristol.

"Ay, ay."

"Come on, then. I know I brought one of 'em down. Sha'n't want no more meat for a month."

"Say, mate, what are they?"

"I d' know. Noo Zealand turkeys, I s'pose."

"Who ever heard of turkey eight or nine foot high!" growled one of the approaching party.

"Never mind who heard of 'em; we've seen 'em and shot 'em. Hallo! where are they? Mine ought to be about here."

"More to the left, warn't it, mate?"

"Nay, it was just about here."

There was a loud rustling and heavy breathing as if men were searching here and there, and then some one spoke again—the man whose voice had startled Don.

"I say, lads, you saw me bring that big one down?"

"I saw you shoot at it, Mikey; but it don't seem as if you had brought it down. They must ha' ducked their heads, and gone off under the bushes."

"But they was too big for that."

"Nay, not they. Looked big in the mist, same as things allus do in a fog."

"I don't care; I see that great bird quite plain, and I'm sure I hit him, and he fell somewhere—hah!"

There was the sharp *click, click* of a gun being cocked, and a voice roared out,—

"Here, you, Mike Bannock, don't shoot me."

There was a loud rustling among the ferns, and then Jem shouted again.

"Mas' Don—Ngati! Why—hoi—oh! It's all right!"

The familiar voice—the name Mike Bannock, and Jem's

cheery, boyish call, made Don rise, wondering more than ever whether this was not a dream.

The day was rapidly growing lighter, and after answering Jem's hail, Don caught sight of him standing under a tree in company with three wild, gaunt-looking men.

"Mas' Don! Ahoy! Mas' Don!"

"I'm here, Jem, but mind the Maoris."

"I forgot them!" cried Jem. "Look out! There was a lot of savages arter us."

The three men darted behind trees, and stood with their guns presented in the direction of the supposed danger, Don and Jem also seeking cover and listening intently.

"Were you hit, Jem?"

"No, my lad; were you?"

"No. Where's Ngati?"

"I'm afraid he has got it, my lad. He went down like a stone."

"But Mike! how came he here?"

"I d'know, my lad. Hi! stop! Don't shoot. Friends."

Ngati, who came stalking up through the bush, spear in hand, had a narrow escape, for two guns were presented at him, and but for the energetic action of Don and Jem in striking them up, he must have been hit.

"Oh, this is a friend, is it?" said Mike Bannock, as he gave a tug at his rough beard, and turned from one to the other. "Arn't come arter me, then?"

"No, not likely," said Jem. "Had enough of you at home."

"Don't you be sarcy," growled Mike Bannock; "and lookye here, these gentlemen—friends of mine!"—he nodded sidewise at the two fierce-looking desperadoes at his side—"is very nice in their way, but they won't stand no fooling. Lookye here. How was it you come?"

"In a ship of war," said Don.

"Ho! Then where's that ship o' war now?"

"I don't know."

"No lies now," said the fellow fiercely; "one o' these here

gentlemen knocked a man on the head once for telling lies."

"Ah," growled one of the party, a short, evil-looking scoundrel, with a scar under his right eye.

"Hear that?" cried Mike Bannock. "Now, then, where's that there ship?"

"I tell you I don't know," said Don sharply.

"Whorrt!" shouted Mike, seizing Don by the throat; but the next moment a sharp blow from a spear handle made him loosen his hold, and Ngati stood between them, tall and threatening.

"Here, come on, mates, if you don't want to be took!" cried Mike, and his two companions raised the rusty old muskets they bore.

"Put them down, will yer?" cried Jem. "Lookye here, Mike Bannock: Mas' Don told you he didn't know where the ship was, and he don't. We've left her."

"Ah!" growled Mike, looking at him suspiciously. "Now, look here: don't you try none of your games on me."

"Look here!" cried Jem fiercely; "if you give me any of your impudence, Mike Bannock, I'll kick you out of the yard."

"Haw-haw!" laughed Mike. "This here arn't Bristol, little Jemmy Wimble, and I'm a free gen'leman now."

"Yes, you look it," said Don, contemptuously. "You scoundrel! How did you come here?"

"Don't call names, Mr. Don Lavington, sir," whined the ruffian. "How did I come here? Why, me and these here friends o' mine are gentlemen on our travels. Arn't us, mates."

"Ay: gen'lemen on our travels," said the more evil-looking of the pair; "and look here, youngster, if you meets any one who asks after us, and whether you've seen us, mind you arn't. Understand?"

Don looked at him contemptuously, and half turned away.

"Who was there after you?" said Mike Bannock, suspiciously.

"Some of a tribe of Maoris," replied Jem.

"No one else?"

"No."

"Ah, well, we arn't afeared of them." He patted the stock of his gun meaningly. "Soon make a tribe of them run home to their mothers. See them big birds as we shot at? And I say, young Lavington, what have you been doing to your face? Smudging it to keep off the flies?"

"'YOU'RE GOING ALONG OF US; THAT'S WHAT YOU'RE GOING TO DO'" (*p.* 382)

Don coloured through the grey mud, and involuntarily clapped his hand to his face, for he had forgotten the rough disguise.

"Never you mind about his face," said Jem grinning. "What birds?"

"Them great birds as we shot at," said Mike. "I brought one of 'em down."

"You! you couldn't hit a haystack," said Jem. "You hit no bird."

"Ask my mates!" cried Mike eagerly. "Here you, Don Lavington, you usen't to believe me when I told you 'bout big wild beasts and furrin lands. We see three birds just here, fourteen foot high."

"You always were a liar, Mike," said Don contemptuously. "You did not see any bird fourteen feet high, because there are no such things. You didn't see any birds at all."

"Well, of all——" began Mike, but he stopped short as he heard Don's next words,—

"Come, Jem! come, Ngati! Let's get on."

He stepped forward, but after a quick exchange of glances with his companions, Mike stood in his way.

"No you don't, young un; you stops along of us."

"What!" cried Don.

"We're three English gen'lemen travelling in a foreign country among strangers, and we've met you two. So we says, says we, folks here's a bit too handy with their spears, so it's as well for Englishmen when they meet to keep together, and that's what we're going to do."

"Indeed, we are not!" cried Don. "You go your way, and we'll go ours."

"That's our way," said Mike quickly. "Eh, mates?"

"Ay. That's a true word."

"Then we'll go the way you came," cried Don.

"Nay, you don't; that's our way, too."

"The country's open, and we shall go which way we like," cried Don.

"Hear, hear, Mas' Don!" cried Jem.

"You hold your tongue, old barrel cooper!" cried Mike. "You're going along of us; that's what you're going to do."

"That we are not!" cried Don.

"Oh, yes, you are, so no nonsense. We've got powder and shot, and you've only got spears, and one gun's equal to fifty spears."

"Look here, sir!" cried Don sternly, "I don't want any

words with such a man as you. Show me the way you want to take, and we'll go another."

"This here's the way," said Mike menacingly. "This is the way we're going, and you've got to come with us."

"Jem; Ngati; come on," said Don.

"Oh, then you mean to fight, do you?" growled Mike. "Come on then, mates. I think we can give 'em a lesson there."

"Mas' Don," whispered Jem, "it's no good to fight again guns, and my shoulder's a reg'lar dummy. Let's give in civil, and go with them. We'll get away first chance, and it do make us six again' any savages who may come."

"Savages!" said Don angrily; "why, where would you get such savages as these? The Maoris are gentlemen compared to them."

"That's my 'pinion again, Mas' Don; but we'd better get on."

"But why do they want us with them?"

"Strikes me they're 'fraid we shall tell on them."

"Tell on them?"

"Yes; it's my belief as Master Mike's been transported, and that he's contrived to get away with these two."

"And we are to stop with three such men as these?"

"Well, they arn't the sort of chaps I should choose, Mas' Don; but they say they're gen'lemen, so we must make the best of it. All right, Mike, we're coming."

"That's your sort. Now, then, let's find my big bird, and then I'm with you."

"Yah! there's no big bird," said Jem. "We was the birds, shamming so as to get away from the savages."

"Then you may think yourself precious lucky you weren't shot. Come on."

Mike led the way, and Don and his companions followed, the two rough followers of Mike Bannock coming behind with their guns cocked.

"Pleasant that, Mas' Don," said Jem. "Like being prisoners again. But they can't shoot."

"Why did you say that, Jem?" said Don anxiously.

"Because we're going to make a run for it before long, eh, my pakeha?"

"My pakeha," said Ngati, laying his hand on Don's shoulder, and he smiled and looked relieved, for the proceedings during the last half hour had puzzled him.

Don took the great fellow's arm, feeling that in the Maori chief he had a true friend, and in this way they followed Mike Bannock round one of the shoulders of the mountain, towards where a jet of steam rose with a shrieking noise high up into the air.

CHAPTER L.

HOW TO ESCAPE?

IT was in quite a little natural fortress that Mike stopped, the way being in and out through a narrow rift that must have been the result of some earthquake, and when this was passed they were in a sheltered nook, at one side of which the face of a precipice hung right over, affording ample protection from the wind and rain. Through quite a cranny a stream of perfectly clear water trickled, and on the other side was a small deep pool, slowly welling over at one side, the steam rising therefrom telling that it was in some way connected with the noisy jet which rose outside.

"There, young Don Lavington, that's where we lives, my lad, and you've got to stay with us. If you behave well, you shall have plenty to eat and drink. If you don't, mind one o' my mates don't bring you down as he would a bird."

Don glanced round wonderingly, and tried to grasp why it was that Mike Bannock was there, the only surmise upon which he could take hold being the right one—Jem's: that Mike was a transported man who had taken to the bush.

He had just come to this conclusion when Jem turned to him.

"Shall I ask him that, Mas' Don?"

"Ask him what?"

"What I think. Depend upon it he was sent out to Botany Bay, and run off to this country."

"No, no, Jem; don't ask."

"He can't have come out here honest, Mas' Don. Look at him, there arn't a honest hair in his head."

"But we don't want to offend him, Jem."

"Don't we? Tell you what we do want, Mas' Don; we want to get hold o' them old rusty muskets and the powder and shot, and then we could make them sing small. Eh? What say?"

This was in answer to something said in a low voice by Ngati, who looked from one to the other inquiringly.

Ngati spoke again, and then struck his fist into his hand with a look of rage and despair.

"Yes, I feel the same," said Don, laying his hand upon the great fellow's arm. "I'd give anything to be able to understand what you say, Ngati."

The chief smiled, as if he quite comprehended; and grasped Don's hand with a friendly grip, offering the other to Jem.

"It's all right, old boy," said the latter. "We can't understand each other's lingo, but we know each other's hearts. We've got to wait a bit and see."

* * * * *

A week passed rapidly away, during which, in his rougher moods, Mike treated his prisoners as if they were slaves, calling upon Ngati to perform the most menial offices for the little camp, all of which were patiently performed after an appealing look at Don, who for the sake of gaining time gave up in every way.

Jem grumbled, but he did what he was told, for the slightest appearance of resistance was met by a threatening movement with the muskets, which never left the men's hands.

They were fairly supplied with food; fish from the streams and from a good-sized lake, Ngati proving himself to be an adept at capturing the large eels, and at discovering fresh supplies of fruit and roots.

But in a quiet way, as he watched his English companions like a dog, he always seemed to comprehend their wishes, and to be waiting the time when they should call upon him to fly at their tyrants and then help them to escape.

"Didn't know I was coming out to look after you, did you, young Don?" said Mike one evening. "King sent me out o' purpose. Told one of the judges to send me out here, and here I am; and I've found you, and I ought to take you home, but I won't. You always liked furrin countries, and I'm going to keep you here."

"What for?" said Don.

"To make you do for me what I used to do for you. I was your sarvant; now you're mine. Ups and downs in life we see. Now you're down and I'm up; and what d'yer think o' that, Jem Wimble?"

"Think as you was transported, and that you've took to the bush."

"Oh, do you?" said Mike, grinning. "Well, never mind; I'm here, and you're there, and you've got to make the best of it."

To make the best of it was not easy. The three convicts, after compelling their prisoners to make the resting-place they occupied more weather-proof and warm, set them to make a lean-to for themselves, to which they were relegated, but without arms, Mike Bannock having on the first day they were at work taken possession of their weapons.

"You won't want them," he said, with an ugly grin; "we'll do the hunting and fighting, and you three shall do the work."

Jem uttered a low growl, at which Mike let the handle of one of the spears fall upon his shoulder, and as Jem fiercely seized it, three muskets were presented at his head.

"Oh, all right," growled Jem, with a menacing look.

"Yes, it's all right, Jem Wimble. But look here, don't you or either of you cut up rough; for if you do, things may go very awkward."

"I should like to make it awkward for them, Mas' Don,' whispered Jem, as the convicts turned away; "but never mind, I can wait."

They did wait, day after day, working hard, ill fed, and suffering endless abuse, and often blows, which would have been resented by Ngati, but for a look from Don; and night by night, as they gathered together in their little lean-to hut, with a thick heap of fern leaves for their bed their conversation was on the same subject—how could they get the muskets and spears, and escape.

There was no further alarm on the part of the Maoris, who seemed, after they had been discouraged in their pursuit, and startled by the guns, to have given up all intention of recapturing the escaped prisoners.

"If we could only get the guns and spears, Jem," said Don one evening for the hundredth time.

"Yes, and I'd precious soon have them," replied Jem; "only they're always on the watch."

"Yes, they're too cunning to leave them for a moment. Was any one ever before so unlucky as we are?"

"Well, if you come to that," said Jem, "yes. Poor old Tomati, for one; and it can't be very nice for Ngati here, who has lost all his tribe."

Ngati looked up sharply, watching them both intently in the gloomy cabin.

"But he don't seem to mind it so very much."

"What do you say to escaping without spears?"

"Oh, I'm willing," replied Jem; "only I wouldn't be in too great a hurry. Those chaps wouldn't mind having a shot at us again, and this time they might hit."

"What shall we do then?"

"Better wait, Mas' Don. This sort o' thing can't last. We shall soon eat up all the fruit, and then they'll make a move, and we may have a better chance."

Don sighed and lay with his eyes half closed, watching one particular star which shone in through the doorway.

But not for long. The star seemed to grow misty as if veiled by a cloud; then it darkened altogether; so it seemed to Don, for the simple reason that he had fallen fast asleep.

It appeared only a minute since he was gazing at the star before he felt a hand pressed across his mouth, and with a horrible dread of being smothered, he uttered a hoarse, stifled cry, and struggled to get free; but another hand was pressed upon his chest, and it seemed as if the end had come.

CHAPTER LI.

NGATI'S GOAL.

JUST as in the case of a dream, a long space of time in the face of a terrible danger seems to pass in what is really but a few moments. Don, in an agony of apprehension, was struggling against the hands which held him, when a deep voice whispered in his ear,—

"My pakeha."

"Ngati!"

Don caught the hands in his, and sat up slowly, while the chief awakened Jem in the same manner, and with precisely the same result.

"Why, I thought it was Mike Bannock trying to smother me," grumbled Jem, sitting up. "What's the matter?"

"I don't know, Jem. Ngati just woke me in the dark, and—— Oh! Ngati!"

His hands trembled, and a curious feeling of excitement coursed through his veins, as at that moment he felt the stock of a gun pressed into his hands, Jem exclaiming the next moment as he too clasped a gun,

"But there arn't no powder and—— Yes, there is."

Jem ceased speaking, for he had suddenly felt that there was a belt and pouch attached to the gun barrel, and without another word he slipped the belt over his shoulder.

"What do you mean, Ngati?" whispered Don hastily.

"Go!" was the laconic reply; and in an instant the lad realised that the Maori had partly comprehended his words that evening, had thought out the full meaning, and then crept silently to the convicts' den, and secured the arms.

Don rose excitedly to his feet.

"The time has come, Jem," he whispered.

"Yes, and I dursen't shout hooroar!"

Ngati was already outside, waiting in the starlight; and as Don stepped out quickly with his heart beating and a sense of suffocation at the throat, he could just make out that the Maori held the third musket, and had also three spears under his arm.

He handed one of the latter to each, and then stood listening for a few moments with his head bent in the direction of the convicts' resting-place.

The steam jet hissed, and the vapour rose like a dim spectral form; the water gurgled and splashed faintly, but there was no other sound, and, going softly in the direction of the opening, Ngati led the way.

"We must leave it to him, Jem, and go where he takes us," whispered Don.

"Can't do better," whispered back Jem. "Wait just a moment till I get this strap o' the gun over my shoulder. It's awkward to carry both gun and spear."

"Wait till we get farther away, Jem."

Crash! a flash of fire, and a report which echoed like thunder from the face of the rocks.

Jem, in passing the sling of the musket over his head, had let it fall upon the stones with disastrous effect.

"Run, Mas' Don; never mind me."

"Are you hurt?"

"Dunno."

Jem was in a stooping posture as he spoke, but he rose directly, as there was a rush heard in the direction of the convicts' lair, and catching Don's hand they ran off stealthily after Ngati, who had returned, and then led the way once more.

Not a word was spoken, and after the first rush and the scramble and panting of men making for the rocks, all was very still. Ngati led on, passing in and out among tree and bush, and mass of rock, as if his eyes were quite accustomed to the darkness, while, big as he was, his bare feet made no more sound than the paws of a cat.

Both Don and Jem followed as silently as they could, but they could not help catching against the various obstacles, and making noises which produced a warning "Hssh!" from their leader.

As they passed on they listened intently for sounds of pursuit, but for awhile there were none; the fact being that at the sound of the shot the convicts believed that they were attacked, and rushing out, they made for the mountain. But as no further shots were heard, they grew more bold, and, after waiting listening for awhile, they stole back to the shed that should have been occupied by Don and his friends; where, finding them gone, they hurried into their own place, found that the arms were taken, and, setting up a shout, dashed off in pursuit.

The shout sent a shiver through Don and Jem, for it sounded terribly near, and they hurried on close to the heels of Ngati, forgetful for the moment of the fact that they were armed, and their pursuers were weaponless.

After a time the sounds from the camp, which had been heard plainly on the night wind, ceased, and for the first time Don questioned Jem as to his injury.

"Where are you hurt, Jem?"

"Shoulder," said that worthy, laconically.

"Again?"

"No; not again."

"But I mean when the gun went off."

"In my head, Mas' Don."

"Ah! we might stop now. Let me bind it up for you."

"No, no; it don't bleed," replied Jem, gruffly. "I mean hurt inside my head, 'cause I could be such a stoopid as to let this here gun fall."

"Then you are not wounded?"

"Not a bit, my lad; and if you'll stop now, I think I'll try and load again."

But Ngati insisted on pushing on, and kept up a steady

walk right south in the direction of the star which had shone in through the doorway.

It was weary work, for the night was very black beneath the trees, but every step was taking them farther from their enemies, and though they stopped to listen again and again, they heard no sound of pursuit.

Morning dawned at last, bringing light to their spirits as well as to their eyes; and for three days they travelled on due south by mountain and lake, hot spring and glorious valley, now catching a glimpse of the sea, now losing it again.

Ngati seemed to have some definite object which he could not explain; and when Don tried to question him, the great fellow only laughed and trudged on.

They did not fare badly, for fruit, roots, and wild fowl were plentiful, fish could be obtained, and with glorious weather, and the dying out of the pain of their wounds, the journey began to be pleasant.

"There's only one thing I'm afraid of, Mas' Don,' said Jem; "and that is that those convicts will smell us out."

But as time went on that fear grew less, and just at sunset one evening, as Ngati turned the shoulder of one of the mountains and stood pointing, Don set up a shout which Jem echoed, for there beneath them in a valley, and about a quarter of a mile from the shimmering sea, lay a cluster of cottages, such as could only have been built by Europeans, and they realised now what had been the Maori's thoughts in bringing them there.

CHAPTER LII.

DON HAS A HEADACHE.

"ESCAPED from the Maoris, and then from a party of men you think were runaway convicts?" said the broad-shouldered, sturdy occupant of the little farm which they reached just at dusk. "Ah, well, we can talk about that tomorrow, my lads. It's enough for me that you are Englishmen. Come in."

"I cannot leave our friend," said Don quietly, as he laid his hand on Ngati's arm.

"What, the savage!" said the farmer, rubbing his ear. "Well, we—oh, if he's your friend, that's enough."

They had no occasion to complain of the hospitality, for the farmer, who had been settled there, with a few companions only, for about four years, was but too glad to see fresh faces, and with a delicacy hardly to be expected from one leading so rough a life he refrained from asking any questions.

Don was glad, for the next morning he rose with a peculiar aching sensation in the head, accompanied by alternate fits of heat and cold.

The next day he was worse, but he kept it to himself, laughing it off when they noticed that he did not eat his breakfast, and, to avoid further questioning, he went out after a time to wander up the valley into the shady woodland and among the tree-ferns, hoping that the rest and cool shadowy calm of the primæval forest would prove restful and refreshing.

The day was glorious, and Don lay back listening to the cries of the birds, dreaming of home, and at times dozing off to sleep after his restless night,

His head ached terribly, and was confused, and at times, as he lay back resting against a tuft of fern, he seemed to be back at Bristol; then in an instant he thought he must be in the Maoris' *pah*, wondering whether there could be any truth in Jem's fancies as to why they were being kept.

Then there was a dull time of blank weariness, during which he saw nothing, till he seemed to be back in the convicts' lurking-place, and he saw Mike Bannock thrusting his head out from among the leaves, his face brown and scarred, and eyes glistening, as he looked from place to place.

It was all so real that Don expected to see the scoundrel step out into the open, followed by his two companions.

And this did happen a few minutes later. Mike Bannock, armed with a heavy club, and followed by his two brothers in crime, crept out. Then it seemed to be no longer the convicts' home, and Don started from his dreamy state, horrified at what he saw, for the scoundrels had not seen him, and were going cautiously toward the little settlement, whose occupants were all away hunting, fishing, and attending to their crops. Don alone was close at hand, and he in so semi-delirious and helpless a state, that when he tried to rise he felt as if it would be impossible to warn his friends of their danger, and prevent these ruffians from making their descent upon the pleasant little homes around.

An acute pain across the brows made Don close his eyes, and when he re-opened them his head was throbbing, his mind confused, and as he looked hastily round, and could see nothing but the beautiful verdant scene, he felt that he had been deceived, and as if the figures that had passed out of the dense undergrowth had been merely creatures of his imagination.

He still gazed wildly about, but all was peaceful, and not a sound save the birds' notes fell upon the ear.

"It must have been fancy," he thought. "Where is Jem?"

He sank back again in a strangely excited state, for the idea that, in his fleeing to this peaceful place, he had been the means of bringing three desperate men to perhaps rob, and murder, and destroy, where all was repose and peace, was too terrible to bear.

One minute he was certain that it was all fancy, just as he had dreamed again and again of Mike and his ruffianly companions; the next he was as sure that what he had seen was real.

"I'll go and find some one," he said hastily; and, rising feebly to his feet, he set off for the farm, but only to catch wildly at the trees to save himself from falling.

The vertigo passed off as quickly as it came on.

"How absurd!" he said, with a faint laugh. "A moment's giddiness. That's all."

He started again, but everything sailed round, and he sank upon the earth with a groan to try and make out whether it was all fancy or a dream.

In a moment he seemed to be back at home with a bad headache, and his mother passing softly to and fro, while Kitty, full of sympathy, kept soaking handkerchiefs in vinegar and water to cool his heated brow.

Then, as he lay with his eyes tightly closed, Uncle Josiah came into the room, and laid his hand pityingly upon his shoulder.

Don gazed up at him, to see that it was Ngati's hideously tattooed countenance close to his, and he looked up confused and wondering at the great chief.

Then the recollection of the convicts came back, and a spasm of horror shot through his brain.

If it was true, what would happen at the little farm?

He raised himself upon his elbow, and pointed in the direction of the house.

"Ngati," he said excitedly, "danger!"

The chief looked at him, then in the direction in which he pointed; but he could understand nothing, and Don felt as if he were trying to get some great dog to comprehend his wishes.

He had learned scores of Maori words, but now that he

wanted to use them, some would not come, and others would not fit.

"Ngati!" he cried again piteously, as he pointed toward the farm, "pakehas—bad pakehas."

The chief could understand pakehas—white men, but he was rather hazy about bad, whether it did not mean good, and he gave a low grunt.

"Bad pakehas. Fight. Jem," panted Don.

Ngati could see that something was wrong, but in his mind it seemed to be connected with his English friend's health, and he laid his hand upon Don's burning brow.

"Bad pakehas—go!" cried Don. "What shall I do? How am I to make him understand? Pakehas. Jem. Help!"

At that Ngati seemed to have a glimmering of what his companion meant, and nodding quickly, he went off at a trot toward the farm.

"He'll bring some one who can understand," said Don to himself; and then he began to feel that, after all, it was a dream consequent upon his being so ill, and he lay back feeling more at ease, but only to jump up and stare wildly toward where the farm lay.

For, all at once, there rose a shout, and directly after a shot was heard, followed by another and another.

Then all was still for a few minutes, till, as Don lay gazing wildly toward where he had seen Ngati disappear, he caught sight of a stooping figure, then of another and another, hurrying to reach cover; and as he recognised the convicts, he could make out that each man carried a gun.

He was holding himself up by grasping the bough of a tree, and gazing wildly at Mike and his brutal-looking friends; but they were looking in the direction of the farm as they passed, and they did not see him.

Then the agonising pain in his head seemed to rob him of the power to think, and he sank back among the ferns.

Don had some consciousness of hearing voices, and of feeling hands touching him; but it was all during a time of

"'NGATI,' HE SAID EXCITEDLY, 'DANGER!'" (p. 395).

confusion, and when he looked round again with the power to think, he was facing a tiny unglazed window, the shutter which was used to close it standing below.

He was lying on a rough bed formed of sacking spread over dried fern leaves, and the shed he was in had for furniture a rough table formed by nailing a couple of pieces of board across a tub, another tub with part of the side sawn out formed an armchair; and the walls were ornamented with bunches of seeds tied up and hung there for preservation, a saddle and bridle, and some garden rools neatly arranged in a corner.

Don lay wondering what it all meant, his eyes resting longest upon the open window, through which he could see the glorious sunshine, and the leaves moving in the gentle breeze.

He felt very happy and comfortable, but when he tried to raise his head the effort was in vain, and this set him wondering again, till he closed his eyes and lay thinking.

Suddenly he unclosed them again to lie listening, feeling the while that he had been asleep, for close beside him there was some one whistling in a very low tone—quite a whisper of a whistle—a familiar old Somersetshire melody, which seemed to carry him back to the sugar yard at Bristol, where he had heard Jem whistle that tune a score of times.

This set him thinking of home, his mother, and Cousin Kitty. Then of stern-looking Uncle Josiah, who, after all, did not seem to have been unkind.

"Poor Mas' Don! Will he ever get well again?" a voice whispered close to his ear.

"Jem!"

"Oh, Mas' Don! Oh! oh! oh! Thank the great Lord o' mussy. Amen! amen! amen!"

There was the sound of some one going down heavily upon his knees, a pair of clasped hands rested on Don's breast; and, as he turned his eyes sidewise, he could see the top of Jem's head as the bed shook, and there was the sound of some one sobbing violently, but in a choking, smothered way.

"Jem! Is that you? What's the matter?" whispered Don feebly.

"And he says, 'What's the matter?'" cried Jem, raising his head, and bending over Don. "Dear lad, dear lad; how are you now?"

"Quite well, thank you, Jem, only I can't lift up my head."

"And don't you try, Mas' Don. Oh, the Lord be thanked! the Lord be thanked!" he muttered. "What should I ha' done?"

"Have—have I been ill, Jem?"

"Ill, Mas' Don? Why, I thought you was going to die, and no doctor, not even a drop of salts and senny to save your life."

"Oh, nonsense, Jem! I never thought of doing such a thing! Ah, I remember now. I felt poorly. My head was bad."

"Your head bad? I should think it was bad. Dear lad, what stuff you have been saying."

"Have I, Jem? What, since I lay down among the ferns this morning?"

"This morning, Mas' Don! Why, it's close upon a month ago."

"What?"

"That's so, my lad. We come back from cutting wood to find you lying under a tree, and when we got here it was to find poor old 'my pakeha' with a shothole in him, and his head all beaten about with big clubs."

"Oh, Jem!"

"That's so, Mas' Don."

"Is he better?"

"Oh, yes; he's getting better. I don't think you could kill him. Sort o' chap that if you cut him to pieces some bit or another would be sure to grow again."

"Why, it was Mike Bannock and those wretches, Jem."

"That's what we thought, my lad, but we couldn't find out. It was some one, and whoever it was took away three guns."

"I saw them, Jem."

"You see 'em?"

"Yes, as I lay back with my head so bad that I couldn't be sure."

"Ah, well, they found us out, and they've got their guns again; but they give it to poor Ngati awful."

Just then the window was darkened by a hideous-looking face, which disappeared directly. Then steps were heard, and the great chief came in, bending low to avoid striking his head against the roof till he reached the rough bedside, where he bent over Don, and patted him gently, saying softly, "My pakeha."

CHAPTER LIII.

DON SPEAKS OUT.

A HEALTHY young constitution helped Don Lavington through his perilous illness, and in another fortnight he was about the farm, helping in any little way he could.

"I'm very sorry, Mr. Gordon," said Don one evening to the young settler.

"Sorry? What for, my lad?" he said.

"For bringing those convicts after us to your place, and for being ill and giving you so much trouble."

"Nonsense, my lad! I did begin to grumble once when I thought you were going to be ungrateful to me for taking you in."

"Ungrateful!"

"Yes, ungrateful, and trying to die."

"Oh!" said Don smiling.

"Nice mess I should have been in if you had. No church, no clergyman, no doctor, no sexton. Why, you young dog, it would have been cruel."

Don smiled sadly.

"I am really very grateful, sir; I am indeed, and I think by to-morrow or next day I shall be strong enough to go."

"What, and leave me in the lurch just as I'm so busy! Why, with the thought of having you fellows here, I've been fencing in pieces and making no end of improvements. That big Maori can cut down as much wood as two men, and as for Jem Wimble, he's the handiest fellow I ever saw."

"I am very glad they have been of use, sir. I wish I could be."

"You're right enough, boy. Stop six months—a year—altogether—and I shall be very glad of your help."

This set Don at rest, and he brightened up wonderfully, making great strides during the next fortnight, and feeling almost himself, till, one evening as he was returning from where he had been helping Jem and Ngati cut up wood for fencing, he fancied he saw some animal creeping through the ferns. A minute's watching convinced him that this was a fact, but he could not make out what it was. Soon after, as they were seated at their evening meal, he mentioned what he had seen.

"One of the sheep got loose," said Gordon.

"No, it was not a sheep."

"Well, what could it have been? There are no animals here, hardly, except the pigs which have run wild."

"It looked as big as a sheep, but it was not a pig," said Don thoughtfully. "Could it have been a man going on all fours?"

"Hullo! What's the matter?" cried Gordon looking up sharply, as one of his two neighbours came to the door with his wife.

"Well, I doan't know," said the settler. "My wife says she is sure she saw a savage creeping along through the bush behind our place."

"There!" said Don excitedly.

"Here's t'others coming," said Jem.

For at that moment the other settler, whose log-house was a hundred yards below, came up at a trot, gun in hand, in company with his wife and sister.

"Here, look sharp, Gordon," he said; "there's a party out on a raid. We came up here, for we had better join hands."

"Of course," said Gordon. "Come in; but I think you are frightening yourselves at shadows, and——"

He stopped short, for Jem Wimble dashed at the door and banged it to just as Ngati sprang to the corner of the big log kitchen and caught up a spear

"Mike and them two beauties, Mas' Don!" cried Jem.

"Then it's war, is it?" said Gordon grimly, as he reconnoitred from the window. "Eight—ten—twelve—about thirty Maori savages, and three white ones. Hand round the guns, Don Lavington. You can shoot, can't you?"

"Yes, a little."

"That's right. Can we depend on Ngati? If we can't, he'd better go."

"I'll answer for him," said Don.

"All right!" said Gordon. "Look here, Ngati,"—he pointed out of the window and then tapped the spear—"bad pakehas, bad—bad, kill."

Ngati grunted, and his eyes flashed.

"Kill pakehas—bad pakehas," he said in a deep, fierce voice. "Kill!" Then tapping the Englishmen one by one on the shoulder, "Pakeha good," he said smiling, and then taking Don by the arm, "My pakeha," he added.

"That's all right, sir," said Jem; "he understands."

"Now then, quick! Make everything fast. We can keep them out so long as they don't try fire. And look here, I hate bloodshed, neighbours, but those convict scoundrels have raised these poor savages up against us for the sake of plunder. Recollect, we are fighting for our homes—to defend the women."

A low, angry murmur arose as the guns were quickly examined, ammunition placed ready, and the rough, strong door barricaded with boxes and tubs, the women being sent up a rough ladder through a trap-door to huddle together in the roof, where they would be in safety.

"So long as they don't set us afire, Mas' Don," whispered Jem.

"What's that?" said Gordon sharply.

"Jem fears fire," said Don.

"So do I, my lad, so we must keep them at a distance; and if they do fire us run all together to the next house, and defend that."

Fortunately for the defenders of the place there were but three windows, and they were small, and made good loopholes from which to fire when the enemy came on. The settlers defended the front of the house, and Don, Jem and Ngati were sent to the back, greatly to Jem's disappointment.

"We sha'n't see any of the fun, Mas' Don," he whispered, and then remained silent, for a shout arose, and they recognised the voice as that of Mike Bannock.

"Now then you," he shouted, "open the door, and give in quietly. If you do, you sha'n't be hurt. If you make a fight of it, no one will be left alive."

"Look here!" shouted back Gordon; "I warn you all that the first man who comes a step farther may lose his life. Go on about your business before help comes and you are caught."

"No help for a hundred miles, matey," said the savage-looking convict; "so give in. We want all you've got there, and what's more, we mean to have it. Will you surrender?"

For answer Gordon thrust out his gun-barrel, and the convicts drew back a few yards, and conversed together before disappearing with their savage followers into the bush.

"Have we scared them off?" said Gordon to one of the settlers, after ten minutes had passed without a sign.

"I don't know," said the other. "I can't help thinking——"

"Look out, Mas' Don!"

Bang! bang!

Two reports from muskets at the back of the house, where the attacking party had suddenly shown themselves, thinking it the weakest part; and after the two shots about a dozen Maoris dashed at the little window, and tried to get in, forcing their spears through to keep the defenders at a distance; and had not Ngati's spear played its part, darting swiftly about like the sting of some monster, the lithe, active fellows would soon have forced their way in.

Directly after, the fight began at the front, the firing growing hot, and not without effect, for one of the settlers went down with a musket bullet in his shoulder, and soon after

Gordon stood back, holding his arm for Don to bind it up with a strip off a towel.

"Only a spear prick," he said coolly, as he took aim with his gun directly after; and for about an hour the fight raged fiercely, with wounds given and taken, but no material advantage on either side.

"Be careful and make every shot tell," said Gordon, as it was rapidly growing dark; then backing to the inner door as he reloaded, he spoke for a few seconds to Don.

"We shall beat them off, sir," said Don cheerily.

"Yes, I hope so, my lad," said the settler calmly. "You see you are of great use."

"No, sir; it's all my fault," replied Don.

"Mas' Don," whispered Jem, as Don returned, "look out of the window; mind the spears; then tell me what you see."

"Fire!" said Don after a momentary examination.

He was quite right. A fire had been lit in the forest at the back, and ten minutes after, as Mike Bannock's voice could be heard cheering them, the Maoris came on, hurling burning branches on to the roof of the little log-house.

For a few minutes there was no result. Then there arose a yell, for the roof had caught, the resinous pine burned strongly, the smoke began to curl in between the rafters, and the women were helped down.

To extinguish the flames was impossible, and would even have been as vain a task had they been outside ready with water.

"How long will she last before she comes down?" said one of the settlers.

"We can stop in here for a quarter, perhaps half an hour longer," said Gordon; "and then we must make a dash for your place."

"Yes," said the settler, "and they know it. Look!"

By the increasing light from the burning house, the savages could be seen with their white leaders preparing for a rush.

Just then Don and his two companions were forced to leave

the little lean-to, whose roof was burning furiously, and it was only by closing the rough door of communication that the besieged were able to remain in the big kitchen.

"It won't last five minutes, my lads," said Gordon. "Be ready, women. I'll throw open the door. We men will rush out and form up. You women run down to the right and make for Smith's. We shall give them a volley to check them, and run after you."

"Ready?"

"Ay."

"All loaded?"

"Ay," came in a deep despairing growl.

"Down with these boxes and tubs then. You, Don, you are young and weak; go with the women."

"No," said Don; "I shall go with you men."

"Brayvo, Mas' Don!" whispered Jem. "What a while they are opening that door! We shall be roasted, my lad, after all, and these wretches 'll pick our bones."

The door was flung open, and the enemy uttered a yell of delight as the little party of whites ran out of the burning house.

"Now, women!" cried Gordon.

"No: stop!" roared Don.

Crash!

A heavy volley from the right, and the besiegers made a rush for the left.

Crash!

A heavy volley met them on the left, fired diagonally from half behind the blazing house.

Then there was a cheer, echoed by a second, and two parties of blue jackets were in among the Maoris, who fled, leaving half their number wounded and prisoners on the ground, while Don and his friends helped the women out into the open, away from the signs of bloodshed, which looked horrible in the light from the blazing house.

"A little too late," said the officer in command of the detachment.

"Too late to save my house, sir, but in time to save our lives," said Gordon, grasping his hand.

"I wish I had been sooner; but it's rough work travelling through the bush, and we should not have come, only we heard the shouting, and saw the glow of your burning house."

No time was lost in trying to extinguish the fire after a guard had been set over the prisoners, the men under the officers' orders working hard with the few buckets at command; but the place was built of inflammable pine, which flared up fiercely, and after about a quarter of an hour's effort Gordon protested against further toil.

"It's of no use, sir," he said. "All labour in vain. I've not lost much, for my furniture was only home made."

"I'm sorry to give up, but it is useless," said the officer.

Jem crept close up to his companion.

"I say, Mas' Don, I thought it was some of our chaps from the sloop at first, but they're from the *Vixen* frigate. Think they'll find us out?"

"I hope not, Jem," replied Don; "surely they will not press us again."

"Let's be off into the bush till they're gone."

"No," said Don; "I'm sorry I left the ship as I did. We will not run away again."

Meanwhile preparations were made for bivouacking, the officer determining to rest where they were that night; and after seeing his men stored in two of the barns, and sentries placed over the prisoners in another, at one of the settlers' places, one log house being given up to the wounded, he joined the little English gathering, where the settlers' wives, as soon as the danger was past, had prepared a comfortable meal.

After an uneventful night, the morning broke cheerily over the tiny settlement, where the only trace of the attack was at Gordon's, whose rough log-house was now a heap of smoking ashes.

The sailors had breakfasted well, thanks to the settlers' wives, and were now drawn up, all but the prisoners' guard, while the officer stood talking to Gordon and his neighbours with Don and Jem standing close by; for in spite of Jem's reiterated appeals, his companion refused to take to the bush.

"No, Jem," Don said stubbornly; "it would be cowardly, and we're cowards enough."

"But s'pose they find us out? That there officer's sure to smell as we're salts."

"Smell? Nonsense!"

"He will, Mas' Don. I'm that soaked with Stockholm tar that I can smell myself like a tub."

"Nonsense!"

"But if they find out as we deserted, they'll hang us."

"I don't believe it, Jem."

"Well, you'll see, Mas' Don; so if they hang you, don't you blame me."

"Well, Mr. Gordon, we must be off," said the officer. "Thank you once more for all your hospitality."

"God bless you, sir, and all your men, for saving our lives," said the settler warmly; and there was a chorus of thanks from the other settlers and their wives.

"Nonsense, my dear sir; only our duty!" said the officer heartily. "And now about our prisoners. I don't know what to do about the Maoris. I don't want to shoot them, and I certainly don't want to march them with us down to where the ship lies. What would you do, Mr. Gordon?"

"I should give them a knife apiece, shake hands with them, and let them go."

"What, to come back with the said knives, and kill you all when we're gone!"

"They will not come back if you take away the scoundrels who led them on," said Don sharply.

"How do you know?" said the officer good-humouredly.

"Because," said Don, colouring, "I have been living a good deal with them, both with a friendly tribe and as a prisoner."

"And they did not eat you?" said the officer laughing.

"There, Mas' Don," whispered Jem, "hear that?"

"I think you are right, youngster," continued the officer, "and I shall do so. Mr. Dillon, bring up the prisoners."

This was to a master's mate, who led off a guard, and returned with the captives bound hands behind, and the Maoris looking sullen and haughty, while the three whites appeared at their very worst—a trio of the most vile, unkempt scoundrels possible to see.

They were led to the front, scowling at every one in turn, and halted in front of the officer, who, after whispering to the master's mate, gave orders to one of the seamen. This man pulled out his great jack knife, opened it, and being a bit of a joker, advanced toward the Maoris, grinding his teeth and rolling his eyes.

The savages saw his every act, and there was a slight tremor that seemed to run through them all; but the next instant they had drawn themselves up stern and defiant, ready to meet their fate at the seaman's knife.

"No, no. No, pakeha. No kill," said a deep angry voice; and as every one turned, Ngati stalked forward as if to defend his enemies.

But at the same moment the man had cut the first Maori's bands, and then went on behind the rank, cutting the line that bound seven, who stood staring wildly.

The next minute a seaman came along bearing a sheaf of spears, which he handed, one by one, to the astonished savages, while their wonder reached its height, as the master's mate presented to each a knife, such as were brought for presents to the natives.

"Now," said the officer, addressing them, "I don't understand you, and I don't suppose you understand my words; but you do my deeds. Then, in the king's name, you are free; and if you ever take any English prisoners, I hope you will behave as well to them as we have behaved to you. There, go."

He finished by pointing away to the north; but instead of going they stood staring till Ngati came forward, and said a few words in their own tongue.

The effect was electric; they all shouted, brandished their spears, danced wildly, and ended by throwing down their weapons before the officer, seizing him by the arms, and rubbing noses with him.

He submitted laughingly till the Maoris picked up their spears, and stood looking on, apparently quite satisfied that they were safe.

"Here, hi, Jack!" cried a hoarse brutal voice. "Look sharp, we want to get rid of these cords; where's your knife?"

"Wait a little while, my friends," said the officer sarcastically; "as soon as we get to the ship, you shall have them changed for irons."

"Whorrt!" cried Mike.

"We were out in search of three convicts who murdered a couple of the guard, and escaped from Norfolk Island in a boat. I have fallen upon you by accident, and I have you safe."

"Norfolk Island! Where's Norfolk Island, mate?" said Mike coolly.

"Never heard o' no such place," said his vilest-looking companion, gruffly.

"Memory's short, perhaps," said the officer.

"But convicts; we're not convicts," growled Mike.

"Gentlemen, p'r'aps, on your travels?"

"Yes, that's it," said Mike with effrontery.

"Ah! well then, I shall have to take you on board His Majesty's ship *Vixen*, where you will probably be hung at the yard arm for inciting the ignorant Maoris to attack peaceful settlers. Forward, my lads!"

"Here, stop!" roared Mike with a savage grin.

"What for?" said the officer sternly.

"Arn't you going to take them, too?"

"Take whom—the Maoris? No; but for you they would have let these people be in peace. Forward!"

"No, no; I mean them two," said Mike savagely, as he pointed—"them two: Don Lavington and Jem Wimble."

"Halt!" cried the officer. "Do you know these men?" he said suspiciously.

"There, I told you so, Mas Don," whispered Jem.

"I know that man," said Don firmly. "I only know the others by their making us prisoners out in the bush."

"Where did you know him?" said the officer—"Norfolk Island?"

"No, sir; at Bristol. He worked as labourer in my uncle's yard."

"That's right enough," said Mike; "and him and Jem Wimble was pressed, and went to sea."

"Ay, ay!" said the officer quickly.

"And they deserted, and took to the bush."

"Hah!" ejaculated the officer. "From the sloop of war. The captain asked us to keep an eye open for two lads who had deserted."

"Hor—hor—hor!" laughed Mike maliciously; "and now you've got 'em; Mr. Gentleman Don and Master Jemmy Wimble."

"If your hands warn't tied," cried Jem fiercely, "I'd punch your ugly head!"

"Is this true, young man?" said the officer sternly. "Did you desert from His Majesty's sloop?"

Don was silent for a moment, and then stepped forward boldly.

"Yes!" he said.

"Ah, Mas' Don, you've done it now," whispered Jem.

"I was cruelly seized, beaten, and dragged away from my home, and Jem here from his young wife. On board ship we were ill-used and persecuted; and I'm not ashamed to own it, I did leave the ship."

"Yes, and so did I!" said Jem stoutly.

"Humph! Then I'm afraid you will have to go with me as prisoners!" said the officer.

"Hor—hor—hor! Here's a game! Prisoners! Cat-o'-nine tails, or hanging."

"Silence, you scoundrel!" roared the officer. "Forward with these prisoners."

Mike and his companions were marched on out of hearing, and then, after a turn or two, the officer spoke.

"It is true then, my lads, you deserted your ship?"

"I was forced to serve, sir, and I left the ship," said Don firmly.

"Well, sir, I have but one course to pursue."

"Surely you will not take them as prisoners, sir?" cried Gordon warmly—"as brave, true fellows as ever stepped."

"I can believe that," said the officer; "but discipline must be maintained. Look here, my lads : I will serve you if I can. You made a great mistake in deserting. I detest pressing men; but it is done, and it is not my duty to oppose the proceeding. Now, will you take my advice?"

"What is it, sir?"

"Throw yourself on our captain's mercy. Your ship has sailed for China; we are going home short-handed. Volunteer to serve the king till the ship is paid off, and perhaps you will never hear of having deserted. What do you say?"

"The same as Jem Wimble does, sir. I can volunteer, and fight, if you like; but I can't bear to be forced."

"Well said!" cried the officer, smiling at Don's bit of grandiloquence; and, an hour later, after an affectionate parting from Ngati, who elected to stay with Gordon, Don and Jem were Jacks once more, marching cheerily with the main body, half a mile behind the guard in charge of the convicts.

CHAPTER LIV.

HOME.

IT was a non-adventurous voyage home, after the convicts had been placed in the hands of the authorities at Port Jackson; and one soft summer evening, after a run by coach from Plymouth, two sturdy-looking brown young sailors leaped down in front of the old coaching hotel, and almost ran along the busy Bristol streets to reach the familiar spots where so much of their lives had been passed.

Don was panting to get back into his mother's arms, but they had to pass the warehouse, and as they reached the gates Jem began to tremble.

"No, no; don't go by, Mas' Don. I dursen't go alone."

"What, not to meet your own wife?"

"No, Mas' Don; 'tarn't that. I'm feared she's gone no one knows where. Stand by me while I ask, Mas' Don."

"No, no, Jem. I must get home."

"We've stood by one another, Mas' Don, in many a fight and at sea, and on shore. Don't forsake your mate now.'

"I'll stay, Jem," said Don.

"Mas' Don, you are a good one!" cried Jem. "Would you mind pulling the bell—werry gently? My hand shakes so, I shall make a noise."

Don gave the bell a tremendous peal, when Jem looked at him reproachfully, and seemed ready to run away, as the lesser gate was snatched angrily open, and a shrill voice began,—

"What d'you mean by ringing like——"

"Sally!"

"Jem!"

Don gave Jem a push in the back, which sent him forward into the yard, pulled the gate to, and ran on as hard as he could to his uncle's house. He had laughed at Jem when he said his hand trembled, but his own shook as he took hold of the knocker, and gave the most comical double rap ever thumped upon a big front door.

There was a click; the door was thrown open by one who had seen the brown young sailor pass the window, and Don Lavington was tightly held in his mother's arms, while two little hands held his, and Kitty jumped up to get a kiss placed upon his cheek.

The explanations were in full swing as, unheard by those in the parlour, the front door was opened by a latch-key, and that of the parlour followed suit, for Uncle Josiah to stand looking smilingly at the group before him.

When at last he was seen, Don started up and gazed dubiously in the grave, stern face before him, recalling in those brief moments scene after scene in the past, when he and his uncle had been, as Jem expressed it, "at loggerheads again,' and his life had seemed to him a time of misery and care. His first coherent thoughts were as to what he should say—how he should enter into full explanations of his movements since that eventful night when he encountered the press-gang. It was better to attack, he thought, than to await the coming on of his adversary, and he had just made up his mind to the former course of action, when all his plans and words were blown to the wind, and there was no need for either attack or defence, for the old man advanced with extended hand.

"Don, my lad," he said quietly, "I've felt the want of you badly at the office. Glad to see you back."

"I ought to tell you, sir——"

"Ah, we'll explain all by-and-by, my boy," said the old man. "I know that you can't have been to blame; and, look here, time back you were as stubborn as could be, and thought you were ill-used, and that I was your enemy. You've been round the world since then, and you are bigger, and broader, and wiser now than you were."

"I hope so, uncle."

"And you don't believe that I ever was your enemy?"

"I believe, uncle, that I was very foolish, and—and——"

"That's enough. P'r'aps I was a bit too hard, but not so hard as they are at sea. You haven't got to go again?"

"No, uncle."

"Then God bless you, my boy! I'm glad to have you back."

Don could not speak, only hold his weeping mother to his breast.

* * * * *

It was some time before Don was able to begin his explanations, and the account of what had passed; and when he did it was with his mother sitting on his right, holding his hand in both of hers, and with his cousin seated upon his left, following her aunt's suit, while the old Bristol merchant lay back in his chair smoking his evening pipe, a grim smile upon his lips, but a look of pride in his eyes as if he did not at all disapprove of Don's conduct when he was at sea.

"But I ought not to have deserted uncle?" said Don, interrogatively.

"Well, my boy," said the old merchant thoughtfully, taking his pipe out of his mouth, and rubbing his stubbly cheek with the waxy end, "I hardly know what to say about that, so we'll let it rest."

* * * * *

"Confound all press-gangs!" said Uncle Josiah that night, as they were parting for bed. "But I don't know, Don, perhaps this one was a blessing in disguise."

"Then I hope, uncle, that the next blessing will come without any disguise at all. But, mother, you found my bundle?"

"Your bundle, my dear?"

"The one I threw up on the top of the bed-tester, when I was foolish enough to think of running away."

"My dear Don, no."

They went to the chamber; Don leaped on the edge of the bed, reached over, and brought down the bundle all covered with flue.

"Don, my darling!"

"But I had repented, mother, and——"

"Hush! no more," said Uncle Josiah firmly; "the past is gone. Here's to a happy future, my boy. Good-night."

THE END.

www.ingramcontent.com/pod-product-compliance
Lightning Source LLC
Chambersburg PA
CBHW050846300426
44111CB00010B/1149